17

The Boogeyman Exists:

..And He's In Your Child's Back Pocket

(second edition)

FOR MORE BY JESSE WEINBERGER

Internet Safety Blog: www.OvernightGeekUniversity.com
For video content: www.YouTube.com/OvernightGeekU

Connect on Social Media

- Facebook.com/OvernightGeekUniversity
- YouTube.com/OvernightGeekU

To hire Jesse Weinberger to speak to your: students, parents, school district, or organization go to OvernightGeekUniversity.com

The Boogeyman Exists:

..And He's In Your Child's Back Pocket

(second edition)

Jesse Weinberger

Disclaimer

Although the author has made every effort to ensure that the information in this book was correct at press time, the author and does not assume and hereby disclaims any liability to any party for any loss, damage, or disruption caused by errors or omissions, whether such errors or omissions result from negligence, accident, or any other cause.

Ordering Information

Quantity sales, fundraising opportunities, and special discounts are available for corporations, associations, and others. For details, contact the author at info@overnightgeek.com

ISBN-13: 978-1539480815

ISBN-10: 153948081X

Printed in the United States of America

Cover Image: iStock Photos

2nd Edition Dedication

This 2nd edition is dedicated to all of my student audiences over the years, especially the kids who have asked me for help and have trusted me with their fears and their stories.

I'm particularly grateful to the smallest audience of all - my own kids - the ones who are forced to listen to me whether they want to or not. They have been my greatest inspiration and the reason I keep presenting and writing. Plus it's just fun to randomly say *herpes* and watch them flinch.

NOTE TO FATHERS

The term *mother* is used synonymously with *parent* throughout this book. There is no disrespect intended on my part to my male audience.

Parenting is far less about your plumbing and far more about your consistency, love, and engagement.

Whenever I say *mother* in this book, please consider yourself (and your plumbing) included.

Table of Contents

INTRODUCTION TO THE SECOND EDITION

Welcome to the 2nd edition of Boogeyman

Completing the 1st edition was every bit like giving birth to a first child. In the beginning, you're excited just to be pregnant and you feel an almost constant sense of anticipation. But somewhere near the end you're grumpy, feel like a bloated walrus, and just need for it to get the hell out. I mean, sure, you end up loving it - but sometimes when you look at it really closely you start to wonder if all that tequila you had the night it was completed was such a good idea. Best to not look too closely.

The 2nd edition is now 3 years old, and like any toddler it has been relentless in pursuing me all over the house - even following me into the bathroom. It's been needy and attention-seeking and like most 3 year olds, it's face is slightly smudged and could have used an extra 20 minutes soaking in the bathtub before I shared it with you. But here it is.

Typically, subsequent editions of a book are meant to delicately correct previous content while adding updated content. I went in a bit of a different direction, like with a hand grenade. In terms of aesthetics you'll notice that the size of the book is physically shorter and narrower. The original size was a bit too large to easily shove into my purse. I realized that maybe this was equally annoying for some of you, well, those of you who carry purses. And hey, no judgment here - rock on with your man purse, Kevin.

But don't worry, no content was sacrificed in the pursuit of purse-ability. In fact, this 2nd edition has grown to over 80k words from 50k words in the original version. In addition, the readability has drastically improved with a new font and layout. I've added a ton more content related to the *parenting* side of digital parenting as a result of the comments and requests I received from parent audiences.

I've had to come to terms with the fact that just like our children, this book will never really be finished. As I write this, a brand new folder sits on my desk containing post-it notes covered in reminders and self-recriminations for the 3rd edition. I've also learned that I can't wait three years between editions, so look for the 3rd edition (God help me) in two years. By then it will be five years old which means that maybe it will be able to pour its own damn juice and I'll be able to pee in peace. See you then.

Love,
Big Mama

SECTION I: UNDERSTANDING THE BASICS

Chapter 1: The Central Issue

Chapter 2: Parenting in Transition

Chapter 3: Be Proactive

Chapter 4: Media Literacy

Chapter 5: How Do Your Children Connect?

Chapter 6: Understanding the Two Major Points of Vulnerability

Chapter 1

THE CENTRAL ISSUE

WE ARE HERE

Thank you for being here and engaging in this discussion. Your willingness to be educated is your family's first line of defense in an always-on digital world.

As parents raising 21st-century digital citizens, if we are to fully comprehend the real digital lives of our children, it is crucial that we continuously and consistently educate ourselves on the specifics of - where they go online, who they interact with, which types of content they consume, and how their personalities can change once they enter the digital sphere. The results will probably surprise you. The perceived anonymity of online engagement can convert the best-behaved child into a creature you would hardly recognize. Even when your child does behave appropriately, the risks of exposure to pornography cyberbullies, and sexual predators still remain.

Believe it or not, there is good news in this seemingly only bad news scenario. Yes, the risks are real and sometimes imminent - yes there is value in

1

tech education and engagement with technology in your family - and yes we can have a very real and lasting impact on the digital safety of our families.

In order to successfully effect real change on the digital landscape for our children, we need all hands on deck. We are here.

THEY ARE THERE

I love traveling to a new school district and presenting to tweens and teens in small groups. These children - our collective progeny – are good kids. But most importantly they're trying to be good. Don't be fooled by the typically negative tone of stories about teenagers on the news. It isn't true. I've met well over two hundred fifty thousand students (mostly 5th to 12th graders). I'm consistently impressed by these kids, they are bright and respectful and funny. Regardless of socioeconomics, geography, or type of school (private, religious, public) - they are **trying**. Ask any middle school or high school teacher, and they will tell you the same thing.

Our kids have more pressure weighing on their (developmentally unprepared) hearts and minds than any other generation in history. It should not be surprising to learn that this generation of children is suffering from anxiety and depression at record and increasing numbers[1]. Speaking as a member of the generation of adults who allowed this to happen - the fault is ours. It happened on our watch. We've made these mistakes out of love, yes (remember that whole hell and best intentions thing?) but the results are undeniable. As parents, we have cultivated and encouraged an environment where we offer our children too much hand-holding and not nearly enough space or encouragement to fly independently, particularly when flying could result in failure[2].

We have high expectations which are effectively unattainable when combined with little usable guidance on how to deliver. We effectively reward and celebrate all things mediocre so that they wouldn't be able to identify an

---

1 Additionally, those children who do reach out for help and are increasingly receiving intense treatment modalities such as prescription medications and inpatient hospital stays. Mojtabai, R., M. Olfson, and B. Han. *"National Trends in the Prevalence and Treatment of Depression in Adolescents and Young Adults."* Pediatrics 138.6 (2016): n. pag.

2 Mastery of any skill is dependent on failure and our encouragement of striving towards the risk of failure. Must read about failure - Daniel Coyle's book: *The Talent Code: Greatness Isn't Born. It's Grown.* London: Arrow, 2010. Print.

actually hard-won accomplishment if it smacked them in the eye. And yet, somehow, they persevere. Even the ones with the hardest and saddest façades still have that glimmer. That spark is part 'hope' mixed with a deep and profound desire to be recognized and actually understood. They want you to SEE them, to actually see them in a real way. Your child just wants to feel accepted by you and by their friends, and in the absence of either of these two - by anyone at all they might find online.

THE THREE PRESSURES: ACADEMICS, FINANCES, AND DIGITAL SOCIAL LIFE

Much like the three Fates of Greek mythology[3] imposing their will on the mortal world- our children are under tremendous academic, financial, and social pressure. These three live in a self-feeding machine of perpetual exhaustion.

Parent-initiated academic expectations, in a vacuum, are not the enemy. However, since your children spend the majority of their time in academic pursuits, it's easy for parents to drift into making the mistake of confusing who the child is with her numerical outcomes. The majority of parents will acknowledge that the overwhelming love they feel for their children is not dependent on their achievements. We say and believe that our love for our children is not diminished by their limitations or affected by their behavior. It is also obvious that we would much rather our children not become convicted murderers - projecting our own hopes and dreams onto that child. It's also true that we can't help but feel proud of our children when they do well by some external standard. We feel proud when that child's name is announced, or printed, or highlighted in some public way. Those achievements generally spring from some quantitative measure - the score on an exam points scored in a game, or a GPA. Even though we can rationally agree that basing the worth of any person on a single exam or outcome is absurd when our own child receives the accolade we feel that flush of pride. When some other child receives the award we think "why didn't my kid do that?"

While you might recognize that your child is more than just a score,

---

3 According to Greek mythology the three Fates had the power to decide how long a mortal would live. Every time a human/mortal was born - Clotho spun the thread of life for that child, Lachesis measured to a specific length, and Atropos cut the thread to mark the end of the life.

he might perceive your quantifiably triggered parental pride as proof of love. Your child may then illogically decide that better numbers = more love; and if they can't produce better numbers that their chances of gaining your love or admiration are doomed.

The fact that financial limitations or extreme privilege can have an impact on the entire life of the family is not news. However, the new social digital pressure (the third Fate) can be influenced by the dollars. If you were a teenager any time before the 90s, what made you "popular" in high school was probably based on who your friends were, which parties you were invited to, or maybe where you sat in the cafeteria. Any of these might be impacted by your socioeconomic level.

In this brave new digital world, an enormous part of whether or not you are popular is based on your quantitative social media scores, literally. Every 8th grader knows who has the most followers on Instagram and how many likes they received on their last post. This is an area outside of financial privilege. If I'm a clever enough 8th grader, then I'll figure out a way to boost those numbers on my next post. However, if I'm a wealthy 8th grader who posts photos of my last trip to Costa Rica where I'm zip lining in the forest, then those numbers will speak for themselves.

These children feel like they're always being judged - and they are: by their parents, by their peers, and by total strangers. These new "standard" pressures don't even include other potential challenging situations such as family stability, mental health concerns, physical health, and learning differences.

Children will go to extraordinary lengths in their quest to be noticed and understood. Wearing the same clothing brands and hairstyles may be a way to blend in while avoiding negative attention. Other children may take the opposite tack and wear heavy makeup and dramatic clothing. Choices in music and recreational activities can define others. Extreme focus on athletic ability and successes are yet another way to find recognition. Your child's digital life follows her along her chosen path of recognition-seeking behaviors. Children and young adults use digital tools to feel connected to their friends and their digital community. For many, connection to an unknown or negative person is better than no connection at all.

This is where we begin to drift into trouble. We need to remember that our sole job as parents is to keep them safe and prepare them for the day they leave. That's all. That's the job.

TAKING THE JOURNEY TOGETHER

As I travel around the United States presenting to parents, children, and school districts, there are moments I look out at the audience and think "these people must think I've gone mad." Sometimes I feel like Chicken Little shouting: "The sky is falling," but then I turn on the news the next morning, and a chunk of the sky falls into my coffee.

The trick to wrapping our exhausted parental brains around these digital risks is to understand that your child is NOT the exception to the rule and your home is NOT the single place on the planet where safety naturally abounds in the absence of guidance and supervision. It makes no difference where you live, how much money you have, or how well behaved you perceive your children to be.

I have personally gathered and compiled hundreds of thousands of lines of data via my live student presentations. The results follow[4]:

- The new age of onset of pornography consumption is 8 years old. The new age of onset of pornography addiction is 11 years old.
  (Why? Too young access to devices + porn is everywhere.)
- Sexting begins in the 4th/5th grade.
  (Why? Too young access to devices + media hypersexualization.)
- Cell phone ownership among children starts solidly in the 3rd grade. Tablet ownership can begin as early as Kindergarten.
  (Why? Parents are unaware the risks of gifting the device.)
- The youngest children are engaging in the riskiest behaviors. I'm far more worried about the current 3rd/4th graders than any other group.
  (Why? Too young access to devices + parents thinking that the required conversations about sexting, should occur when the child goes through puberty but actually need to occur when the device is gifted.)
- Between 45% to 68% of the middle schoolers I've met have zero limitations imposed on the amount of time they spend online - meaning that they can

---

4 The data I've collected supports the results from a study by the University of New Hampshire *"The Nature and Dynamics of Internet Pornography Exposure for Youth"* which showed that very young children are becoming addicted to online pornography with their first exposure as young as 8 years old. I have met the parents of some of these children - most recently the parents of a 9-year-old girl whose parents were forced to remove wi-fi from their home and place all devices into a lockbox at night. As a result the child stole her friend's iPod Touch and used a neighbor's unlocked wi-fi signal in order to continue to consume porn

game, surf, chat for as many hours as they like.

(Why? Parents of younger children are especially unaware of the extent of the risks.)

As a society of parents, we need to mind our own corners of the web with ruthless diligence. But you are here, and I am here. And together we can make a real difference in your child's experience of their digital world.

PERSONAL NOTE TO PARENTS

Right about now, you might be feeling like a crappy parent - *like all of this was going on and you had no idea - and good gravy you've really screwed the pooch this time - and why on earth did you think YOU were going to be a good parent - you have absolutely ZERO skills.....*

If your internal dialogue sounds like a drunk 70s gym teacher screaming at the kid flinching during dodgeball, you need to be nicer to yourself. There are days when parenting is like rubbing your knuckles against a cheese grater while being swarmed by bees. And no one told you that the bad days were going to suck as much as they do. And some days the only positive thought you can come up with is the fact that at least no one in the house has lice or butt worms. And yes that's a thing.

We all screw up as parents. I screw up daily - even knowing what I know - I still allow my two kids (now in college and high school) to drag me into a negotiation[5]. I don't even notice it happening, and then BAM there I am explaining myself. Here's the thing. It's not like they came shooting out of your vaginal canal along with a manual. That would have been awesome - first the baby, then the placenta, then the manual! (Let's just hope it's not spiral bound - ouch!) The point is there is no manual. So, of course, we're going to screw it up. The best we can do is stick together, teach each other, and give ourselves a break when we fall short.

---

5 NEVER negotiate with terrorists. Only a heartless 9 year-old villain willing to inflict terror to further his evil ends would ask you for an M17 video game in front of your mother-in-law.

THE LEAST YOU SHOULD KNOW

You probably aren't aware of your child's "real digital life." Once you do, it may surprise you.

This generation of kids is under more pressure than any other generation in history. Your children just want to be acknowledged - preferably by the ones they love, but potentially by anyone.

The digital risk and digital behavior statistics I've gathered from my own student audiences reflect exceedingly young participation in pornography consumption (8 years old), pornography addiction (11 years old), sexting (4th/5th grade), and cell phone ownership (3rd grade).

I couldn't even get out of the first chapter without at least one "vagina." Buckle in, it's gonna get weird.

CONVERSATION STARTERS & ACTION ITEMS

With friends

- Email a few close friends (preferably the parents of your child's friends) and talk to them about these statistics.
- Did they know about these trends?
- Have they ever had an experience related to digital use which instigated a change in how the family uses technology?
- Ask your friends how they handle digital rules in the home or at school. Do they even have rules?

With spouse and/or babysitters

- Speak with the childcare providers and babysitters who spend the most time with your children (including grandparents). Use the following questions as a starting point to spark a deep conversation on this topic:
- Is there a time of day when your child seems to be spending the most time on a device?
- Is there a sense of which apps or sites are the child's favorites?
- Are there any specific areas of concern which can be identified?

Chapter 2
PARENTING IN TRANSITION

"BEFORE DIGITAL" PARENTING

The literal birth of humanity comes from the actual first pregnancies. It would be hard to imagine that even cave women did not have a very similar experience - other than pain meds (praise the gods of epidurals!) When I was pregnant in the BD (Before Digital) era, my parenting concerns were the same as every other mother's throughout the ages: health, education, safety, financial stability, and the overwhelming desire to raise children who contribute more to the world than they take. Other than the obvious differences in education, environment, and access to medical care, not much has changed throughout the BD years for mothers.

With my first child, I didn't understand what it meant to be a parent – who does? It never occurred to me that from that singularly dramatic moment forward, an entire chunk of my heart would separate from my body and walk around without me. I did not know that there would be moments in the very near future when my ability to control every single aspect of his environment would fail.

My first major parenting panic attack came when my first child was headed to kindergarten. It's an odd thing. I had already spent the first five years of his life buckling him in and out of safety seats and harnesses....out of the high chair (click), into the carrier (click), into the car seat (click-click). If the beginning of his life had a soundtrack, the bass line would be made up of a continuous "click-click" human beat box. Then he started kindergarten which meant taking the school bus. Suddenly I was supposed to just toss him like a loose marble into a giant yellow tin can, driven by God knows who. You don't think about the fact that school buses don't have seatbelts until you wave goodbye to that first child. The wheels on that bus almost drove me directly into a straitjacket. No click-click. Can you understand that? NO CLICK-CLICK.

But as parents this is what we do - we over focus on details and miss the larger issues. On the neurotic end of the parenting continuum, we overuse hand-sanitizers and under-emphasize imagination. We forget to cultivate compassion with the same zeal we focus on flash cards of famous scientists. On the loosey-goosey-free-range opposite end of the parenting continuum, we fill the closet with cute outfits and forget to fill the shelves with books. While every other kid on the soccer team is wearing the approved uniform, yours is wearing a hot pink tutu because well, she's expressing herself. The crazy is compounded by mom's total lack of self-awareness in justifying this Future-Sociopaths-of-America behavior by saying 'well, sometimes you just have to pick your battles.' (Barf.)

As mothers, we simultaneously long for more control and more independence. We can't wait until he can pour his own juice and then wish we had those chubby fingers to hold, long after they've gone lean and have stopped being so eager to hold ours. And our children feel the same; participating in a constant pushing and pulling. On some days we're on different rhythms, and every time I pull, my son pushes me away. Then when he pulls and wants more from me, I encourage him to be more independent. These things will never change. Each resulting milestone is wonderful in a heartbreaking sort of way.

Parenting from the beginning of time to the indefinable future will always be made of equal parts love and fear. Love for that child and fear of the loss of that love. Grasping and letting go. Wash. Rinse. Repeat.

PARENTING IN THE 21ST CENTURY

I worry for my friends with young children. The entire landscape of parenting has changed; some for the better, much for the worse. AD era (After Digital) parenting holds all of the issues from the BD era, plus a full slate of gooey new ones. The year my (now college age) son was born, I purchased my first cell phone. My husband and I both considered it an amusing extravagance. Soon the extravagance transitioned, first into a helpful tool and then into a required part of living in a so-called civilized society.

Our parenting gadgets have changed drastically. Every mom-to-be for the past 30 years has had a baby monitor listed on their shower wish list. Since then, baby monitors have evolved becoming more feature-rich and technologically sophisticated. Currently, in our quest for full-time baby surveillance, we buy video wireless baby monitors connected to wi-fi. This particular technological advance has now made it possible for the "boogeyman" to hack your wi-fi signal and watch your child[6] (and the inside of your home) from across the world with the same ease that you watch from two rooms away. Oops.

Are you still living through bath time with a sweet little baby? I remember stressing over bath time. Was the water too hot? Were the bubbles chemical free? Those concerns seem quaint and old-timey. (Since the first edition of this book "cruelty-free bath bubbles" has become a thing. What the hell does that even mean??) Today's AD era parents have much larger concerns. You might have taken an adorable photo of your baby covered in bubbles, aww so cute...but did you know that your precise location may be attached to that image? If the EXIF data is intact on the photo[7], you've made it

---

6 In 2016 as a result of numerous reports of hacked baby video monitors New York City's Department of Consumer Affairs issued a public alert to parents which stated in part "Video monitors are intended to give parents peace of mind when they are away from their children but the reality is quite terrifying - if they aren't secure, they can provide easy access for predators to watch and even speak to our children." In some cases, parents were waking up in the middle of the night to hear strangers speaking to their children.   Find the entire statement along with best practices here https://www1.nyc.gov/site/dca/media/pr012716.page

7 Check the settings on your smartphone's camera app and look for the LOCATION setting. Make sure there is NO tick mark in this box. Every photo has EXIF data embedded within the image file. When the location setting in the camera is set ON, the EXIF data will also include the location where you were standing when you took the photo. In our bubble bath example - the latitude and longitude of the bathtub's location is recorded and saved as part of the photo file. Most social media sites like Facebook strip out the EXIF data (mostly because it makes the resulting file smaller), but all sites and modes of transmission do NOT automatically strip out EXIF. Once a recipient receives your photo (via a myriad of potential methods) it's a very simple process to backwards extract the

easy for the boogeyman to get his creepy hands on your baby by accidentally providing him with the latitude and longitude of the exact location where that photo was taken. Oops.

The new Amazon Echo and Echo Dot devices have brought futuristic robot interfacing into our homes. By beginning your statement with the device trigger word "Alexa," you can wake the robot and issue countless commands to the device which sits in your home and is listening at all times[8]. Once a command triggers Alexa, she can answer questions, play music, order Amazon products and much more. Amazon keeps each of the Alexa requests in the cloud where they remain until the owner realizes that they can and should be deleted. The new device has already been a part of several news stories. In Texas, a 6-year-old girl ordered a $160 dollhouse and sugar cookies from Alexa[9] without her parent's permission or knowledge- adorable. In Arkansas, murder investigators subpoenaed the home's Amazon Echo[10] - hoping to gain insight of what could be heard inside the home at the time of the killing. Oops.

Parenting-born anxiety has always existed and shows no signs of being spirited away by the just-right cocktail of medication and a tequila chaser (I've tried). Parenting anxiety is just fear for the child you love made tangible; this will exist as long as parenting exists. The speed and acceleration of technological development are outpacing our knowledge and ability to create a harbor of safety in our homes. Digital life has evolved and devolved to mimic and reflect the reality of our brick-and-mortar life. And why wouldn't it? Much like the real world, the digital world has its underbelly. Would-be criminals and predators have existed since cave people. There was definitely a cave-man called "Pauly-the-Spear" selling protection to the other poor cave slobs who were just trying to sell mammoth tusks on the corner. Theft, murder, sex crimes, drugs, and pornography have existed through the ages. And while this is not a new story, there are clear distinctions. Within the brick and mortar BD era/real world, an 8-year-old would not walk to the corner store and buy a pornographic magazine. And why not?

EXIF data from a photo and thereby learn precisely where the photo was taken.

8 See list of best practices settings for Amazon Echo in Chapter 14: Resources.

9 *6-year-old orders $160 dollhouse, 4 pounds of cookies with Amazon's Echo Dot*, by Jennifer Earl January 5, 2017, cbsnews.com

10 *Prosecutors Get Warrant for Amazon Echo Data in Arkansas Murder Case*, by Erik Ortiz December 28, 2016, nbcnews.com

Porn consumption among children in the Before Digital Era (aka Real World)

Intent: The BD era 8-year-old doesn't have the desire to buy a girlie magazine because he doesn't even know what that is.

Cost Barrier: He doesn't have any money of his own.

Social Acceptance: You probably wouldn't let him walk to the corner store alone in the first place, and even if you did the store clerk wouldn't sell him the magazine.

Parenting: It would never occur to you to have a pornography conversation with your 8-year-old.

How has the landscape changed? Let's look at the same scenario as if it occurred in the current digital era.

Porn consumption among children in the After Digital Era (aka Online World)

Intent: The 8 year old knows that porn exists because he's probably already seen it, probably accidentally at first. His experience of porn is screen based and easy to access. Given the level of digital immersion among the very young - he wouldn't even consider purchasing printed content. He probably doesn't realize that paper porn exists.

Cost Barrier: There is no cost barrier - online porn is free and two clicks away from wherever he is online.

Social Acceptance: Porn access and consumption among children is pervasive as is the social acceptance among children. They don't see the big deal.

Parenting: It would STILL never occur to you to have a pornography conversation with your 8-year-old because you've underestimated both his ability and his intent to easily access online porn.

In the AD era world, there is an immense ease of access to content of all kinds including pornography. Despite your 8-year old's initial lack of intent; it is incredibly easy for him to happen upon pornography with one benign click. (Kids call it "BoobTube" for a reason.) Everyone has access to anything, at any time. The cost barrier no longer exists since so much of this content is freely available online. The social acceptance issue is not a factor since "all of his friends" are seeing the same content. In terms of parenting, mom and dad don't realize just how much porn is available and actively consumed by very young children.

There are a handful of slides in the middle of my parent presentation which show just how easy it is to reach pornographic material via any web-enabled device. The reaction from the audiences is palpable and silent as they attempt to comprehend the scale of the problem. Your child can easily access porn online - usually within 2 or 3 clicks, and on virtually any platform. YouTube has dedicated porn channels. There are porn stars who have profiles on Instagram, there's porn on Music.ly, Twitter, Snapchat (definitely Snapchat), and generally speaking any platform or app where uploading photos or videos is an option for the user.

THE 'GOOD JOB' GENERATION

I'm a first generation American. My mother was born in Cuba and came to this country just before I was born. I didn't speak English until I was around five years old or so (and eventually learned English with the help of Sesame Street and the Electric Company[11].) There's something that happens when you've been raised by immigrant parents at the lower end of the socioeconomic scale my parents weren't particularly "nice" - at least not as compared to American parents. Being a parent in the late 60s/early 70s in addition to having just arrived in this country without speaking the language and working like a three-legged farm animal makes you, well, tired.

I can vividly remember my mother telling me (in a very matter-of-fact way) "You know, there's really nothing special about you, at all. You're not even really that cute. So whatever you want in this world you'd better be ready to work and sweat and scratch and claw for it. The world doesn't owe you a thing, so if I were you - I'd study harder." Gee...thanks, Mom. And looking back now I can honestly say that the parenting perspective of 'you're NOT special' is infinitely better than the world we've created for our children where every kid is special and deserving of accolades and trophies and medals just for showing up. I was taught to expect failure and to learn from it. I was taught to shake it off and move on, because no one had the time to coddle me through it - whatever the "it" of the day happened to be. To this day, I tie my shoes the

---

11 The amazing programming from The Electric Company still exists! You can find old videos and updated content at www.pbskids.org/electriccompany

wrong way because I taught myself - true story.

When my son was a toddler, my mother caught me saying "good job" to him constantly. I didn't even think about it. I mean, he was a toddler and super cute (I used to lick the excess baby food off of his face - seriously.) So I said "good job" to him, who cares? One day she had apparently had enough and said in her robust espresso-strength Ricky Ricardo accent - "why on earth do you keep saying 'good job' when he hasn't done anything worth praising? He's not supposed to kick the cat or throw his napkin on the floor, stop praising basic expectations."

Wowie zowie. Lordy, my mother was right AGAIN!! And that was the moment that I began to carefully examine the language and motivators that parents use with their children, knowingly or not.

HOW WE ARE COMPLICIT AS PARENTS: PARENTING

In terms of digital safety, as parents, we are complicit (by action or omission) in creating a potentially unsafe environment for our families. The biggest single error we can make as parents is to NOT engage, to NOT dig deep and educate ourselves on the reality of their digital landscape. Parents avoid digging deep for many different reasons. The most typical driver of parental avoidance is a simple one: it's easier to NOT parent - when you use the word "parent" as a verb. And in defense of all of these parents - "parent" didn't even become a verb until the mid-20th century.

If your own parents were born any time before 1945 your childhood was markedly different than your child's life experience. True, this can be said for any gap of time larger than 15 years. However, this particular gap includes a colossal leap forward in technological advancements not seen since the industrial revolution. In fact, until the mid-1950's the concept of "parenting" as an activity one should strive to be good at - did not exist either. Before Dr. Spock,[12] there was no concept of parenting self-help because "parenting" (as a verb) wasn't even a thing. Spock was the one who started us on the road of examining our actions as parents and measuring outcomes in all facets of child rearing. Moreover, engaged parenting did not become an expectation of fathers until much later still.

---

12 Dr. Benjamin Spock - (not Mr. Spock from Star Trek) was a pediatrician who was the first health care professional to ever examine the psychological wellness of children and family dynamics.

So here we are in the 21st century, expected to **do stuff** as parents - in an environment which can feel like a medieval gauntlet where your odds of success are pretty bleak. As a result, we can't possibly parent as our parents did, which basically amounted to keeping us alive and hoping for the best. The moment you buy your children a phone or tablet your tiny 21st-century window of free-range parenting slams shut.

It's easier to not parent. But we know that it's far easier to do and say nothing which would upset your child in terms of digital safety - or anything really. Maybe you are, or you know this type of parent; the one who is fine with everything, who doesn't set rules or expectations, the one who justifies their own hands-off approach with "everyone else has a phone and I didn't want my 11-year-old to feel left out." As the parent of a college student I can tell you with 100% certainty that when a parent's desire for a child to "fit-in" surpasses the focus on the child's well-being, your results are going to stink. The same issue of fitting in versus well-being is going to keep coming up throughout the child's life. And if you find it impossible to say 'no' to a 10-year-old's request for an Instagram account - good luck saying 'no' to that same child when she's 15 years old and wants to drink alcohol to fit in[13]. When you ignore your better parenting instincts for your child's desire to fit in, you're actually saying that you agree with the child's assessment that their perceived peer pressure is more important than their well-being. You're telling your child that you don't have any defined value systems in place but rather that the groupthink is what guides your family and your parenting. You may not articulate that view or even recognize it as such, but every time you give in or change your mind based on your child's wheedling or the actions of other parents - you show your child that your family does not have a defined set of values[14].

---

13 The "but everyone else does it" rationale when spoken by parents is one of the 6,397 things which can throw me into a murderous rage. Uncontrolled anger aside, the data is on the side of being LESS permissive. Parents who allow their children to watch them drink frequently and permit their children to try alcohol and consume alcohol underage produce children who drink more, drink more recklessly, and have more negative health and social consequences later in life. There is no debate. Here are a few studies:

* Abar, Caitlin, Beau Abar, and Rob Turrisi. *"The impact of parental modeling and permissibility on alcohol use and experienced negative drinking consequences in college."* Addictive Behaviors 34.6-7 (2009): 542-47.

* Komro, Kelli A., Mildred M. Maldonado-Molina, Amy L. Tobler, Jennifer R. Bonds, and Keith E. Muller. *"Effects of home access and availability of alcohol on young adolescents alcohol use."* Addiction 102.10 (2007): 1597-608. Web.

14 Parenting with integrity. What are your defined values? Have you ever considered that question? Parenting with integrity means that you take a long hard dispassionate view at your

Growing up at the speed of tech. During the Q&A session at the end of a presentation to an audience of K-12 educators, a teacher asked me how he could encourage his seven-year-old daughter to be *more* interested in the iPad he had just gifted her - rather than her Barbie dolls with which she was obviously obsessed. This teacher had just heard me speak at length about specific and general risks and how young children don't **need** devices. Essentially my response was: *Don't speed up the pace of childhood.* How does it make any sense to try and transition this little girl's tactile, imaginative, in-real-life playtime to a screen... especially when she's shown a repeated and clear preference for the dolls?

This is where we need to be ruthlessly self-aware of our own complicity. Are you introducing the technology to your child because it's convenient for you? Which I comprehend from the parenting sanity side. There's nothing better for a peaceful long car trip than Netflix. They get sedated and you avoid the urge to toss yourself out the window onto oncoming traffic. Just know, however, that the child's willingness to get sedated will extend out of the realm of the car and will leech into the vacation. There's value in boredom and being forced to interact with your siblings. Some of the most memorable moments of any family trip come via anxiety, fighting, and managing personalities. Your child's first exposure to tech comes from you, just be sure to wait until they're older - as old as you can manage.

Mocking kids for behaviors we've allowed. Full recognizing that there is an incredibly long list of things that make me angry; this one has got to be in the top three. Somehow it's become perfectly acceptable to malign, misjudge, and complain about millennials[15]. It's become the easy punchline, the low-hanging fruit of social observances. You'll hear that millennials are lazy, have no focus, are unmotivated with no social skills, and we should be terrified to see them take the baton in our race to social self-immolation; if indeed they aren't too stupid to reach back for the baton in the first place. Let's

---

family and who you ARE as a unit. Maybe in your family you value time together more than anything else and as a result the house is usually a train wreck. And that's okay with you because you value the time together. Maybe you're a family who needs structure and you invest the time and effort into plans and schedules because everyone is happier and healthier when you live within the plan. How would you define your family? First take a critical view of what exists now - you can't begin to improve what you're too afraid to define. Then define your best case scenario - is your family even capable of that best case scenario? Even tiny movement towards your goal should be viewed as successes shared by the entire family.

15 You are a millennial if you will reach adulthood (21 yo) in the early part of the 21st century.

first assume that every one of these criticisms is exactly accurate and that it even makes sense to levy judgment on an entire generation based solely on their year of birth - like a hastily written horoscope meant to ring true for hundreds of millions of people.

Even if this preposterous set of givens were true - consider: Whose fault is it? Unlike the rest of the animal kingdom - children are born utterly helpless and requiring a tremendous amount of emotional and physical care. So where should the fault lie when these so-called snarky, lazy, unmotivated, overly-sensitive narcissistic sacks of meat are still living in our basements when they're 30 years old? It's our fault. Stop blaming your children for behaviors you've allowed in the first place. Part of our job is to create an environment where good habits can flourish because the structure will not accept mediocrity. Creating this structure takes forethought, planning - and a truckload of other verbs. For example, if you "say" that you want your children to eat more vegetables but you don't cook them every night and put them on your child's plate like a normal part of their lives - what do you think is going to happen? Are you imagining that somehow - the child who has never eaten anything green (besides sour apple gummy bears) is suddenly going to bounce off the school bus begging for brussel sprouts? Uh, no - that's not happening. It's the same with digital safety. If you make a rule that no devices are allowed at the dinner table (ever) and your child continues to bring the device to the dinner table - that's **your** fault. If my mother had told me 'no phones at the table' and I did it anyway I can pretty much guarantee that she would have shoved that phone into my eye socket, making it a permanent part of my skull - but on the plus side, I'd be able to take pictures by pulling my earlobe.

Creating a sociopath - special snowflake edition. Actual snowflakes fall out of the sky already special. The special-ness is baked in. Humans aren't that lucky. We have to grind our snowflakes into special-ness with hard work. Without the hard work, your kid is just a chunk of snow - hopefully not yet yellowed by life.

Stop telling your children how special[16] they are. They're special to YOU, nobody else cares. Nobody. Nobody cares that your kid won the 35th place trophy - out of 35 places - that just means he lost the best. Every kid

---

16 They're not special - they're filled with potential. If they harness that potential and work really hard they can create something amazing. But specialness is not an inherent trait - it's earned with hard work. You have to like do stuff, kind of a lot.

knows that the only thing they prove is that they were able to maintain a pulse for six consecutive weeks. Your child knows these trophies and accolades are garbage; you insult their intelligence when you display them and encourage mediocrity. These phony accolades murder your child's natural instinct to strive and work towards a goal. They know dishonest and baseless praise when they see it even when you've crammed it all into the Cabinet of Mediocrity for all to see.

If everybody is special, then nobody is special - that's just math. Someday your child is going to have a boss or a mother-in-law who hates his guts for absolutely no reason. That's life, and our children are nowhere near equipped for this reality. If you provide a constant stream of praise and encouragement it all becomes equally meaningless.

The trick is to provide what scientists call "accurate praise" or positive feedback which reflects reality. Researchers[17] asked over 300 students at South Korean elementary schools (as well as their parents) to rate how much the parents typically understated or overstated their school related praise. Children who perceived their parent's praise as accurately reflecting their performance tended to have a higher GPA and lower levels of depression symptoms than students who received too little acknowledgment or an excessive dose of praise. The study's co-author Young-Hoon Kim says that American and South Korean parents have a tendency to overpraise their children.

If your kid is acting like a jerk - tell him. Tell him that you expect more from him - tell him where he went wrong, specifically. Don't tell your daughter that her friends are being mean just because "they're jealous" - that might be the reason, but encourage self-awareness in this process. What might she have done to incur the hormonally-laced wrath of the middle school goblins? And if jealousy is the cause - why does she insist on continuing to call these people friends?

In the grand scheme of life, it's highly unlikely that any of our children are really all that special. And if you have more than two kids then you can pretty much count on at least one of those kids being *really not* special. I'll let you decide which one.

---

17 Lee, Hae In et al. *"Understanding When Parental Praise Leads To Optimal Child Outcomes"*. Social Psychological and Personality Science (2016): 194855061668302. Web.

Instant gratification in all things. If you're the default parent[18] in your home, you'll be familiar with the following scenario. You're driving your child somewhere - a practice, a doctor's visit, the 35th loop that same day back to the school to pick up a forgotten item, etc. Your child tosses out a random request from the back seat: "Do you have a fine-tipped Sharpie marker, magenta, neon?" The request hasn't hit the ether and you've already pulled the aforementioned, highly-specific-writing implement from some human orifice. Then, something spills all over the back seat. That's okay - that's why you carry an entire roll of paper towels in your left boot. The right boot? Funny you should ask, that one holds the hand sanitizer, band aids, granola bars and a Gatorade - the good flavors only, please.

Heaven forbid these kids do a single thing on their own or [GASP] be forced to wait. Waiting? What is this foreign and offensive word? Our children don't wait - for anything - ever. They either get it NOW or it isn't worth waiting for in the first place.

Do you remember wondering? Do you remember not knowing? Do you remember not remembering the name of some famous person, or the capital of Missouri, or the formula for calculating force? Not remembering is *so last century*. Recently a fourth-grade teacher told me that (in her opinion) there was no point in having students memorize the state capitals when they could just Google the answer at any point in their lives[19]. Your ability to remember (sans Google) that Jefferson City is the capital of Missouri and that it lies on the Missouri River is an independent piece of data which has inherent value and makes you NOT AN IMBECILE in life. Being an educated human means making connections between seemingly disparate pieces of information and subjects. If you aren't well educated you won't even know what you are supposed to "Google" in the first place. In reality, subjects are not kept in discrete silos like they are during the school day. When you're an adult you don't get all of your math[20] needs out of the way during the first 45 minutes of your morning followed by all of your writing needs during the second 45 minutes of your morning.

---

18 The default parent is the person your child runs to first when life gets: bloody, scary, really real, sticky, or covered in vomit. If you're not sure who the 'default parent' is in your house - it isn't you.

19 As a result, I may or may not have (allegedly) tried to strangle that teacher. The facts are blurry- but I have a vague memory of law enforcement explaining to me how much they don't appreciate strangulation regardless of the level of stupidity one is forced to endure. Who knew?

20 And by the way: Math is Life - if you didn't realize this, you haven't been paying attention.

Now, digital instant gratification mimics the real-world instant gratification we cultivate and enable for our children. So who cares? Why does it matter if they get answers immediately? Who cares if you walk around with a roll of toilet paper in your bra because your child prefers that quilted super soft brand to the toilet paper in public bathrooms? It matters, kind of a lot. (And we'll ignore the fact that you're raising a ghoulish, thumb-sucking, adult child that the rest of us will have to deal with later- thanks.)

We've entered a weirdo place in human history where the only things that truly matter are the ones we can experience immediately. Literally right NOW. And some of these new "life features" are clearly beneficial to humanity as in communication and medical care. I'm not suggesting that we go back to telegrams and bloodletting.[21] Just like you, I totally prefer the immediacy of email and antibiotics. But there is a heretofore unnoticed and unintended consequence to instant gratification in all things. If **now=good** then **later=bad** or at least **later=inefficient** or not worth the effort. In this brave new universe of now-now-now:

1. Have a question? Google it for an answer, don't bother trying to drag it out of your brain.

2. Taking a photo? See it immediately, post it immediately, get feedback (or not) from friends immediately.

3. Having trouble with that algebra problem? Don't waste your precious time experiencing the troubleshooting process of a long math problem (which is a crucial part of the learning process.) Just hover your phone over the problem and you'll see the breakdown of the steps.

None of these modern conveniences alone signal the end of civilization - and frankly, they're each pretty amazing. However, our societal focus on "instant" in all things diminishes our human need for delayed gratification. Without time[22], space, and failure[23] - we cannot grow.

---

21 If you don't know what bloodletting is - you haven't read enough classic fiction. Stop everything you're doing and read anything by Dickens, Chekhov, Tolstoy, Austen, any of the Brontes, or Shakespeare. And no, Fifty Shades of Trash doesn't count.

22 Dr. Angela Duckworth has done an immense amount work in studying what she calls "GRIT" - what makes a person more successful than another. Delayed gratification is a major part of what makes you grittier than your spouse for example; and includes personality characteristics like working hard NOW for a reward which may only come (if at all) in the very distant future. World class musicians, professional athletes, Nobel winners, prolific writers - these are all by definition "gritty." Gritty people spend their days honing their craft, beating on it until they're exhausted and

At every step of their young lives we show our children that: instant, fast, now is the ideal. So how can we logically expect them to see the joy in reading an exceptionally long book, take dozens of practice ACT tests and study for countless hours with no guarantees, save and invest their unspent allowance for potential long-term gain, or increase their violin practice time to 2 hours per day because it will reap long-term expertise? "Work now for possible gain later" seems terribly old-fashioned in an environment where our first instinct is to ask "Isn't there an app for that?"

HOW WE ARE COMPLICIT AS PARENTS: SOCIAL MEDIA USE

As parents we need to act as an example for our children - easier said than done. We are enormously fallible humans who can't be expected to behave perfectly all the time or even most of the time. As parents, we're still learning[24].

And by the way, why don't our children ever emulate the good things they see us do? I have yet to come upon my daughter in the bathroom on her knees cleaning the heck out of the toilet because she's imitating me. But I lob a single well-deserved swear word out the car window and all of a sudden I'm getting calls from the preschool that little miss is doing a profanity-laced Dora the Explorer open mike at the playground….and she's killing.

The truth, however, is that it matters. Our kids watch us all the time - they copy the crappy stuff and ignore the good stuff. If you live your life in mid-selfie[25] so will your child. If every meal, experience, and interaction in your life need to be posted and laid before your online community for praise and (hopefully) quantifiable adulation - your child will behave the same way. If you live your life through the filter of a screen - so will your child.

Your social media presence and the photos, posts, check-ins with or about your children on Facebook or Instagram could be putting the safety of your entire family at risk. Generally speaking - in two minutes or less with just

---

all for a reward which may never come. Grit it where passion and work ethic meet. Grit is the anti-instant gratification.

23 Recommended reading: *The Talent Code* by Daniel Coyle

24 Expecting that we can act as a beacon for correct speech and behavior at all times for our children is an unreasonable expectation and will only lead to more parental anxiety. Do your best and be nice to yourself.

25 If you're over 40 and you're taking duck pout selfies, please stop. You're embarrassing yourself. Over 30s...tick-tock.

your child's first name and the name of his/her school - I will have your home address. Within 3 minutes (depending on which social media platforms are being used) I will be able to figure out where your child's bedroom sits within your house. If you're feeling creeped out right now - that's the appropriate response. Here's the even creepier bit - *you* are the one helping me to find your child.

A significant amount of the compromising data I find online about a child comes from the parent's Facebook page or Instagram profile. I understand that you're proud of your children - I mean they're sooooo special, right? Your well-intentioned pride can become a source of data which can be used by someone willing to hurt you or your family. Here are some privacy basics when you're using Facebook:

Cover photo. Your cover photo (the landscape oriented photo you've uploaded which appears at the top of your Facebook profile) cannot be anonymized, meaning that anyone can see that photo regardless of any other privacy settings you might have in place. This cover photo should NEVER be a photo of your family or your children - particularly when that photo of your child potentially leaks additional breadcrumbs of data like school name, sports, and location.

Profile photo. Your profile photo is the one which represents you - as an avatar of sorts - within the Facebook world. Every time you post, comment, or like - the profile photo you've chosen appears to the left of that activity along with your username. Your profile photo should be set as viewable to *Friends of Friends* (at the most visible end) and to *Only You* (at the most restrictive end). Here again, you NEVER want your profile photo to be a photo of your children or a photo which reveals additional pieces of personally revealing data. If you were, for example, to comment or like a post from your local news station - you've exposed that profile photo to the public.

Segmenting posted content with lists. Facebook allows you to create "lists" to segment and control your exposure on a post-by-post basis. Any content you've posted with a privacy setting of "public" can be seen by anyone who finds that post or your profile - whether that user is one of your "friends" or not. Facebook allows you take that privacy setting a step further by creating specific lists made up individual people you add to each list. (You can add any friend to multiple lists.) Then you can allow or disallow an entire list on any given post. For example - I have a list called "sketchy" - these are people I've friended for a number of different reasons but I don't consider them my actual friends.

Here's how this might work according to content typically posted by parents:

- Posting personal photos of you and your family - assign the privacy setting to each of these individual posts to ONLY a list you could call "Family"; leaving "Acquaintances" or "Sketchies" out.

- Posting a link to the promotion of a local car wash your children are involved in - in this case you might want ONLY your "Family" and "Neighborhood" lists to receive this content, but definitely not your "Sketchy" list.

Remember that if you post anything to your general "Friends" list - you're exposing your content to every single person you've ever friended - even that totally weird guy from high school you mercy-friended because you felt guilty.

Tagging your child or spouse in photos. Any time a photo is posted by a Facebook "Page" [26] the content is easily accessible by anyone whether they have a Facebook profile or not[27]. These images are also Google indexed and may be searched and found via Google Images. Let's say that a local ice cream shop takes a cute photo of your child and uploads it to their Facebook Page. You see the photo and tag yourself and your child, or your spouse, in the photo. You've now successfully made the connection (to the public) of your child's name, your connection to your child, your connection to your spouse, and you've provided a potential gateway to whatever other breadcrumbs of data you're giving out.

This is especially risky with baby photos or any professional photographs posted by the photographer on *their* Facebook Pages. If they tag the parent of the child in the photo, someone who might want to do you harm would have all of the information they need. Plus shoving your newborn into a

---

26 Facebook *Profiles* belong to individuals while *Pages* belong to companies or organizations like schools and businesses.

27 You do not need a Facebook account to access *Facebook Pages*. You will be able to see all of the content as a non-user, you just won't be able to engage with the Page via likes, comments, etc. This means that anyone anywhere can see the content (about your family) posted on any *Facebook Page*.

flower pot is just sad for everyone involved.

Check-ins. "Checking into" a physical location in real life is a relatively common feature in many social media platforms and can take many forms. It's the equivalent of you walking into a local bar and holding up a sign with your name and yelling "I'm HERE!!" Checking-in has the added feature of providing your "friends" (on Facebook) and "followers" (on Instagram, Twitter, etc.) with your current and precise location. But wait, don't forget you're still holding up that sign right. That's great for the creepy guy watching or just a garden variety thief who can go to the Facebook page of that bar and figure out who has just checked-in, because 1)you've just shouted into the universe that you're NOT at home 2)since your profile is associated with your check-in you can be located IRL at the bar and Capt. Creepy can pretend to know you and 3)Gross.

REALITY FROM THE CHILD'S PERSPECTIVE

When an adult first learns about live streaming apps,[28] a disgusted snorting sound closely follows, along with comments related to the monumental hubris involved in broadcasting one's life (or maybe that's just me.) However, we would be missing the much larger and foundational point of how children and young people view assessing personal value; where "personal value" is defined as what "what value do I add to the world and how is that judged?"

Generationally the concept of assessing value based has moved **away** from:

what I identify as my personal shortcomings via introspective[29] self-reflection followed by reputation management (asking myself what I am actively doing which is good and increases good[30] while being

---

28 Live-streaming platforms/apps give users the capability to point a camera at themselves (generally on a cell phone) and broadcast the day-to-day minutiae of their lives to whomever might be watching.

29 Recommended reading: *The Road to Character* by David Brooks. "In The Road to Character, he focuses on the deeper values that should inform our lives. Responding to what he calls the culture of the Big Me, which emphasizes external success, Brooks challenges us, and himself, to rebalance the scales between our "résumé virtues"—achieving wealth, fame, and status—and our "eulogy virtues," those that exist at the core of our being: kindness, bravery, honesty, or faithfulness, focusing on what kind of relationships we have formed."

30 Benjamin Franklin began every single day with the same item at the top of his daily agenda - a simple task - to ask himself "What good shall I do this day?" At the end of each day he asked himself "What good have I done today?"

mindful to represent myself in a way I can be proud of)

and **towards:**

> using a quantified measurement of what **others** think about the content I've posted on social media - where the calculation occurs entirely externally and my sense of personal value is determined by everyone and anyone other than me.

Our children have outsourced their self-esteem to a social media audience and a mathematical algorithm where more always equals better and where niche interests and human values don't translate to amassing numbers as readily as say, a bathroom sexy booty-pop pic or a video of a hamster eating a tiny slice of pizza.

When your child's sense of personal value is derived from the quantifiable value in a new friend/follower/fan (more = better) and they believe whatever they see (lack of media literacy) - we've reached dangerous and risky territory. This is where the boogeymen live - this is what they're counting on. They're counting on the fact that your 12-year-old son is trying to build up his Instagram following or that your 15-year-old daughter is trying to become a famous and well-paid YouTuber extraordinaire. Your children aren't picky. Every "plus one" is equal to every other without any vetting or thought. They don't really look too deeply into who that person "really" is - hey, it's one more subscriber or fan. What difference would it make? If any single follower is equal to any other single follower and your child measures his own personal value and self-esteem on these calculations - your child becomes vulnerable to any influence which seeks to encourage reaching their quantifiable goals even if those influences are graphically violent, hypersexualized, or unkind.

Take one guess where the boogeyman is hanging out? Not in a bar on a Saturday night with other normal adults...he's hanging out on a Minecraft server chatting up your kid.

THE LEAST YOU SHOULD KNOW

Before Digital Era (BD Era) parenting and After Digital Era (AD era) parenting are markedly different in terms of safety risks.

Pornography consumption among children as young as 8 years old differs in terms of intent, cost barrier, and social acceptance.

We are accidentally (and accidentally-on-purpose) complicit as parents when you consider:

- It's easier to NOT parent.
- We may give our children mixed messages and encourage too-young tech exposure, speeding up the pace of childhood.
- Mocking the millennials generation for behaviors we have cultivated and allowed is counterproductive and hypocritical.
- We're raising a generation of 'special snowflake sociopaths'.
- Removing all obstacles from your child's path and reinforcing the presumption of value for instant gratification will have lifelong aftershocks, especially where their education is concerned.
- We need to set an example for our children that there is more value in a life lived largely off of a screen.
- On Facebook the cover photo cannot be kept private, your profile photo and cover photo should never be a photo of your family or children, and you should create "lists" to segment your friends.
- Parents should refrain from both tagging children/spouses in social media posts and checking into public places.

If a child spends an hour or more per day using social media, chances are that the child is using their quantifiable social media outcomes as a calculation of their own personal value.

CONVERSATION STARTERS

Ask your child: Do you ever wonder what happens to all of the information we provide online? Do you ever wonder who can see your Amazon Echo requests or Google searches? If all of your Google searches were printed and handed out to every person you knew would that change your search behavior? Why or why not?

Ask your child: Very few things in life can be considered 100% good or 100% bad. I was searching on YouTube for a repair video and saw some crazy stuff. Has that ever happened to you? Do you think YouTube is mostly good or mostly bad, or what percentages of each? How about Snapchat or Instagram?

Ask your child: If you could choose between working really really hard now for a chance to be considered the best at something by all of your classmates or not working very hard at all for a chance to get a reward just for participating, which would you choose? Have you seen situations like this at school or on a sports team?

ACTION ITEMS

Take a critical view of your home's weaknesses in terms of hackability. First focus on any devices which allow you or others to "enter" your home and are connected via Wi-Fi. For example video baby monitors, Amazon Echo, digital security, or webcams.

Pay attention to the ways that you, your spouse, and other parents give praise to children. How often is that praise actually earned with hard work versus just showing up, or for basic skills or expected behaviors?

The next time you're in a situation where everyone in a group dives for their smartphones to find the answer to a question, pull the breaks and get your friends or family members to try and come up with the answer by discussing it. Can you go at least five minutes before checking to see if you're right?

Do whatever you can to purposely delay gratification with your children by creating rewards and incentives which are earned after an extended amount of time AND effort. Even a request for a snack can be delayed for a few minutes. They won't die while they wait, I promise.

On that next car trip try to pause for at least 30 minutes every few hours for a tech blackout. Use the time to play a memorization or recall game just to get their brains moving. Your teens will pretend to hate it. That's okay. If teenagers don't use up their daily allotment of hate, they turn into goblins.

Go through your own Facebook profile and make sure that your cover photo, profile photo, post privacy settings, tagging, and check-ins all conform to the suggestions in this chapter.

Remember to give yourself a break - parenting is hard.

Chapter 3

BE PROACTIVE

I've been teaching Internet Safety for almost 10 years and have presented to well over three hundred thousand students, parents, and teachers. I have been invited to school districts in the aftermath tech-related suicides and helped law enforcement understand how particular social media platforms and gaming apps are used by predators to attract and lure victims into engaging in risky behaviors. I have taught countless teachers and parents how to identify and address digital issues in their school buildings and their homes.

As a result of witnessing how these situations and their consequences have changed the lives of real families, here are a few truths I want to share with you:

- The digital landscape is in constant flux. Every day brings a new untested variable.
- Your child's digital health is critical to his overall healthy development.
- Constant parental engagement and continuous parent education are the keys to success.

All technology is helpful, right?

The word "technology" is defined, simply, as any tool which increases efficiency. When chimpanzees cleverly use two different types of sticks to increase their ant consumption, they're engaging in technology use. One type of stick angers the ants and the second is used for "ant-dipping." The ants swarm the stick, the chimp pulls out the stick, rubs the ants off in his fingers and then eats them[31]. Until our genetic cousins build "an app for that" they'll keep using the two-stick-ant-mass-murder technology, because it works.

Remember that "increasing efficiency" is required to consider any tool a "technology". So, the ant-dipping process is considered a technology because the two-stick method is infinitely more efficient than trying to eat the ants one-by-one. But perhaps more importantly, ant-dipping fits the "technology" definition because it improves and replaces **a process which was already part of the chimp's life - eating ants**.

This is where the discussion goes off the rails and triggers more questions than answers. The difference between humans using digital tools versus digital tools expanding by using humans - depends upon how well those humans can engage in self-reflection. The blind presumption of increased human efficiency via digital use is at the core of this argument.

In order to understand the impact digital tools have on our lives we will apply the following two criteria to a few of the most popular online websites and services.

1. Does the digital tool increase my level of efficiency? Does it make my life easier? Does it help me complete tasks from my to-do list in a simpler or quicker way?

2. Does this increased efficiency impact a life process I was already engaging in before I began using the digital tool?

There is no doubt that: Facebook[32], Amazon[33], Netflix[34], and Uber[35] are four of

---

31 Möbius, Yasmin, Christophe Boesch, Kathelijne Koops, Tetsuro Matsuzawa, and Tatyana Humle. *"Cultural differences in army ant predation by West African chimpanzees? A comparative study of microecological variables."* Animal Behaviour 76.1 (2008): 37-45.

32 As of the March of 2017 on Alexa's "Most popular websites of 2017" Facebook is the #3 most popular website in the US and the #1 most popular app in the United States. NOTE: Once an independently run web analytics ranking website, Alexa was purchased by Amazon in 1999. The data and the analytics are widely accepted as accurate despite its corporate ownership.

33 As of the March of 2017 on Alexa's *"Most popular websites of 2017"* Amazon is the #1 most

the most used sites/apps/services in the world. In fact, these four appear and reappear within the Top 10 on hundreds of data driven ranking lists. But why? Are we in a collective trance or are these apps and sites really improving our lives in a real way? Using Facebook, Amazon, Netflix, and Uber - let's explore our litmus test.

QUESTION #1: Does the digital tool increase my level of efficiency?

Facebook: No[36]. On so many different levels, no. Can it deliver cat videos, angry political rants by so-called friends, and photos of your neighbor's broken toe posted immediately after a photo of her lunch? Yes, it can do all of those things. Do any of those things increase your efficiency? No.

Amazon: Yes, if you consider the amount of time, gasoline, and effort saved by not leaving your house to shop. Amazon also allows you to create automatically purchased and shipping subscriptions for items you regularly purchase. For example: You could create a purchasing subscription for your monthly vitamin purchase. The efficiency here is obvious - the purchases show up every X number of days without any user intervention. They just show up, precisely when you need them.

Netflix: No. First of all, binge-watching. And let me make it clear - I LOVE NETFLIX - like in an addictive-I-have-issues kind of a way. But does it increase my efficiency? No.

Uber: Yes. There's nothing better than knowing precisely when that car is going to roll up, and what it's going to cost - not to mention the added efficiency of not even needing access to your wallet at the time of the ride. As an Uber user, you pay electronically via the payment you've already chosen in the

popular shopping site in the US, and Nielsen listed the Amazon Shopping App as the 10th most popular app in the US in 2016.

34 As of the March of 2017 on Alexa's "*Most popular websites of 2017*" Alexa shows Netflix as the #9 most popular website in 2017, as well as the #2 most popular ecommerce site in the US

35 Uber is the world's dominant ride hailing app in 107 countries. 'Dominance' was defined by data analysts when an app successfully fit both of the following criteria: 1) an app was the most popular taxi ride app in the country AND 2) a minimum of 1% of the Android devices in that country had already downloaded the app. Source: SimilarWeb.com, a web analytics provider.

36 When Facebook and other social media platforms are used to mobilize people into activism or via community engagement, there is an obvious increase of efficiency - but for the average shlub, this is a big NO.

app. This is a HUGE efficiency.

QUESTION #2 Does the increased efficiency impact a life process I was already engaging in before beginning to use the digital tool?

Facebook: No. Before Facebook you were NOT staying up all night trying to figure out "52 Shocking Ways to Repurpose Your Spouse's Pillow Drool". Before Facebook there was no need for Facebook.

Amazon: Yes. Amazon replaces real-world shopping (and much more).

Netflix: No. Despite the awesome-ness of Netflix - it's not providing any real added efficiency to watching television and movies at our leisure.

Uber: Yes. Uber replaces the need to hail a cab or call and wait for a cab to arrive from their dispatch location. Uber also replaces the need to pay at the time of the ride.

This simple thought experiment reveals a final scorecard of two noes each for Facebook and Netflix and two yeses each for Amazon and Uber. Netflix and Facebook use will not plummet because of my simple analysis - least of all from me personally. However, you regain your power as a consumer just by asking the questions and in the process taking a proactive view of the environmental variables (of which digital devices is just one) which you choose to allow in your life.

Every single act you take as a human is a choice. You make the choice to get out of bed at some un-godly hour to drive your kid to 5am ice time for hockey practice (no thanks). That's a choice you are making. You could choose to **not** do that. (And none of us would blame you.) As users of digital tools living in an increasingly digital world it's easy to forget that we can choose to NOT, or choose to SHUT OFF, or choose to DELETE, just as readily as we can blindly and DOWNLOAD, INSTALL, or ALLOW any single one of these variables to enter your home and your life.

In our most aware trance state we perceive that all digital tools are probably helpful or useful and that they're meant to enhance our lives. At the deepest trance state (aka sheep), there really isn't any thought given at all to the digital tools - we just bump around the digital universe like a ping pong ball bumped along the whim of the artificial intelligence algorithms which manipulate what we view while tracking what we click.

As parents, our own digital behavior will inform our children's digital behavior. If you are the sort of person who always needs to have the latest smartphone and buys every cool digital gadget you see, your children will see value in that behavior and its resulting device acquisition. Your device engagement and purchase behavior reflects a belief that the devices themselves have inherent value independent of its human usefulness.

We need to move away from the "just because it's cool" rationale for engaging with technology, especially when our children are watching. There's nothing wrong with loving tech, I do too. But unless you are a computer engineer, deep engagement in digital tools for their own sake makes absolutely no sense. By blindly presuming that all digital tools are helpful and by believing we're "supposed" to want them, we assign value to the device itself rather than focusing on the improvements and value it might bring to your actual human life and relationships. There's a big difference between waiting all night to be the first in line to get the new iPhone for no apparent reason other than you have to have before everyone else versus waiting all night to be the first in line to get the new GoPro because you and your son are going to start filming every hike you are planning to take this summer.

IT'S NOT MY JOB....

To make life even more infuriating there are countless times when digital tools make our lives significantly more difficult - and for some mind-boggling reason I haven't yet discovered- we're okay with it, or maybe we're all just sleepwalking. So here's your wakeup call.

A few months ago I took one of my children to the doctor for a well visit. The appointment had been made 6 months prior (by me on an app). We walked into the lobby and a staff person flagged us down and ushered us into the check-in area. Then we were directed by a second human to a digital kiosk so that I could "check myself in". I looked at the kiosk, I looked at my daughter, then I looked at the woman behind the counter and I said "No". I felt my daughter sigh in an audible manifestation of dread.

Woman behind the counter: *(looking at me confused)* "I'm sorry?"

Me: *(A bit louder)* "I said No.... No, I'm NOT doing this...No, I'm not checking myself in."

Woman: *(in her best talking-to-a-preschooler voice)* "Oh, it's quite easy, I know that the technology can seem scary, but it's very easy"

Daughter: *(sigh/moan reaching DefCom 7 level)*

Me: "I'm not 'afraid of the technology' *(including finger air quotes).* See the thing is: I DON'T WORK HERE. You, however DO work here. And since I don't work here, I would like for YOU to check me in."

Daughter: "MooooooooooooM" *(Translation : Imagine the sound a moose would make if he were just like chillin' in the woods and suddenly found himself on the receiving end of an angry and unexpected rectal exam.)*

It wasn't the digital kiosk per se that made my fragile psyche snap; it's the presumption that technology in all things and in all places can only be an improvement. It's the expectation that a company or service provider tells us to use a machine and we just do it, no questions asked. It's our willingness to just enter personal information onto a screen, just because someone told us to. It's the assumption that as consumers we're morons - because we kind of are morons.

I love technology. But not when it's used to dumb down the masses into thinking we're improving our own lives, when actually we're just getting scammed into increasing a company's bottom line at no financial or actual benefit to ourselves. Consider the following:

- When I go to the airport I print off my own parking tag, then use a kiosk to check myself in at the specific airline and print off my own baggage claim check - followed closely by stripping half-way down and taking my baggage apart for security. If I'm lucky there will be NO human intervention requiring digging around my under-carriage for the sake of "security" because everyone knows that there's nothing more dangerous than a ticking flapdragon.
- Most major cities allow me to pay for a parking meter with a credit card at a street kiosk - removing the need for a human to go around and collect cash from the meters. The "expired" meters send out a signal to the parking police reducing the time and staff required to patrol those meters.
- At the grocery store I check out my own groceries and bag them myself.
- Most big box retailers provide self-serve stations all over the store so that I can run my own price checks.

How stupid have we become as consumers? The self-serve "conveniences" of I-can-just-do-this-quicker-myself is a giant scam on consumers with two typical outcomes:

- As a consumer, **you** do the job which a paid employee would normally do, effectively increasing the company's profits earned on the back of **your** time and energy. When you check out your own groceries, you are allowing the grocery store to hire less people and make more money.
- When the day comes that you need assistance in a retail store, there's no one around to help because so much of the staff has been made redundant by technology.

If you have strong opinions about the high levels of unemployment in your community but willingly use and contribute to the proliferation of self-serve digital devices, stop complaining about the unemployment rate, because it's partly your fault. When given the chance, say 'no'to the so-called tech conveniences. Use the self-serve digital kiosks and checkout machines only when it is a convenience for **you**. And say 'no' when it isn't. Bring on the revolution!

CURRENT STATE OF THE UNION

We are all digital citizens whether or not we choose to fly the flag or sing the national anthem. Even if you are the most stubborn of all the Luddites, or you refer to the microwave as that "dagnabbit contraption"... like it or not you are living in a digital world.

Your local print newspaper is getting thinner and thinner. Some print dailies have died altogether only to be reborn as online-only versions. Your doctor probably stores your medical records in digital form. An email alert sends you the results of your child's strep test and the data gets added to your family's online medical profile. Depending on your car's manufacturer, your smartphone is capable of coordinating communication between your calendar, the airport, and your car. You may even receive an alert offering to start your car's engine the moment that your plane lands at the airport.

It doesn't matter how you feel about it, the day has arrived. In many ways, the data which represent our lives, are being condensed down to file-size. Digital is everywhere - and it's a global phenomenon. Consider this:

- More people in the world have a mobile phone, than a toilet.
- More people in the world have a mobile phone than access to clean

drinking water

These statistics sound like the punch line to a late-night comedian's joke which begins with a lead-in about some poor guy in a poverty stricken nation looking for water who posts his discontent on his Twitter timeline.

#WTH #ThereWasJustAPuddleHereYesterday

It would be funny except that it's true. There are people in the developing world without access to a reliable source of clean water[37] and sanitation, who do have access to mobile phones. And yes, the argument can be made that launching satellites[38] and mobile towers is far more sustainable and logistically simpler than digging and installing hundreds of thousands of miles of pipe to bring water to the hundreds of millions who need it globally. Moreover, there is tremendous value in bringing Internet access to every corner of the world when that access brings content, education, and connection which adds to human life rather than detracting from it.

The list of opportunities which make ubiquitous internet access overwhelmingly valuable to humanity is the same list which creates the digital risks inside of your own home. We stand on the crest of the perfect storm due to the almost complete lack of barriers to entry in becoming a part of the global digital society.

- You can purchase a phone at any point in the cost spectrum
- Cell towers and satellites cover most of the planet (except that one pesky corner of your kitchen)
- Devices are fairly simple to use

These statistics and the massive scale they illustrate should not surprise us. They reflect our own behavior in the smallest and most mundane daily scenarios. Connection to our mobile phones is a connection to our actual lives both real and digital.

A frequent criticism of the digital age is that people have become increasingly isolated. While it's true that isolation and connection are choices we make as humans, it is also true that immersive overuse of digital devices

---

37 If you would like to become involved in this incredibly worthy cause go to Water.org.

38 In fact, satellite and tech company extraordinaire OneWeb has committed to bringing Internet access to every single unconnected school on the planet by 2022 and to "fully bridge the Digital Divide by 2027, making Internet access available and affordable for everyone," by launching over 2,600 satellites. Learn more here www.OneWeb.world

encourages more immersive overuse of digital devices. It's a hamster wheel, and you're the hamster. Computer engineers, guided by behavioral psychologists create user scenarios (customized just for you) in which you will feel compelled to click, comment, share, and like. The addictive features of bait and reward are all there.

This is where parenting comes in. As parents, we have to be the guard dog at the gate rather than throwing our hands up and blaming it on the device we purchased or the app we allowed the child to use in the first place.

It's disingenuous, at best, to blame our social isolation on digital devices. It's our own fault. We are willing participants in a digital world where we can't find a single silent or stimuli-free space. Phone calls from work when you are off the clock, Facebook updates from friends which expect your supportive involvement and a constant barrage of notifications about: the weather, a movie premiere, a celebrity death, or news stories about the latest tragedy. It's all out there and it's all pounding on our doors waiting to be let in. And we choose whether to fling the doors wide open, slam them shut, or find some livable point in between.

If you feel as though your children constantly have their heads bent over a glowing screen in a mindless trance, you are not alone. This is the reality in most homes and cities around the world with little connection to affluence, culture, or geography. Although owning digital devices presupposes one's economic ability to purchase them we've already seen that the vast majority of humans on the planet own at least one digital device. And in most cases that one device is a mobile phone.

Your child is a "digital native", rather than his "digital immigrant" parents. Digital natives have never known a world without digital immersion. Their reality and their brain structures have been changing to accommodate this new environment. Consider for a moment that the typical 21-year-old entering the workforce has consumed (on average) 5,000 hours of video game playing, 250,000: emails, instant messages, and texts, 10,000 hours of cell phone use and 3,500 hours of time online. As our current generation of toddlers grows into their young adult years, those numbers will rise dramatically. They don't notice their full immersion any more than fish realize that they are surrounded by water. Similarly, our children do not realize that they are digital natives. Amidst their total immersion, they cannot see the distinction between "real world" and "technology".

A modern K-12 education requires and expects your children to use digital skills for their education. Kindergarteners are using iTouch devices in the classroom to drill math facts and play phonics games. Unsurprisingly, when teachers introduce a new app, students do not need an explanation of how to click or where to go next. Even our youngest children instinctively understand the concept of tapping a screen to exact a desired response.

Starting in elementary school, children are expected to engage with technology when completing homework assignments and projects. Younger students might simply be required to bring in a printed copy of a digital photo. Digital literacy expectations rise as they get older. Your third grader might be expected to begin engaging in simple online research. In middle school and high school, your children will be expected to become savvy and critical consumers of digital content and collaborate in teams in creating multimedia projects.

Don't confuse your child's uncanny ability to figure out how to use a smartphone with the specific digital skills and competencies they will need to be successful in a 21st century digital classroom. The School Librarian (a teacher who has a Master's degree in Library Sciences or its equivalent) is singularly equipped to teach all of these skills, preparing them for a lifetime of effective critical thinking. Unfortunately, most schools do not have the requisite time or staff (aka the School Librarian) to effectively teach students how to be successful in this area.

In fact, there is a new staffing and facilities trend in K-12 buildings across the country which is particularly worrisome. It makes me violently queasy to watch schools diminish the role of the School Librarian and indeed the school library itself. Some schools no longer have credentialed librarians (and yes it matters, quite a lot). They've been replaced with warm bodies who can check out books and read stories to the little ones (a job which could be successfully completed by a 4th grader). Then there are the schools libraries which have been emptied of many or most of the actual books (remember those??) and replaced[39] with "maker areas" filled with 3D printers and empty study areas. This is absolutely maddening. Put simply, critical thinking =

---

39 PS I have no issue with 3D printers and open study areas. Bring it on! But which mouth-breathing simpleton decided that there is an educative equivalency between books/critical thinking expertise and "maker areas"? These two are not interchangeable any more than divorcing George Clooney to marry a well sharpened pencil instead. Are you a school administrator thinking about getting rid of your: library, books, or (actual) librarian, in order to make room for something else like 3D printers? Here's an idea, stab yourself repeatedly in the foot with that sharpened pencil until the feeling passes. Hey, you can just 3D print yourself a new foot.

education. A well-stocked school library and a credentialed School Librarian are absolutely CRITICAL to the complete education of our children. If you see this trend brewing in your school fight it with every bit of energy you have. It matters.

In the absence of an actual critical thinking curriculum delivered by an educator who really comprehends critical thinking, students are expected to "just know how" to complete online research for assignments, vet content sources critically, and use photos and content responsibly. Parents lack the digital skills needed to process the firehose of content (accurate, inaccurate, irrelevant, and biased) provided by a basic Google search.

This is where the educational gap widens between where a child's digital skills are expected to be versus where they actually are. Unless you are relatively tech savvy, this could prove to be a significant area of risk for your child's academic future. If you find yourself at a deficit in this area, accompany your child to the local library and ask a librarian to teach you how to use online tools for academic research.

Do you remember taking standardized tests and filling out the paper bubble sheets with a pencil? Do you remember pencils? The 2015-2016 school year hit a tipping point in computer based standardized testing versus paper based testing; for the first time the majority of states[40] were delivering K-8 standardized testing via a computer screen versus paper and pencil. Computer based testing presupposes that students possess higher than average digital skills: the critical assessment of content by choosing a valid fact source, copying and pasting content from the web while completing an essay, citing those sources, and using digital tools to manipulate text. All of the exact tools I need to write this book, and precisely the digital skills your child has never learned.

Before I get to the data I need to take a break for a personal Public Service Announcement:

I HATE computer based standardized testing. HATE HATE HATE.

Why does my eye-twitch at the mere mention of computer based standardized testing? Here's the short list:

---

40 *"Pencils Down: The Shift to Online & Computer Based Testing"* Ed Tech Strategies November 5, 2015.

- Students have wildly varying digital skills, impacting their ability to complete the exam within the time frame - meaning that 'paper versus computer' has an impact on scores- defying the very definition of the word *standardized.*
- Children who suffer from test anxiety may feel that the computer version is an "unknown variable" which is the worst possible scenario for managing test anxiety.
- There are entire communities who don't have consistent access to the exact device which will be used on test day - undoubtedly impacting test confidence and scores.
- When a student uses paper they have the ability to actively work, think, and take notes on top of the paper questions. They can use standard testing strategies like: underlining important words in the question ("despite", "majority", "list 4 causes"), marking parts of a reading comprehension paragraph which might be important later, and crossing off answer choices in the process of elimination. None of these comprehension and testing skills can be implemented on a screen.

But hey, maybe I'm just being too picky (not the first time I've heard that, thanks). Maybe the data coming OUT of the computer based tests will be the same or even better than the paper and pencil version of the test. Since these kids play video games all day and scroll through Instagram all day, maybe, the computer testing will enhance their outcomes. Um, NO.

In 2005, The National Center for Education Statistics set out to examine the data resulting from an experimental computer based test versus paper based test scenario. The pool of students took the exact same test/assessment in either paper or computer format. The eighth graders who took their math assessment on paper had "significantly" better results than the students who took the same exact assessment on a computer screen. Not surprising at all.

Similar disparities between paper versus computer testing resulted from the 2014-2015 national PARCC exams. In this case, the data was not generated in an experimental environment but from the actual national testing of students. The PARCC data showed a more pronounced difference in computer versus paper outcomes in both Language Arts and middle and high school math assessments. In Illinois[41] for example 32% of high school students

---

41 *"PARCC Scores Lower for Students Who Took Exams on Computers"* by Benjamin Herold,

who took the PARCC Language Arts assessment scored "proficient" versus 50% of the students who took the same exam on paper. These are not small differences.

The anticipation of the arrival of state-mandated computer based standardized testing is a big reason why many school districts have begun implementing 1:1 (One-to-One) Technology Programs which provide each student with a dedicated device for their academic use. A well-planned and well-executed 1:1 program can do wonders for a child's education and there are almost endless ways to make it a relevant and exciting part of the student's education. However, if the device is merely being used as a replacement for paper and pencil, then what's the point? The entire 1:1 implementation has to justify use of the device by using our criteria for app engagement earlier in this chapter: Does it increase the student's efficiency while replacing a less efficient way of completing a task?

As with any new technology there will be unintended consequences from implementing a 1:1 program which could never have been predicted in the absence of quantifiable data outcomes. One of the most definitive negative consequences comes from paper note taking versus screen note taking. (Guess which one wins?) If you walk into any university lecture hall you will see students typing out notes on a computer screen while the professor lectures. Sounds like it would be way more efficient, but hold on. It turns out that the exact opposite is true. Multiple studies have shown results similar to the study done by Mueller[42] and Oppenheimer in 2014 which showed that when students use a keyboard to take notes that they may be "impairing learning because [laptop] use results in shallower processing." In fact, three separate studies showed that students who typed out their notes tended to merely transcribe everything heard versus processing the information and reframing it into their own words - which is critical to the learning process. Even when students were warned against not transcribing verbatim notes, the results remained the same: as compared to the pen note takers, the typists has "worse" results on recall[43] based test questions and "significantly worse" results on conceptually[44] based

Education Week, Feb 3, 2016.

42 *"The Pen is Mightier Than the Keyboard: Advantages of Longhand Over Laptop Note Taking"*, Pam A Mueller, Daniel M. Oppenheimer, 2014, Psychological Science

43 Recall questions as for basic memorization of dates or names.

44 Conceptual questions require a student to compare or analyze data such as "How do Japan and Sweden differ in their approaches to equality within their societies?"

test questions.

There can be enormous value in using tech in the classroom - when lessons are developed mindfully and safeguards are implemented consistently. A largely digital future requires an army of digital workers. We need the computers, we need the programs, and we need the programmers. Despite what sci-fi movies might claim, the machines are not yet ready to take over. For the foreseeable future, humans will be required to imagine, create, program, and maintain a new generation of digital systems. Our children need to be educated in order to become those digital workers. But until they get there, it's up to us to supervise the process in their lives and in our homes.

It is uncommon to find a home that has zero web access, even if just via a smartphone. Therefore, the digital aspect of your child's life demands some sort of parent-imposed structure and acceptable-use rules. Just remember that your rules only extend to the end of your driveway. Your child may be clear on the "no YouTube without parent supervision" rule, but does that rule apply when he's playing at Bobby's house as well? It is well worth the effort to try to build consensus among your parent community. Invite other parents over for a cup of coffee or glass(es) of wine to discuss your agreed upon rules. Getting together as a group of parents sends a united message to your child's friend group.

HEALTHY DEVELOPMENT OF CHILDREN

My student audiences are a practical road map of healthy child development gone astray at the hands of immersive and constant tech use. Whether it affects the day-to-day management of child life (ie. bedtimes are extended or obliterated because of all-night bedroom device usage), the normalization of hyper-sexualized content (via so-called "family channel" programming or via covert pornography consumption) - our children bear the scars of these artificially placed obstacles to healthy development.

Imagine that you notice that your child keeps scratching his wrist. You ask to see what he's scratching, and he shows you a big red, raw patch of skin. What do you do? You probably begin asking questions: Do you remember bumping it? Were you outside? Where outside? What were you doing when you first noticed it? Does it hurt or just itch?

This is basic parent triage. You are trying to figure out the trigger of the itch by ruling out some variables and including others. As you get down past the obvious ones (soap allergy- no, bug bite - no) you go to the more unlikely choices (allergy to a neighbor's pet?). You start with the data you know and get down to the root cause. At the end the complete solution might be: poison ivy, topical medication, no more playing in that part of the yard until we remove all of the poison ivy. It would be a mistake to just determine that it was poison ivy and provide the anti-itch cream without removing the actual cause. If you don't remove the massive patch of poison ivy in your backyard all you've done is temporarily solved a problem which will undoubtedly keep happening.

Your child's device use needs to become a part of your child's health triage. When a child spends a significant amount of time focused on a screen you have to view the device as an environmental variable (positive, negative, or neutral) in all facets of their well-being. Especially when the symptom of excessive tech usage comes disguised as something seemingly unrelated.

We can all bear witness to a child's changed behavior as a result of not having slept enough. In the toddler years, a missed nap could mean the derailment of your entire adult evening. The need for quality sleep continues throughout their development and well through the high school years. It's not a genius deduction to guess that a child who is falling asleep at school needs more rest - and chances are that teachers and coaches are noticing your child's sluggish demeanor. Finding the cause for that lack of sleep, however, is the "itchy wrist" triage scenario all over again. You notice your daughter is falling asleep at the breakfast table (itchy wrist), you determine that the trigger is lack of sleep (poison ivy - not too difficult). However, it isn't enough to send her to bed at an earlier time if you've still allowed her to take her phone with her into her room. You've let her continue to have access to our metaphorical patch of poison ivy in the yard. The phone is still in the bedroom and the lack of sleep will undoubtedly continue.

However, lack of sleep in particular can manifest in ways which would seem to point to a much larger or complex cause. Adolescents who get insufficient sleep and/or poor quality sleep: are far more likely to engage in increased risk taking behaviors[45], are positively related to delinquency because

---

45 Telzer, Eva H., Andrew J. Fuligni, Matthew D. Lieberman, and Adriana Galván. *"The effects of poor quality sleep on brain function and risk taking in adolescence."* NeuroImage 71 (2013): 275-283.

of the connection to lack of self-control (interestingly regardless of parenting practices and neighborhood impacts)[46], impact their own ability to learn, pay attention, and process emotional inputs[47].

Imagine, for a moment that the scenario described above were to continue to a critical point. Our imaginary daughter continues to impact her waking life by getting insufficient and poor quality sleep - despite mom and dad sending her to bed earlier (but allowing the continued 24-7 access to her phone). Soon enough those potential negative outcomes could deteriorate to a crisis point and any combination of: increased delinquency, lack of self-control, diminishing ability to focus and remain attentive, and worsening emotional processing.

Now the scenario has changed. As the imaginary parent faced with addressing these new and worsening child behaviors, it might make sense to engage a physician or mental health professional for help. Very few, if any, of those medical professionals will begin their assessment by asking "How much and how well are you sleeping?" And far fewer of those adolescent "patients" will admit to staying up all night surfing Instagram. Medical professionals might provide a psychiatric referral for the "acting out" behaviors. Mental health professionals might prescribe medications. All of this medical, school, and parental intervention and we still haven't removed the metaphorical poison ivy patch from the backyard.

There are many other digital parenting issues to contend with besides sleep deprivation. The point is this: When your child spends a significant amount of time on a screen, that screen has now become a variable of his environment and we need to take a bottom-up approach to figure out how it might be impacting his health and development. The ideal scenario is one where you don't wait for the itch to happen before you triage the environment. This approach requires you to ask core questions about who you are as a family, what you believe to be true, and how your home and life ought to be mindfully arranged as a result.

---

46 Meldrum, Ryan C., J. C. Barnes, and Carter Hay. *"Sleep Deprivation, Low Self-Control, and Delinquency: A Test of the Strength Model of Self-Control."* Journal of Youth and Adolescence 44.2 (2013): 465-77.

47 Tarokh, Leila, Jared M. Saletin, and Mary A. Carskadon. *"Sleep in adolescence: Physiology, cognition and mental health."* Neuroscience & Biobehavioral Reviews 70 (2016): 182-88.

CHANGING LANDSCAPE OF RISKS

Since the first edition of this book the landscape of risks has expanded into new areas and deepened in old ones. All of these risks can be categorized into two simple buckets: access and time. For example, device use has increased and much younger children own a personal and dedicated device as young as two or three years old. The fact that a two year old has access to a device increases his risk level. The cleanest way to minimize risk is to minimize access as much as humanly possible. When the child does have access, then limiting the amount of time they remain on the device is the second best way to minimize risk. Delay access, minimize time.

All of the old risks still exist and perpetrators are getting more and more sophisticated by using technology in new and novel ways. There have been solved and unsolved cases of sexual predators using GPS to locate victims, sexting is still happening in all of the same places plus kids are using vault apps to hide their porn without getting caught, SD cards can hold thousands of images and are used by both kids and sexual predators to hide content, cloud storage apps (like DropBox) are used by both kids and sexual predators to hide and share content, etc.

New cootie categories abound. Here are just a few:

Wi-fi enabled devices such as the Amazon Echo, home surveillance systems, and interactive dolls and toys (with data gathering artificial intelligence) which we willingly purchase provide the opportunity for would-be hackers to break into those devices - and then exploit the access into our homes and our data.

Wi-fi enabled personal devices like fitness bands which are Bluetooth (wirelessly) connected to our smartphones. These can provide a "weakest link" scenario when travelling through an airport for example. A hacker would need far less time to successfully hack into your fitness band, versus directly hacking your smartphone, which would then provide backdoor access into your smartphone.

The popularity of Augmented Reality (AR) video games like Pokemon GO will continue to grow by adding a hologram-esque digital aspect to the real world. We will see the expansion of these offerings into consumer applications (think: HGTV wallpaper superimposed on your wall). Microsoft's

Hololens[48] is the leader in this space.

Virtual reality apps and devices do the opposite of augmented reality by bringing the user into the virtual world. These games and VR in general should not be used by children because of the neural consequences both known and unknown. (And by the way, the #1 category of visited content while wearing VR glasses is pornography, because of course it is.) The Samsung Gear VR has been the frontrunner in VR category.

Digital cameras can be anywhere and where you least expect them. Camera fashion accessories are a new trend like SnapChat's Spectacles[49] - a pair of sunglasses with a small video camera on the glasses which automatically uploads videos to your SnapChat account of whatever you're looking at.

In an effort to capture as much of your online time as possible, social media apps are spending more of their time and money into building psychometric models which analyze your mile high pile of click data (where you clicked, when you clicked, how often you clicked) in order to use predictive analysis to guess what you will do next. Then they will sell your predictable eyeball behavior to the advertiser who pays the most.

PARENTAL ENGAGEMENT & EDUCATION

New apps and social media platforms spring up daily making it exhausting and confusing work to try and keep up. You need to accept that this education is required and valuable[50]. I am often asked to speak to someone's spouse (or worse ex-spouse) in an attempt to convince the unwilling party that their child requires some level of digital limitation or discipline. My answer is always the same: if your ex-wife doesn't think there is an issue, and doesn't see value in this process, there's nothing else to be said[51].

---

48 *Microsoft HoloLens: Mixed Reality Blends Holograms with the Real World,* YouTube video https://www.youtube.com/watch?v=Ic_M6WoRZ7k

49 SnapChat Spectacles https://www.spectacles.com/

50 If you don't believe and embrace the truth that engaging in your child's digital safety is necessary and valuable, please give this book to someone else. Don't waste your time.

51 After a parent presentation, a father of an elementary student asked for a private word. His frustration and anxiety were obvious in his demeanor. Despite repeated conversations with his ex-wife and mutual agreements that their 10-year-old would NOT be given a smartphone, mom purchased the phone anyway. Dad was having a hard time enforcing the tech rules during the times that the child was in his custody because mom didn't enforce the rules at her house. According to dad, mom would not hold to the subsequent agreements of forbidden apps, hours of usage, etc. I asked Dad what he thought would happen if the phone accidentally fell into the washing machine.

I've been a developer and programmer for the past 20 years. I've personally worked and advocated for 1:1 technology programs at school districts. Your children need technology for their education and in order to participate effectively in an expanding digital landscape. Do not give up on technology. Do not throw out the baby with the digital bathwater. There are ways to incorporate technology into your family life safely and mindfully without letting it take over.

But this digital parenting process kind of sucks. Education is the only option. It's time-consuming and you might not be a techy person and it's hard, but it is what it is. It's another thing you are going to have to do and success means showing up consistently. We need to keep showing up and learning and engaging with our kids. Can you do it? Of course you can. Remaining one step ahead is the only chance we have of crossing this minefield alive. Don't give up now.

#BeFierceBeUnafraid

He just blinked at me several times before saying "She'll buy another one?" I replied "What if the second one fell into the toilet, accidentally of course? How many phones need to accidentally die in your home before they stop being purchased?" He smiled and said "I'm going to guess two." Alrighty then. (P.S. Proceed at your own risk.)

THE LEAST YOU SHOULD KNOW

Don't presume that all technology is helpful or will improve your life.

The definition of technology requires that the digital tool increases your efficiency and that the efficiency impacts a life process you were already engaging in before using the digital tool.

Our digital engagement is a choice we make. The depth and breadth of our children's digital engagement is also a choice we make.

Digital engagement for its own sake is mindless sheep behavior.

When you encounter self-serve digital kiosks in stores, at the doctor's office, and at the airport - refuse to use them unless you personally derive a benefit. Say no when it doesn't.

There are people in the developing world without access to a reliable source of clean water and sanitation that do have access to mobile phones.

Isolation and connection are choices we make as humans. It is also true that immersive overuse of digital devices encourages more immersive overuse of digital devices. It's a hamster wheel and you're the hamster.

Your child is a *digital native* you are a *digital immigrant.*

A modern K-12 education requires and expects your children to use digital skills for their education. Most schools do not have the time and staff to effectively teach children how to be effective in this area.

Many schools are diminishing the role of school libraries and credentialed school librarians this is a massive lack of judgment on the school's part.

High stakes standardized tests are migrating to a computer-based format from paper and pencil. The data resulting from completed computer-based testing shows that students tend to do better on the paper and pencil version.

Paper and pencil note-takers learn and retain more than keyboard note-takers.

Your child's digital device is a part of his environment and should be considered a variable impacting his health.

When you take a critical view of your family digital environment, build and safeguards, and create a proactive philosophy about choosing which digital activities and tools to adopt - you take control of your family's digital health.

There are new and expanding digital risks including Wi-Fi enabled devices like the Amazon Echo, augmented reality games and apps, virtual reality games and devices, and the expansion of psychometric analysis which helps tech companies design highly addictive environment tailored to individual users.

The only complete solution to digital health is Parental education and engagement

CONVERSATION STARTERS

Ask your child: I find that one minute seems to fly by when I'm on Facebook, do you find that time goes by faster when you're online? Why do you think that is?

Ask your child: Which social platforms do you like best? Why? Which platforms are the most popular at school? *Note: this is not the time to reprimand your child for having a social app you didn't approve of. First hear what he/she has to say and then remind them to please check with you first.*

Ask your child: Do different platforms represent different parts of your life? For example: Do most of your sports friends hang out on Twitter versus your friends from school?

Ask your child: Did you know that in some parts of the world, people have mobile phones but don't have access to water or sanitation? What do you think about that?

Ask your child: If our entire community lost power for an entire week, how would that change the ways in which you communicate and connect with your friends? Would that bother you? *Note: Listen intently for even a subtle message of relief in this answer. It might be an indication that your child is eager to take a step back from the digital madness, but doesn't know how.*

ACTION ITEMS

Take some time to review your own personal digital use and apply the two main efficiency questions. Which ones should stay in your life? Which ones should go?

Refuse to use self-serve and digital kiosks as much as you possibly can. Let's start a revolution!

Speak to the administrators at your child's school. Have a conversation about the dangers of diminishing the role of libraries, credentialed Librarians, and the foundational need for teaching students practical media literacy skills.

If you do not understand the basics of online research begin here: *Librarian's Guide to Online Searching*, 3rd edition by Suzanne Bell

Contact your local school administrators and ask when/if online standardized testing will come to your state or school. Ask about the availability of devices within the district to accommodate all test subjects. If there is a shortage of devices, students will need to be tested in shifts; this means that some students may be tested far earlier or later than others.

Make sure that your children are taking notes in class with paper and pencil rather than by typing them verbatim on a keyboard.

Make a list of any devices which are wi-fi enabled in your home as a mode of communication between the inside of your home and an outside source, like an Amazon Echo or a home security system. These connections can provide a backdoor entry to would-be hackers.

Chapter 4

MEDIA LITERACY

There's a hilarious and horrifyingly accurate television commercial where a beautiful young woman is meeting up with a supposed French model she has only communicated with online. The man who turns up to meet her is clearly past his prime, overweight, sloppy, and is sporting a decidedly unsophisticated fanny pack. Even after seeing the man in real life the young woman remains undaunted - still believing that he's a French model because she "read it on the internet."

Like most comedy, what makes this particular punchline so funny is the underlying truth. At some point, if only for a moment, we have all been duped by an online hoax or an absurd claim. However, extending that single comical truth (in this case: internet=truth) to imply that the product itself holds any merit (in this case: therefore buy insurance from our company) is one presumption too far. A well-delivered punch line does not confer credibility.

As adults, we have honed our critical thinking skills as a result of our inevitable and repeated experience that products (and people) tend to fall woefully short of their promise. We understand at some primal level that those commercials and those messages are total garbage. I mean, we do, don't we? Well, yes and no.

Yes, we do get it, during these intentional conversations which require analysis. If we break down the billowy curtains, the unsexy fanny pack, and the beautifully packaged guilt trips which can only be assuaged by buying **this** product - then yes, we get it and it's obvious. We see it when we choose to be mindful, when we choose to question, and when we choose to refuse to be someone else's pawn.

And no, we don't really get it. When the messages are coming from multiple sources and devices at a rapid-fire pace it can be easy to get sucked in. Our always-on 24-hour cable news environment has exacerbated this already accelerating rate of mindless acceptance. But even on our best, sharpest, and most mindful day we might still be duped by our personal biases and knee-jerk positions.

Do you find that cable news stations are biased against your political beliefs? You might be experiencing what some researchers call the "hostile media effect[52]."Researchers found that if your political beliefs lean decidedly in one direction (significantly conservative or liberal for example) that you will be more likely to identify media bias which benefits the opposite side. In other words, let's say you self-identify as a conservative - when presented with a purposely unbiased news story it's quite likely that you will find some bias against your position. It gets even more interesting when you consider that when your liberal counterparts watch the same exact news story - it's quite likely that they will find bias against their own liberal position. Neutral participants in the study also provided feedback which placed them (just like their self-identified positions) right in the middle of either end of the spectrum; they saw the unbiased news story as neutral. The implication here is clear; your personal bias or lack of bias will be supported by your equally biased perception of the content you consume.

Complicating the "truth" landscape even further is our accidental belief that algorithmic truth = truth. It doesn't. An algorithm by definition is any systematic (or programmatic) process for solving a particular type of

---

52 Vallone, Robert P., Lee Ross, and Mark R. Lepper. *"The hostile media phenomenon: Biased perception and perceptions of media bias in coverage of the Beirut massacre."* Journal of Personality and Social Psychology 49.3 (1985): 577-85.

mathematical problem. Algorithms power satellites and run power plants, they run our lives. They are the reason that Netflix knows which movies to suggest for you versus your husband. Google is Google because of its highly honed highly specific algorithm.

Even Amazon seems to really "get you" when it says "Hey Suzie, people who bought that cat mug also really liked these snarky and smart cat t-shirts." That's when you blush because Amazon is clearly in love with the real you, the inner crazy-cat-lady-you. Before you decide you're going to run down the beach towards Amazon with your arms outstretched in a slowly drawn out sunset romantic montage with Yo-Yo Ma on cello playing in the background, just know - it's not love, it's just math. "But wait," you say.... "stop crushing my dreams....Amazon anticipates my every need, it understands what I love....it seeeeees my soul." Yeah okay, slow down Suzie.

The Amazon algorithm is adaptive to you specifically. The more you use it, the more it learns about you, specifically. It records your every click, every product you search, how long you spend on each product, which ones you buy and which ones you don't, which e-books you've purchased, which ones you've read - and on which page you stopped reading. Then it lays all of that data over the data from every other Amazon user, ever. Amazon predicts what you might like, based on your accumulated data and the probability that you're similar to other people with the same weirdo idiosyncrasies.

WHAT IS MEDIA?

For the purposes of our discussion, I am defining "media" as informational and entertainment content in all its forms regardless of delivery system. The idea of informational content has existed since the printing press was invented in the 1400s. Any written, photographic, video graphic, or audio content is considered "media." How you receive that content is where this discussion really begins.

If you receive a printed newspaper at your home or office, the paper itself is the delivery system. Now consider that you can choose to receive your copy of the New York Times online. In fact, you could print off a copy of a particular article and end up on paper even though you started out via a digital interface. Or, you can choose to download the audio version of the New York Times via Amazon or Audible. In addition, you can follow specific stories, or indeed the entire publication, via social media by following the New York

Times page on Facebook (where you are instantly rewarded with public commentary of the content - both sane and astoundingly unhinged.) But wait there's more....you can also follow @NYTimes on Twitter where you can gather pieces of New York Times articles - 140 characters at a time.

The actual media in this example is the content of the article - the words and the images. The delivery system is the variable which complicates the consumption of its raw content.

DIGITAL CONSUMPTION REQUIRES MEDIA LITERACY SKILLS

Media literacy is the ability to analyze and evaluate[53] media messages. In this way, media literacy (as a skill set) is a very large subset of the larger category of "critical thinking." Media literacy is critical thinking applied to media consumption.

My "Don't Be a Sheep[54]" student presentation begins with a lesson on media literacy. It sounds counterintuitive to begin an internet safety presentation with a study of media messages rather than the more typical dangers associated with internet safety like cyberbullying or sexting. However, much like the sheep that follow each other off of a cliff - our children confuse trends with personal mandates. Peer pressure requires your child participate in an online world where everything they see is believed to be true.

Development of our critical thinking skills demands that we continuously ask ourselves the following two questions when considering any point of fact:

- Is it true?
- How do you know?

The path to a safer digital life for your family is paved in skepticism. Push your children to prove to you and them **why** they think something is true and **how** they know that thing to be true. Cultivating a healthy sense of skepticism helps to both encourage curiosity in your child as well as encouraging application of the skills when it comes time to question if that unknown person on their Minecraft server might not really be a 13-year-old who lives nearby, but rather

---

53 Some definitions of media literacy include the ability to create and access in addition to evaluation and analysis. For the purposes of our discussion here I will focus on the evaluation and analysis of messages being consumed by K-college audiences.

54 Why "sheep?" Did you ever wonder why sheep in particular require some guy with a stick or an entire army of dogs to herd them? Because they're stupid. Read the story of a sheep who decided to take a header off a cliff and was followed by 1500 of his sheep buddies (while their Turkish shepherds stopped for breakfast) . A total of 450 sheep died, decimating the local sheep farming community.   http://usatoday30.usatoday.com/news/offbeat/2005-07-08-sheep-suicide_x.htm

an adult posing as a child in order to gain their trust.

During the media literacy portion of my student presentation, we begin by analyzing advertisements aimed at their young demographic and their wallets. We explore questions like:

- If Abercrombie and Fitch sell clothing why are their ads filled with primarily naked models?
- If you are a young man who wears Axe body spray, will half-naked angels really come hurtling across the cosmos just to smell you? Does the transgalactic travel make the angel's clothes fall off, or is it just the Axe?
- If you are a young lady, teen and fashion focused magazines presume that your singular role in life is to find a man and only by wielding a cartoonishly perfect body, hair, nails, and face, will you successfully keep him[55]. Is that true?
- Will that mascara really make your lashes SO long that you could dust the ceiling fans just by tossing your head backward and blinking? Or should we pay far more attention to the fine print right on the screen which clearly states "Model is wearing fake eyelashes?"

After these discussions, the students don't miss a beat, and you can feel the veil being lifted. It's extraordinary to see the transformation in children who just a moment prior had never given a thought to the hidden and manipulative messages in mass media.

Until that moment, these 12 to 18-year-olds had never heard: "You don't have to believe everything you see and hear. You have the choice to disagree and the right to show your discontent with your purchasing power."

WHY MEDIA LITERACY EDUCATION?

American teenagers spend 31 hours a week watching TV, 17 hours a week listening to music, 3 hours a week watching movies, 4 hours a week reading magazines, 10 hours a week online. That's 10 hours and 45 minutes of media consumption a day. Like much of the rest of the digital conversation, this risk is about scale. In addition[56]:

---

55 Every parent should watch the films made by The Representation Project including Miss Representation

56 "Daily Media Use Among Children and Teens Up Dramatically from Five Years Ago" by the Henry J Kaiser Family Foundation

- 64% of young people say the TV is on during meal time
- 45% say the TV is left on "most of the time" even if no one is watching
- 71% have a television in their bedroom
- 50% have a video game console in their bedroom

It's no surprise that about half of heavy media users say that they usually get fair or poor grades, mostly Cs or lower. The answer to the risk of over-exposure is not to remove all media and become Amish. Not being able to watch Game of Thrones and Netflix are both deal breakers for my potential Amish conversion – plus I don't churn anything particularly well.

The answer is education. Media literacy education is critical in getting a child to "think about why you believe the things you believe." During my presentation, I tell students that I think UGG boots are hideous and that Starbucks coffee tastes like burnt monkey hair which coincidentally is the same smell which comes wafting out of a well-worn pair of UGGs[57]. So the question for your child is: Do you buy UGG boots because you genuinely like them? Or do you buy them because all of your friends have them? You should only buy the things you buy and think the things that you think because you've actually analyzed your thought process. Are you actually deciding or just blindly following the rest of the sheep off of the cliff?

This issue of self-analysis as related to media becomes more and more critical as the child reaches the tween years and is allowed to consume more adult-esque content.

WHAT IS TRUTH?

Imagine yourself experiencing a common modern scenario. You're surrounded by people you know fairly well, perhaps in the break room at your office or with cousins at a family gathering. Someone raises a question or claims a fact which is patently absurd or at a minimum you suspect is incorrect. Maybe it's that weird guy in accounting who makes an equally weird claim, probably involving a conspiracy theory. He's totally into conspiracy theories - and the mating habits of squirrels, not chipmunks, squirrels. Super weird.

While trying to not make eye contact with Captain Conspiracy he

---

57 I've cracked the code on UGG-rot. Take two dryer sheets and shove them into the bottom of each boot when you take them off - you can keep using and reusing the same sheets for a while. This solution will magically kill the "Foot Funk" scent hovering like a grey cloud of despair in your entryway. Because no amount of Febreze is killing that.

launches into his latest bizarro tirade, something about how Starbucks is a front for the CIA to deal with global overpopulation. He explains that every time you buy a Starbucks you're drinking irradiated nanomolecules which can be tracked from space. The CIA will have access to every Starbucks customer and on the day that those lines at the DMV are just way too long, the CIA will flip a switch and about a billion or so people all over the world will just drop dead[58].

As a New Yorker, I can tell you that when some guy who thinks he's Napoleon gallops onto a packed F Train during rush hour on his invisible horse, you should try your best to completely ignore him. Not everyone got that memo. There's always that ONE person in your office, let's call her Madam Fact Checker, who begins to passionately hammer away at Captain Conspiracy's theory. After trying to field a rapid succession of logical questions - Captain Conspiracy shouts "Don't believe me? Google it!".

Then in a scene reminiscent of a sunset duel in a Western town, both Captain Conspiracy and Madam Fact Checker whip out their phones and proceed to Google "CIA Starbucks Nanomolecules". Within seconds they both shout "AHA!" and hold their phones aloft as proof. Wait....what? How has Google provided each of these people with the so-called proof to prove the validity of entirely opposite positions of the same argument? Stay tuned, more on that in a minute....

If you have an unanswered question or concern (ie: Marijuana legalization - good or bad?) Google cannot provide you with answers. Google is merely supplying you with the content upon which you are meant to base your own answer. There is a significant distinction between these two perspectives. Google does not provide answers. Google provides data upon which you determine your own answer.

The Google algorithm actively learns how to respond to you specifically via adaptive artificial intelligence which means that it learns more about you the more you use any part of the Google ecosystem. By your interaction with Google products, you teach Google more and more about you - what you like, what you hate, where you go, what you listen to, where you place value, what you purchase, where you purchase and how much you spend. Then Google uses this aggregated data about you to inform its other sites like YouTube and Google Maps, presuming for example, that you must mean

---

58 I wrote this while on line at the DMV, and I hope the CIA has their finger on the switch. (I drink Dunkin Donuts.)

"funny CAT videos" as soon as you start typing "funny" into the YouTube search bar. You've taught your personalized Google algorithm, via your search and click behavior that you're aggressively working towards your Crazy Cat Lady Certification.

As Google learns more about you specifically, it will begin to filter and alter the results to your search queries based on the history of what you have clicked on in the past. Therefore, your Google search results to "funny" will be very different than someone else's. Moreover, users who view Google merely as a repository of answers may very well be duped by the following widely accepted myths.

MYTH 1: ALL SEARCH RESULTS ARE EQUAL

As far as Google is concerned, every link it offers you in the search results is considered equal, which creates a false equivalency as users presume accuracy and lack of bias. Google makes no distinction within search results in terms of accuracy or bias. All search results are given roughly the same value and the likelihood of whether or not it appears at the top of your search results is largely determined by your prior search/click history[59]. Most active web users live somewhere at the crossroads of speed and suspended disbelief. *I just need the answer quickly and if that answer is delivered by a wacky website based on lies painted over with exaggerated conjecture - then that's okay, I guess.* Google presumes that we just want it quickly and we want to be proven right. So it delivers - brilliantly.

MYTH 2: HIGHER EQUALS MORE IMPORTANT OR MORE ACCURATE

The search results at the top of the screen are perceived to be the most important or most relevant. But remember, your personal search and click behavior history has a major impact on which results appear at the top of the list. Compounded by the false equivalency issue in Myth #1, this becomes a self-feeding cycle which only serves to reinforce the beliefs you already hold to be true, whether they are objectively correct or not. You believe that the moon

---

59 Google's search algorithm is proprietary knowledge and closely guarded and only approximate guesses can be made based on search experimentation. It's enough to know that they change the algorithm constantly and the biggest contributor to the search results output is your previous search and click behavior.

landing was a Hollywood conspiracy and you Google search for proof. You find some completely unsupported (wacky) content to support that claim and leave satisfied to be proven correct. Later, you search for proof on another unrelated conspiracy theory and Google delivers results supporting the conspiracy rather than debunking it because it assumes that this is what you want to see, which then leads to additional conspiracy theory searches and click behavior history, which then leads you back to the beginning. Google's algorithm isn't a conspiracy itself, this is all about revenue.

You've probably noticed the ads which pop up on the right hand side of your Google search and on hundreds of millions of websites. In 2015, 89% of Google's income[60] came from advertising revenue. Google sells space to advertisers who have chosen a particular advertisement to appear when a user just like you searches for a particular order of words (aka search string). For example, Captain Conspiracy is probably seeing ads for designer tin foil hats. The advertiser pays[61] Google for the pleasure of showing the ad to all of the users who enjoy a good conspiracy theory, multiplied by the total number of times the ad is shown and/or clicked on.

It makes perfect sense that Google wants to give you more of what it knows you prefer based on that pesky search and click behavior history which you are constantly accumulating[62]. This is similar to the if-you-liked-that-you-might-like-this algorithm that online retailers like Amazon use to judge you and provide additional items for purchase. There is no conspiracy here either, just the desire to sell more advertising space (Google) or more cat t-shirts (Amazon).

---

60 According to Alphabet, Google's parent company, in 2015 Google reported total revenue of $75 billion. Advertising revenue amounted to 89% of that total or, $67 billion. The remaining $8 billion was earned by Google via "other revenue" including: Google Playstore, Chromebook, Android, and Cloud applications and programming. Interestingly of the $67 billion in total advertising sales, 77% or $53 billion was earned via Google owned websites including: Google search, Gmail, Google Maps, and YouTube. Learn more at http://abc.xyz/investor/index.html

61 It should be noted that I'm a huge fan of Google - this section is not meant to be a diatribe on Google. Google is a for-profit company and they're exceedingly good at what they do. From my somewhat limited and unusually optimistic point of view - Google does a great job at engaging with communities, and paying it forward - as it were. But Google is not Gandhi. As of Feb 2017, Google was responsible for answering to 1,892 stockholders and 62k employees in more than 40 countries worldwide. In an effort to sustain and increase profits they do precisely what they should be doing which is mainly to sustain and increase your attention via its myriad services and products.

62 By the way this adaptive artificial intelligence programming is true for Facebook content and advertising, most larger online retailers like Amazon and 3rd party advertising providers (not Google) like the ads you see on the bottom and sides of sites like CNN and Fox News

In the process of trying to keep its users happy and clicking (more clicks = more ad revenue AND more data) your personalized search algorithm keeps providing you with what it presumes you want to see more of. What this means is that you will rarely be presented with content which stands in opposition to your current opinion, or rather your tracked record of clicks and searches.

Think for a moment about the impact of this self-pleasing, self-congratulatory content delivery system. Where is the opportunity to learn a different perspective, exercise compassion or empathy, potentially change your mind, or expand your thought process? To electronically filter out oppositional content in a personalized way is dangerous to our ability to be critical consumers of content. These adaptive content delivery algorithms create an environment where you already know everything you need to know and everything you enjoy seeing/hearing/reading is what you already enjoy seeing/hearing/reading. Novelty is not part of the equation.

This is terrifying and one of those moments where I'm convinced that I'm being punked. (Does anyone else see what's going on here?) If we all continue to believe what we already believe and our children presume that the answer to all of their questions magically appears at the top of a list of search results- then why even send them to school?

Content and search delivery based on this adaptive algorithm is stabbing critical thinking to death - in the eye, with a spork, dipped in lemon juice.

AND NOW, BACK TO OUR REGULARLY SCHEDULED PROGRAM...

Whatever happened to our "CIA Starbucks Nanomolecules" duel? Last time we tuned in, our renegades Captain Conspiracy and Madam Fact Checker were in mid-duel and had proudly held up their phones with Google proof to support their utterly opposite positions. What inevitably follows begins as a rational discussion and ends as a gooey pile of stupid with a thick swath of imbecility slathered over the top. The discussion will ultimately become a debate of which sites and content can and cannot be trusted.

Madam Fact Checker will at some point lose what teeny bit of sanity she was holding onto while she screams "ConspiraciesRUs.com is NOT A VALID SOURCE OF FACTS!!" Now who looks like the crazy person? Seriously, there isn't an oxygen tank big enough to dive down to the bottom of that kind of stupid - just pet Napoleon's pretty invisible horse and move on.

Competing truths

If you've ever been in a casual gathering like a book club, or a friend's night out - you've probably heard someone complain about their spouse only after they've prefaced their negative comment with a positive disclaimer. *"He's a great husband and I love him- but I absolutely despise hearing him breathe. All of that in-and-out and in-and-out is so annoying."* This is cognitive dissonance in action.

Cognitive dissonance is the stress you feel when you have two contradictory beliefs at the same time, or when you learn new information which clearly contradicts one of your already held beliefs. Using our example from above - you love your husband dearly AND he's a good husband AND you'd like to smother him with a pillow when he breathes. Your brain tries to automatically bring your beliefs in line in order to reduce that contradictory stress. That's the subconscious reason we use the prefaced disclaimer "I love him, but." I need to prove to myself that I really love my husband before I tell you how much I'd like to murder him in his sleep.

Cognitive dissonance is the natural human phenomenon of our brains trying to lessen our stress level by trying to rectify two opposing thoughts. The algorithmic truth provided by Google or Facebook (based on your click history) complicates this reality even further.

1. We create and accumulate our own click history.
2. Our click history becomes our algorithmic truth.
3. If we even consider an opposite point of view which somehow makes it past our own cognitive dissonance filter....
4. ....our click history would only confirm the half of the argument we already believe to be true.

The digital deck is stacked against expanding our minds to consider and accept a new point of view.

HYPER-SEXUALIZATION OF CHILDREN

The hyper-sexualization of children occurs everywhere your children live and breathe. In 2002, retailer Abercrombie and Fitch began selling thongs[63] for little girls (around age 5 and 6) with designs that said "eye candy" and "wink wink". If you pay attention, the trend of not allowing children to remain children is pervasive. When children are presented as sexual beings in the media, in commercials, in print ads, in movies – we are normalizing that behavior for them.

Although the conversation about hyper-sexualization tends to focus on young girls, this affects young boys just as much. If young girls are meant to be the objects of sexual attention, then young boys are meant to desire and seek out those objects of sexual attention. At a time when young boys should be focused on play and their limited social sphere, they do not have the physical and emotional maturity to care about which girls in their class are wearing thongs.

In fact, boys as young as 10 and 11 years old (around 5th grade) are using Axe body products; a brand which focuses its entire marketing message on the idea that young men who use their products will have sexy half-dressed babes knocking down their door, in an almost uncontrollable mind haze. Such is the pull of the product that these young ladies will not be able to help themselves; simultaneously reinforcing the stereotype of young women as mindless sexual drones, while positioning young men to desire taking advantage of their temporary insanity.

Seventeen Magazine is a great example of normalizing hyper-sexualization. If you take a look at their media kit[64] you will find that they "sell" their advertisers access to the teen market beginning at age 12. In fact one of their targeted demographics is the 12 year old to 15 year old female market. Now if you move to the editorial part of their print and online magazine you will find a significant amount of sexualized content among the vapid and typical "sexiest nail polish" articles which are just as likely to appear in the adult version of Cosmopolitan Magazine. Much of the content focuses around topics like how to flirt the right way, how to become a great kisser, and knowing when you're ready to have sex.

Seventeen Magazine is not doing anything wrong. Their job is to turn the largest profit they can. They are neither required nor expected to exhibit

---

63 *Abercrombie's sexy undies 'slip'*
http://money.cnn.com/2002/05/22/news/companies/abercrombie/
64 Seventeen Magazine Media Kit: www.seventeenmediakit.com

any sort of moral compass. They do not have a duty to present developmentally appropriate content to your children. That's your job as a parent. You can also teach your children to vote with their wallets by modeling that behavior yourself.

The gender stereotyping[65] which occurs in these types of publications borders on comedy. The impossible Photoshopping of photos of "super models" who look far more super after the computer is done with them, make young women feel that they will never reach that level of perfect beauty. And they're right. No one can. The woman in that photo on the cover of that magazine doesn't look like that in real life. As adults we buy into this nonsense as well. My own makeup drawers are filled with creams and serums which are meant to lift, firm, and thicken everything gravity hates.

There is a wonderful short video by Dove[66] which shows the time-elapsed process of a lovely young woman transforming into a goddess by the end with the help of Photoshop artists. Her neck is elongated, her eyes are impossibly large, and any creases on her face which allow her to blink, speak, or sneeze are removed. Sharing this media literacy content with your children, regardless of their gender provides them with a healthy dose of cynicism, helping them to learn to judge content and situations critically.

THE TRASHIFICATION OF AMERICA

We may not enjoy it, but as parents we are forced into the role of content gatekeepers[67]. Every time some new vomit gets published I think of my student audiences and wonder whether they will have the personal fortitude to be their own content gatekeepers, especially when their own parents may not be.

In America we place a high value on trash. Not the literal trash that you put out on the curb (albeit a fair argument there as well). Rather, the trash that we consume in everyday media. It's infuriating as a parent to navigate the seas of sewage when you share the muck with the Kardashians and the Honey

---

65 Check out the great guide for discussion with your children about gender stereotyping by Common Sense Media. Tips for Battling Stereotypes by Caroline Knorr www.commonsensemedia.org/blog/tips-for-battling-stereotypes

66 Dove film: "Dove - Evolution Commercial"

67 Common Sense Media has a great online tool which offers reviews of all types of media. If you're not sure whether your child should watch that television show or read that book, take a peek at their website.

Boo-Boos of the world. Turn on an episode of Here Comes Honey Boo-Boo, but rather than watching the screen, watch the face of the person you're with. There is a hazy, horrified, glazed quality which overtakes the viewer.

My husband and I were flipping channels and he stopped briefly on this horrendous bit of programming – mostly because he knew I would freak out and he likes to poke at the bear in the cage. In the midst of my horror, I realized that watching these train wrecks is equal parts catharsis, glorification, and self-denial. When we watch Honey Boo-Boo eat an entire plastic barrel of cheese balls the shock is mixed with the assurance that at least your kid is better than that. True. Understood.

Most often reality television is an exercise in running through a compilation of mental checklists:

- I don't save cat carcasses in my freezer – check (Hoarders)
- My husband doesn't have make moonshine to support our family - check (Moonshiners)
- My daughter doesn't ever utter the phrase "You'd better Red-Neckognize" - check (Here Comes Honey Boo Boo)

The trouble is that we're rubbernecking everywhere. Although the insanity occurs in a more organized tune-in-next-time sort of way on the television, tabloid magazines and check-out stand news is just as bad. The column inch is measured by the percentage of crazy. And we buy it, we buy all of it. Is it possible, that we've become addicted to the catharsis? I don't think that we're genuinely engaged in the content, are we? Please don't say that's the case because that might just be worse. Do we just enjoy watching the pain of someone else's struggle? Can it be a socially systemic schadenfreude[68]? No, I'm going to choose to believe that we're watching the accident in slow motion, and it's impossible to look away. We are raising children in an environment which glorifies the crazy. We watch it, point at it, tsk-tsk it. But isn't it possible that we're creating what we hope to avoid?

Bottom Line

Parenting is not a passive sport. They see every single thing we do and say, and don't do and don't say. Homeland Security uses that phrase "If you see

---

68 Schadenfreude is a German word, which means the "malicious enjoyment of someone else's misfortune" which the entire marketing foundation of America's Funniest Videos.

something, say something". Don't assume that your children understand what it has taken you a lifetime to learn as an adult. Use the questionable media all around you as a teachable moment. Once you've made your point – follow-up with one of the following:

….and that's why we don't watch this crap
….and that's why we don't buy this product
….and that's why your Uncle Vinny is in jail

THE LEAST YOU SHOULD KNOW

Adults are naturally skeptical about advertising and product claims; children have not had the time to build these skills.

The 'hostile media effect' means that you might see political bias against your own position even when it does not exist.

Media literacy is applied critical thinking and begins by asking two questions: Is it true (or compelling)? How do you know?

Teens consume massive amounts of content on a daily basis.

When you do a Google search, your search results are different than someone else's for the same search request. Your results are tailored just for you and do not reflect objective fact.

The real truth comes from looking at unfiltered, uncustomized search results critically, analyzing their sources and coming up with your own conclusions.

The more you use Google products (search, Maps, YouTube, Gmail, etc) the more Google learns about you and your click behavior. Your future searches will reflect what Google thinks you will like, not necessarily what is available or what is correct.

Myth #1: All Search Results are Equal.
Google makes no distinction between search results in terms of accuracy or bias. For Google, every search results just equals ONE more search result. But those results are not equal in terms of accuracy or bias.

Myth #2: Higher equals more important or more accurate.
Similar to Myth #1, Google's physical organization of search results implies that the results at the top of the list are objectively the best, or the most accurate. Google's algorithm is not seeking accuracy but rather gambling on the best chance you will click on one of those top search results listed based on

your click history. Google knows what you like and will give you more of it.

Cognitive dissonance is a normal human phenomenon which makes it difficult to hold two competing thoughts at the same time. Our brains attempt to reduce this stress attempts by choosing to believe one side of the argument at the expense of the other.

The hypersexualization of children occurs in the content all around us. Print advertisements, movies, and television are rife with images of adult sexuality in addition to the intentional sexualization of young children.

CONVERSATION STARTERS

Pick a particularly absurd television advertisement and ask your child what he thinks. "Do you think that product works the way that the ad promises? Why or why not? Does that product solve a problem which people actually have?"

Ask your child - "Did you know that each user gets a different set of Google results based on their click history?"

Ask your child - "How do you think Amazon is able to suggest items for purchase? How does Amazon know so much about a user? Does that concern you at all? Why or why not?"

Ask your child - "If you were forced to choose between either television and movies OR access to the web - which would you pick and why?"

Ask your child - "When you do a Google search - how do you decide which results to click on? Do you ever skip a result because of the website it comes from? Why or why not?"

Ask your child - "How do you decide which websites are good sources and which aren't?"

Ask your child - "Which brands do you think do the best job of accurately depicting the lives of real people? Which are the worst? Why?"

Ask your child - "Did you ever thinking about the money kids spend as an opportunity for activism? Did you ever consider buying or not buying from a company because of the choices the company makes? What do you think would happen if a large number of teens stopped buying from a major brand?"

Ask your child - "If Google could go through your online personality based on your click history and habits, what do you think it would say about you? What sort of person does Google think you are? What does Google think you like, dislike, or show a specific interest in? Do you think that's an accurate representation of who you really are?"

ACTION ITEMS

Watch television together. Illustrate media bias when you see it. Point out ridiculous connections when you see them: the Nike ad with the cheetah. Will purchasing Nike shoes make you run as fast as a cheetah?

There is a significant amount of media literacy education work being done by organizations like Common Sense Media, Miss Representation, Amy Poehler's Smart Girls, and A Mighty Girl.

When your child comes home with a story generated from the official middle school rumor mill - ask him the two questions: *Is it true?* And *How do you know?* This is a great opportunity to emphasize the need for independent verification and skepticism.

Read what your child is reading. The content your child consumes is helping to form your child's thoughts just as much as you are. What is this other parent teaching your children?

Use parental controls wherever possible on movie and television content over a certain age. You can set age restrictions on Netflix, Kindle, and dish or satellite television devices.

Chapter 5

HOW DO YOUR CHILDREN CONNECT?

Hard-boiled science fiction devotees will defend the genre, with their lives if necessary. Discussion and debate can become heated among fans of *Back to the Future*, *Dune*, or *Star Trek* when a point of fact (in a totally fictional scenario) is misinterpreted or misunderstood. Good science fiction feels plausible - it could happen. Great science fiction feels predictive. But the best of the best can only be judged across time and in hindsight.

One of my personal favorites is *The Matrix*. This 1999 film starring Keanu Reeves is consistently and deservedly listed within the top 25 sci-fi movies of all time. The movie gives us a peek into a dystopian future where the computers have taken over and have enslaved humanity. The sentient computers need the heat and electrical activity from human bodies as an electrical source. A system of interconnected computers - "The Matrix" has created a simulation of a typical human world. The enslaved humans imagine themselves living a normal life, going to work, having children, when they are actually floating in goo-filled pods connected via electronic cables to an elaborate electrical system which simultaneously fuels the simulation and provides the computers with an electrical source which is required for the computers to maintain control.

Remember that this movie was released in 1999. Google had only launched in 1998 when no one really even knew what the Internet was, let alone how to search it. Facebook went live five years after the movie, in 2004. The first iPhone was released eight years after the movie release in 2007. When writing the screenplay, the Wachowskis[69] could never have anticipated how their movie and its concepts would mirror the coming technological trajectory. *The Matrix* changed the way that I viewed the world in general and added to my already advanced sense of skepticism. I am a New Yorker after all.

Whenever I hear anyone use the words "connect to the Internet" I imagine that person stepping into a goo-filled pod and willingly losing all sense of awareness and independent thought after plugging their brain into "The Matrix" where the only sense of reality is artificially customized and contrived.

As users of technology, we are connecting into the larger connection, willingly and constantly. Understanding the basics of how connection happens is the first step in identifying and preventing risk.

WHAT IS THE INTERNET

Did you know that the "Internet" and the World Wide Web are not synonymous? In conversation, we might use the terms interchangeably, but there is a vast difference between the two. The Internet is a massive network of networks which connects hundreds of millions of computers together for the purpose of communication. The World Wide Web is just one way of accessing information over the medium of the Internet.

Consider a parallel analogy of global transportation. The global infrastructure (aka the Internet) of transportation in the United States includes interstate highways, local roads, train tracks, airports, and shipping ports. Using one or many of these different forms of transportation you can literally travel anywhere in the world by hooking into other parts of the global transportation infrastructure.

If the Internet is the infrastructure of transportation, then the World Wide Web

---

69 Formerly called the "Wachowski Brothers", now just the "Wachowskis" siblings who have written and directed other amazing sci-fi films like Cloud Atlas and the Netflix series Sense8.

is the national highway system. When you say 'I need to take my kids to school' everyone understands that you're going to travel on a road, probably in your car. In your entire life, you might never avail yourself of the other parts of the infrastructure of transportation: planes, trains, or boats.

WHAT IS A BROWSER?

A browser is a collection of code which allows your device to turn all of the gobbledygook code (HTML, Java, PHP, etc) into a pretty website with buttons in the appropriate places. Typical browsers include Google Chrome (by Google), Internet Explorer (by Microsoft), Firefox (by Mozilla), or Safari (by Apple).

You probably begin your travels on the World Wide Web by opening up a browser which interprets all of the code and provides it to you in a form which is easy to use. Access to a browser gives you the *keys to the kingdom*. Once you have the opportunity to type a web address into a browser screen, you have access to most things online.

If you find yourself going to a .com or other web address it means you are already in the browser. If you can input a web address and "go there" - this is a browser.

WHAT IS A SEARCH ENGINE?

A search engine is made up of two basic functions: gathering and indexing the websites and content on the World Wide Web and organizing that data into a functional and efficient format for a user searching for content. Google is a search engine which sends digital spiders out into the world wide web looking for new webpages, sites, and content. New content is added and indexed while deleted content will be removed from its massive database. The purpose of a search engine is not to provide you with answers, but rather to provide you with content upon which you base your own answer. Most popular consumer search engines: Google, Bing, Yahoo.

WEB ADDRESSES VS EMAIL ADDRESSES

Any address with the @ symbol in it (betty@ebay.com) is an email address. If you think you have an email address and the "@" symbol is not present, you probably have web address instead. Web addresses and email addresses cannot contain spaces and they are **not case sensitive**, which means that using capitals or lowercase doesn't make a difference in the results. So please for the love of chocolate stop saying "all one word" when you read off your email. It makes my eye twitch. It has to be all one word or it wouldn't be a web address or an email address.

These email addresses are all the same:

Betty@ebay.com   BETTY@EBAY.com   Betty@Ebay.com

These websites are all the same:

Www.EBAY.com   www.Ebay.com   WWW.ebay.com

UNDERSTANDING "INTERNET CONNECTIONS"

In order to create a digital connection you need a device and a signal. Remember that your device might be accessing the "internet" without providing access to "the web." For example, satellite and cable television boxes provide internet access to the system when it updates your guide. But that same "box" will probably not open up a browser to surf the web. For the sake of this conversation as it relates to child safety we will focus on the most commonly used devices and points of risk.

How your children access the web via a web browser

Accessing the web via a browser means that the sum total of the content on the web is accessible to your child. Unless you use specific software to limit incoming risks your child will be able to access any content available anywhere on the web. If your child is connecting to the web via a browser he/she is probably using one of the following devices. Other than a desktop computer or gaming system, the rest of these devices connect via a wi-fi signal meaning that the child will have access to the web any time there is a usable signal within range.

Laptop or Desktop. This is the original and traditional device for browser use. Browsers will be the most fully functional on a desktop or laptop and will probably not see any design or programming distortions - these distortions are diminishing over time. Connects: via hard wired modem cable or wi-fi signal.

Tablet. The tablet world includes all of the iPad and Samsung (and other brands) as well as supposedly child-safe tablets. If a so-called "child-safe" tablet has browser access and/or access to the Android, Apple, or other app stores, it is not child-safe. Connects: via wi-fi.

e-Reader. Kindle and other e-readers contain browsers within their programming and act very much like a tablet with access to additional specialized content like e-books, audible books, and almost unlimited video content (on the Kindle). The Kindle has excellent parental controls if you choose to use them. In the absence of those controls this is true, unfettered browser access. Connects via wi-fi.

iPod Touch. Ah, the the hidden jewel among your child's belongings. This is one of those devices that mom and dad forget to watch out for. The iTouch operates just like an iPhone without the ability to dial out via a cell carrier. Besides open browser access, the iTouch also has open access to YouTube unless you lock it down. The iTouch allows your child access to the entire universe of the Apple appStore, which means that they can participate fully in every social media app like Instagram, Facebook, and Twitter. Connects via wi-fi.

Game Console. Game consoles (like Xbox and PlayStation) provide your children to connect to the Internet on the gaming side (players connecting with each other in LIVE play) as well as on the browser side. Your child will have access to the web, YouTube, and other web apps via the gaming interface. Connects: probably via wi-fi but can also be hard wired via cable.

Smartphone. This is the most typical place where your child will use a browser for surfing the web as well as engaging in social media via downloaded apps such as Twitter, Instagram, and Snapchat. Smartphones do not require the use of a wi-fi signal. By virtue of the fact that it's a cellphone – its signal is self-sustained by 3G/4G. However, a smartphone without a data plan is essentially an iPod Touch which can do everything via a wi-fi signal. If you have a disused smartphone lying around the house, it's still fully web enabled via a wi-fi signal. NOTE: My general recommendation: NO smartphones for kids before 9th grade.

Smart TV. These next generation televisions are a hybrid of computers and flat screen televisions. Integrated internet access is part of its core programming making browser access available right on the screen. In addition, smart TVs provide access to third-party services like Netflix and Hulu without the need for additional equipment. Smart TVs are by definition wi-fi enabled, making any home networks accessible by the device as well making it possible to access any files, photos, videos, and music contained on that central network.

Device manufacturers, like Samsung, encourage users to remain loyal to the brand by creating features which operate within its ecosystem. If you own a Samsung smartphone as well as a Samsung SmartTV for example, you can go to YouTube on your phone, pull up a video - and broadcast it via the television. Any video content can be broadcast from a Samsung phone through a Samsung SmartTV.

Heading even further down the rabbit hole...smart TVs like Samsung's have voice recognition capabilities. Similar to the Amazon Echo, you can speak to the television and it will respond to your commands. As we've already seen (Chapter 2: Parenting in Transition) these voice command activated devices need to be listening all the time in order to hear when you happen to utter a specific command. In 2015[70], Samsung came under fire for their so-called privacy policy which made it clear to users that if the voice recognition tool is not blocked, that Samsung could be listening. In fact, Samsung's privacy policy was referred to as Orwellian in yet another nod to the almost predictive value in George Orwell's sci-fi classic *1984* - where Big Brother might be watching and listening whether you knew it or not. Samsung's policy[71] states:

> *"Please be aware that if your spoken words include personal or other sensitive information, that information will be among the data captured and transmitted to a third party through your use of Voice Recognition."*

But wait, we're not done. Samsung's SmartTV also contains the ability to use facial recognition and gesture controls. How do they achieve this miraculous feat? Glad you asked....the television has a camera at the top aimed at you.

---

70 *"Samsung smart TV policy allows company to listen in on users"*, by Andrew Griffin, 9 February 2015, Independent, http://www.independent.co.uk/life-style/gadgets-and-tech/news/samsungs-new-smart-tv-policy-allows-company-to-listen-in-on-users-10033012.html

71 Samsung's SmartTV privacy policy. http://www.samsung.com/sg/info/privacy/smarttv/

From Samsung's privacy policy:

> *"Your SmartTV is equipped with a camera that enables certain advanced features, including the ability to control and interact with your TV with gestures and to use facial recognition technology to authenticate your Samsung Account on your TV. The camera can be covered and disabled at any time, but be aware that these advanced services will not be available if the camera is disabled."*

Samsung is not the enemy and my attempt to educate parents should not be interpreted as any intention to demonize Samsung in particular. In fact, in 2017, Vizio[72] agreed to pay $2.2 million[73] to settle charges with the Federal Trade Commission because Vizio was collecting the viewer data of 11 million Vizio television owners without the consent of the owners. Sony, LG, and others are right on pace to collect massive amounts of user data because there's value in it.

As consumers and parents we need to get educated and to implement safeguards. The job is yours - as a parent - to control which of these devices enters your home and how to protect yourself (in this case) by disabling all of those voice and facial recognition features.

For detailed guidance on how to be safer in a home with a smart TV, take a look at this 2017 guide by Consumer Reports "How to Turn Off Smart TV Snooping Features[74]."

TEXTING & CHAT

SMS (Short Message Service) is the technical term for texting which transmits via mobile phones. Even the simplest non-web based flip phone will allow texting. Texting via a mobile phone lives within the native software on the

---

72 *"VIZIO to Pay $2.2 Million to FTC, State of New Jersey to Settle Charges It Collected Viewing Histories on 11 Million Smart Televisions without Users' Consent"* https://www.ftc.gov/news-events/press-releases/2017/02/vizio-pay-22-million-ftc-state-new-jersey-settle-charges-it

73 Forgive me for being cynical, but $2.2 million is barely a slap on the wrist for a company like Vizio. There's no question that the derived and actual revenue value of the data exhaust of 11 million television owner's user data multiplied by the number of days of Vizio got away with collecting the data FAR outweighs the paltry $2.2 million dollars they settled to pay.

74 Consumer Reports *"How to Turn Off Smart TV Snooping Features"*
http://www.consumerreports.org/privacy/how-to-turn-off-smart-tv-snooping-features/

device. However, there are many other ways your children can engage in texting without a cell phone. In addition, there are a myriad of ways that your children can "chat" with friends (as well as strangers) via their devices which is similar to texting but exists outside the realm of the cellular structure.

Native texting. This is the behavior most commonly associated with the term. Your child is hunched over their cell phone with their fingers moving at the speed of light. You might also notice a Pavlovian response once your child receives a text and they must rush to read it.

Texting via app. There are smartphone apps (which also operate on the iTouch) which make it possible for your child to text outside of the traditional texting via mobile structure. A common example is Kik which is not safe or appropriate for children.

Texting within a game. There are many benign videogames which feature in-game chat, bringing serious risks to children. For example, Clash of Clans seems like a great game for kids. Once you've downloaded the app you "create a clan." Very quickly you will find that the best and most powerful clans are open to strangers. Once the clan is open, so is the opportunity to chat with clan members, both known and unknown. This is a serious risk for sexual predation.

Texting or messaging within an app. Many social apps such as Facebook, Instagram, Twitter, and SnapChat provide the capability to DM another user. A "DM" is a direct message within the app - a so-called private message between users which does not appear on their activity feed. You need to be logged into the child's account in order to see the content and source of the DMs your child might be receiving and sending.

SHARING FILES, VIDEOS, AND LIFE.

Filesharing. Children have figured out that file sharing apps like DropBox, Google Drive, and Apple's iCloud are all great ways to share files and content. In this case, the platform itself is benign in terms of safety. The main question is related to the content itself.

In 2017 I was asked to present at a school where a group of 10th grade boys set up a DropBox account to share photos. Independently they cajoled female classmates to send them nudes and many girls complied with the requests thinking that their particular photo was only being shared with one boy, and never expecting what would happen next. The boys uploaded all of those nude photos into a single DropBox and began charging others for access to the account. For X dollars a classmate would be sold the username and password to enter the DropBox and view all of the images.

Blogs and vlogs. Sites like Tumblr and YouTube encourage kids to create a play-by-play repository of their lives. The rise of famous YouTubers has duped kids into thinking it's simple to get rich by merely creating a YouTube channel and speaking into a video camera. Children perceive these activities as connecting with an audience when really they're reaching out for any sort of acknowledgment. Your child has no business having their own YouTube channel unless you engage the services of both a PR firm to manage their message and a personal security firm to manage their safety.

Livestreaming. The most useless and infuriating on this list- livestreaming is when a user points a camera at themselves, probably on their phone, and live streams everything (and nothing) happening in their life. That's it. Underwhelming? Yes, you'd think. The hubris involved in just engaging in this app would be hilarious if it weren't so sad. The security risks are far less funny. Kids who are livestreaming are giving away massive amounts of personal information whether they realize it or not.

I've seen live streams where the child is live streaming while wearing a shirt with her school's name clearly visible, or outside of the front door of her school, etc. There is no way to do this safely. It's not appropriate for kids, it's stupid, and just the idea that your child is **so** important that millions of people might want to watch her paint her nails is ludicrous and just one more way that you are lovingly cultivating a sociopath. The most popular live streaming apps are: Live.ly, HouseParty, YouNow, and Periscope. Other apps have livestreaming capabilities embedded in the core app like: Facebook, Instagram, and SnapChat.

THE LEAST YOU SHOULD KNOW

The terms *Internet* and *World Wide Web* are not synonymous.

A browser like Internet Explorer allows you to surf the web.

A search engine like Google indexes part of the world wide web and organizes that content in a usable format. Search engines do not index the entire web.

Your child can access the web by using a browser via many devices like a laptop, tablet, e-reader, iPod Touch, game consoles, smartphones, and smart televisions.

Texting and chat can also occur across a multitude of devices and platforms like smartphones, via texting app, within a game, and within a social media app.

New risks to children include file sharing platforms, blogging platforms, and live streaming apps.

CONVERSATION STARTERS

Ask your child: Did you know that the Internet is not just made up of the World Wide Web?

Play this game in order to get your children to reveal every method they can think of to connect. Tell your children that you are going to see how resourceful they can be to get a message out to their friends and classmates. The point of this exercise is to assess what your child perceives his communication options to be.

Ask your child: You need to get an emergency message out to your friends – how would you do it? They might answer: "I would text them". Then ask: OK I've just magically removed your ability to text – what's your second choice? They might answer: "I would Instagram". Keep going until they run out of ideas. When they start to run out of apps and devices prompt them to think of any device they have for communication. Continue until they run out of ideas.

Ask your child: Of all of the electronic devices in the house which is your favorite? Why?

Ask your child: Do you ever chat with players while you're playing a game? Can you show me how that works?

ACTION ITEMS

Watch The Matrix (Rated R).

If your child has access to a Kindle, check out the parental controls.

Re-evaluate your child's use of an iPod Touch.

No smartphones under 14 years old.

Download the Consumer's Guide to smart TV settings. You can find it here http://www.consumerreports.org/privacy/how-to-turn-off-smart-tv-snooping-features/

Chapter 6

UNDERSTANDING THE TWO MAJOR POINTS OF VULNERABILITY

Identifying and managing risk is an integral part of life. From the bottom to the top of the food chain, every single living species assesses and mitigates risk for its survival. This primal survival instinct gives every species in the animal kingdom the option of fight or flight. Porcupines can either shoot its quills or run, squid can either spread its ink or swim away, humans can either shoot you with pepper spray or run away.

The human brain is a constant stream of calculating and recalculating your fight or flight response even when the stimulus isn't particularly threatening. As a human community we are forced to accept a certain amount of risk in daily life. For example, there are inherent risks in choosing to fly on an airplane. If you are terrified of flying you could override your silently brain-crushing anxiety (with the help of pharmaceutical drugs) because you've decided that attending your grandmother's 100th birthday is worth your temporary vulnerability.

In order to live a healthy human life we have to being willing to accept exposure of our vulnerabilities or become captives of our own mental siege against all risk. Individuals determine their own acceptable level of risk based on their own criteria - both conscious and subconscious. One person's relaxing zip lining expedition is another person's afternoon of torture.

All digital risks are made viable in one of two possible scenarios: incoming vulnerabilities and outgoing vulnerabilities. Incoming vulnerabilities are those which are coming in towards your family in various ways. Outgoing vulnerabilities are connected to the content that your family puts out into the web. The trick is to restrict the open availability of the first and educate your family in an effort to prevent the second.

Imagine your family lives in an old medieval castle. The castle has great potential against intruders, provided its defense is kept up and advance with new technologies. The castle dwellers also need to constantly be reminded to pull up the drawbridge before they go to bed - automated drawbridge lowering technology hasn't been invented yet. Whether you live in a castle or a cramped city apartment, the two keys to mitigating risk are prevention and education.

Incoming vulnerabilities

Incoming vulnerabilities exist on their own without any user action. The resulting risks take advantage of weak points in your defenses. Just like the rat holes in your aging castle, you must first identify all of the incoming weak points before you can plug them up. In an incoming vulnerability scenario, you have not done anything to give a predator any information or access to your devices; you are a true innocent bystander. These incoming vulnerabilities can be divided into four basic risk categories, remote access, brain access, data exhaust, and external influences.

Remote Access

On August 10, 2014 Marc and Laurent Gilbert[75], a Houston couple, were doing dishes while their children slept. They began to hear the voice of a strange man cursing and making lewd comments in their 2 year old daughter's bedroom. When they entered daughter Allyson's room, they heard a 'European accented

---

75 ABC News Story: *Baby Monitor Hacking Alarms Houston Parents*

voice' calling Allyson "an effing moron" and telling her "wake up you little slut". The voice then started swearing at Marc and Lauren.

The live voice, belonging to a male hacker, was coming out of the Gilbert's high-tech video baby monitor which was equipped with a webcam. The hacker was able to access the baby monitor from a remote location by hacking the Gilbert's wi-fi signal, and found a virtual backdoor into Allyson's bedroom.

Video baby monitors, security video systems, and other remote access video devices like the video eye on your Kinect, the embedded camera on your smart television[76], the integrated webcam in the lid of your laptop, and the front and back of your tablet. In addition, that fitness tracker you're wearing, which is Bluetooth enabled and connected to your smartphone could be the weakest point of entry into your smartphone or your home wi-fi.

SOLUTION: Use a cable rather than wi-fi to connect that video enabled device - like the video baby monitor or video surveillance equipment. Cover your laptop, tablet, and smart television cameras with a piece of electrical tape when you're not using them. Don't wear your fitness tracker while you're at the airport, coffee shop, shopping mall or some other places where massive numbers of humans congregate (aka where hackers are actively seeking an easy mark).

Brain access

This particular incoming vulnerability allows serious risks to reach our families via their passive and reactive digital use. Much like a lab rat feeling compelled to pick up that smartphone after a text notification is an unfortunate sign of the times.

Both children and adults engage in these behaviors and cannot seem to resist checking email and social media throughout the day. In 2016, 95% of Americans owned a cell phone[77] (77% owned a smartphone) and 46% of people said that they could not bear to live without their smartphones[78]. 78% of teens and 68% of parents reported checking their phones at least once an hour[79].

---

76 CNN article: *Your TV might be watching you*

77 *Mobile Fact Sheet,* Pew Research Center, January 12, 2017. http://www.pewinternet.org/fact-sheet/mobile/

78 *US Smartphone Use in 2015*, Pew Research Center, April 1, 2015.

http://www.pewinternet.org/2015/04/01/us-smartphone-use-in-2015/

79 *Technology Addiction: Concern, Controversy, and Finding Balance*, Common Sense Media, May

Beyond all of the other obvious negative outcomes our constant device overuse is affecting our ability to get a good night's sleep[80]. Lack of good quality and quantity sleep is extremely detrimental to maintaining physical and mental health.

We've willingly placed ourselves in a constant loop of brain changing stimuli: behavior - reward - behavior. Our device use (behavior) triggers responses from our online and audience via notifications (reward) and we respond with additional device use (more behavior). We act like lab rates because we make the choice to engage in a lab rat environment. Continuation down this road will lead to addiction - how could it not? The good news is that the choices we make have a causal effect on which digital risks will reach our brains. We can choose to opt out at a level which makes sense for our families.

SOLUTION: The solution here is the simplest and the most difficult to implement - *limit time and limit access.* Your goal is to limit the raw number of minutes spent on devices and limit the number of times you post in one day. Secondly, limit access: limit which platforms your children use, limit the total number of platforms you and your children access (choose one or two favorites, dump the rest), limit access to your phone before bed (no devices one hour before bed), and have the entire family limit notifications after X o'clock each day by using the *Do Not Disturb[81]* settings on your cell phone.

Data Exhaust

Data exhaust[82] is the data you leave behind when you engage with digital tools. It is both the literal record of your online activity as well as the extrapolated connections between those data sets. These are the data which fuel the algorithms which operate and financially support Google, Facebook, Amazon - and most of the money making side of the World Wide Web. If you're using the web, you're creating data exhaust. The use of this data exhaust by companies is almost inevitable when engaging with digital tools.

3, 2016. https://www.commonsensemedia.org/technology-addiction-concern-controversy-and-finding-balance-infographic

80 See Chapter 2: Be Proactive for more on digitally induced insomnia and its potential effects.

81 I LOVE LOVE LOVE the Do Not Disturb settings on my smartphone (available both on Android and iPhones). My phone is scheduled to go into Do Not Disturb from 4pm in the afternoon until 10am the next morning. This means that zero notifications, text messages, or phone calls will come to the phone during the blocked time frame. You can also customize the settings to just accept messages or calls from your "favorite" contacts, etc.

82 See Chapter 10: Understanding Social Media for more on data exhaust

SOLUTION: The only possible way to limit this risk is to limit your time and depth of engagement. The more you use digital tools the bigger your data exhaust.

External Influences

The Internet is an awe-inspiring, beautiful, massive, diverse, roiling ball of human potential, pock marked with giant pus-filled cavernous chasms of hatred and porn. So just like anything else in life - it's not all good or all bad. But somehow we've convinced ourselves that we only have those two choices - to accept or reject it completely. These choices are neither feasible nor effective.

We've already seen that the average American teenager consumes a massive amount of content daily (almost 11 hours per day consumed mostly simultaneously versus consecutively.) Adults are also over consuming online and video content. The overuse is a problem, but what about the content being consumed? Your family is at the mercy of the external influences which enter your home via websites, social media, games, and video content. Binge watching HGTV is problematic from an effective time use perspective and time spent not engaging with your family. But binge watching graphically violent or sexualized content comes additional risks beyond time spent.

Let's do a quick thought experiment. Estimate the number of hours you spend with your family in active communication. Okay, now remove from that number any communications related to daily tasks (*Brush your teeth! We're going to be late! Brush your teeth!*) How much time is left? Now compare that final total to the amount of time your child spends in digital content consumption and communication with outside influences (both unknown and unknown).

SOLUTION: This is another place to apply the time and access solution. Limit the time by reducing the raw number of minutes you and your children spend in content consumption. Limit access by restricting entire platforms and by implementing age-level restrictions on platforms like Netflix.

Making these changes should open up vast tracts of time in which you can now watch content together and engage in actual conversation with your children about what you just watched. The movie doesn't need to be controversial or deep. Invent alternative plot lines, remove entire characters, come up with different endings - the conversation doesn't need to make any sense. The point is to get into the habit of purposely processing what you just watched, imagining other outcomes, thereby taking the potential sting out of future content by adding a dose of skepticism.

Pull up the drawbridge, prepare the fire pots.

Allowing the existence of these incoming vulnerabilities in your family means that you've accidentally gone to bed and forgotten to pull up the drawbridge. But you're smarter than that now. You've hard-cabled the security cameras, stopped using those annoying fitness trackers in public places, limited time and access to devices - improved your sleep, and limited time and access to external influences, improved your family's communication and cultivated a healthy skepticism.

We've pulled up the drawbridge and stopped up the rat holes. Now, it's time to fill the moat with piranhas and prepare to catapult the fire pots.

Outgoing vulnerabilities

Right about now you could begin to feel pretty smug about the safety of your castle. I mean, only a real psycho is going to try to get across that piranha-filled moat. But wait. Your family might still be at risk if you accidentally help a would-be predator gain access to the castle.

It's not easy being single in the Middle Ages, so you maybe you set up a dating profile on "NoblesOnly.com" - a dating site which caters only to the noble medieval class, because honestly - who dates peasants? You meet the absolutely perfect love of your life on the site and send him an invitation for dinner at the castle. You send the archers home early and personally lower the drawbridge for your new soulmate. Congratulations, you've just let FireBody_27 into your castle, and you're about to find out that the "fire" in his username is far less a physical description than a reference to the 27 charred bodies he keeps in steel drums in his basement.

Outgoing vulnerabilities are the ways in which we accidentally help "the bad guy" via digital engagement. These outgoing vulnerabilities can be divided into three basic risk categories, web-enabled gadgets, data sharing, and seeking connection.

Web enabled gadgets

The Internet of Things (IoT) is a large and growing market of gadgets and equipment which require an active connection to the Internet in order to exist. Most pieces of equipment purport to create efficiencies[83] where none are required, and solve problems which don't exist. There are whole-house lighting, hvac, multimedia and door locking systems controllable by your smartphone. So you can tap a key and instantly blast Guns n Roses in the garage while you listen to Bach in the bathtub.

There are wi-fi enabled keyless entry systems which allow you to unlock your house with your smartphone. Let's say your son forgot his key or you're late letting the babysitter into the house - you could unlock the house remotely from your phone. Never mind the fact that the wi-fi connectivity makes it hackable, or that anyone in possession of your phone can unlock your house.

Devices like the Amazon Echo[84] propose to make your life easier by taking voice commands to play music, order products from Amazon, or to run a Google search. Never mind the fact that the device has to be listening all the time in order to hear the trigger command in the first place or the fact that (again) it's wi-fi enabled requirement makes is vulnerable to hackers.

SOLUTION: Be very careful about the wi-fi enabled gadgets you willingly bring into your home. If you're even considering buying one of these devices, read all of the privacy settings and the company's entire privacy policy before you take the plunge. In addition, you must read Pew Research Center's 2017 report called "The Internet of Things Connectivity Binge: What Are the Implications[85]?"

Resist the temptation to use wi-fi-enabled remote home systems. If you need to turn the lights off roll your butt off the couch and use the wall switch - it might be all the exercise you get all day. Use an actual metal house key versus a digital key- I know that sounds terribly retro but hey, it's your castle.

---

83 Review the section in Chapter Two: Be Proactive on how to determine if a gadget or app actually adds value to your life.

84 See Chapter 2: Parenting In Transition for more on Amazon Echo and privacy settings

85 Pew Research Center's 2017 report called "The Internet of Things Connectivity Binge: What Are the Implications" http://www.pewinternet.org/2017/06/06/the-internet-of-things-connectivity-binge-what-are-the-implications/

Data sharing

Data sharing refers to the content which you and your children willingly share via some digital platform. Content is the oxygen which gives life to social media. As users, we comply by the truckload. We over-share, over-click, and over-comment. Since it is the most popular social media platform on the planet, consider the following Facebook statistics:

- There are 300 million photos uploaded per day or 208k per minute (Source Gizmodo)
- Every 60 seconds: 510k new comments and 293k status updates are posted (Source: The Social Skinny)
- Every seconds, 5 new Facebook profiles are created (Source: AllFacebook)

Full engagement in social media means both creating content and consuming other people's content. During that much content development and consumption, we're bound to become overly comfortable and accidentally give out too much information about ourselves and our families.

On Facebook, in particular, parents should be careful to never use a family photo as their cover photo since this photo cannot be limited by any privacy setting. For example, changing your Facebook cover photo to a photo of your son wearing his sports uniform where the name of his school is clearly visible makes it far easier for FireBody_27 to learn even more about you than you've already told him. In addition, your profile photo should not show images of your children, your city, location or place of employment. Any other key personal details should be reserved strictly for those individuals who you have "friended" on the platform. Your child's social media profiles (on Facebook and elsewhere) should also be stripped of any personalized information which could be viewed by anyone.

Reviewing privacy settings on social media platforms is always the first step to encouraging safety. However, the conversation about safety on Facebook, for example, presupposes that the child will implement the privacy settings as well as not allowing "friend" status to just anyone who asks.

SOLUTION: Limiting time and limiting access will work beautifully here as well. In terms of data sharing, limit how much time is spent in content creation and content consumption while limiting access to your content by anyone you don't know.

Seeking connection

Last time we visited the castle, you were trying to outrun FireBody_27 and hoping you wouldn't be the reason for the change in his handle to FireBody_28. You can't ever really know what the outcome will be when you choose to seek connection with people on a screen[86] rather than in person. This search for human connection, via digital engagement is really the main risk which informs all of the rest. Adults and children may be using social media and engaging in digital tools in order to feel like a part of something bigger, to feel a sense of connection with other people.

Beyond the fact that your children are lying about their age and using dating apps (like Tinder and Hot or Not) this particular risk of seeking connection occurs on other non-dating apps and platforms. There are apps which supposedly help teens find new friends which are actually a haven for sexual predators and human sex traffickers. Live streaming apps (like HouseParty and Live.ly) are also used by teens who, in the process of attempting to make connections, are actually giving out mountains of detailed information about themselves to whoever chooses to tune in and watch.

SOLUTION: Become an example for your family of what it means to cultivate human connection- off of a screen. Create real-life scenarios where your child can connect with their friends without technology. Collect all phones at the door in a basket - they'll recoil at first, and then they'll love it.

Seek connection as a family engaging in new activities which you can bond over. Try something you've never done before - something completely out of your family's comfort zone. If you tend to be cave dwellers - go zip lining. If you're outdoor people, challenge neighbors to a bowling match.

If, as an adult, you choose to use a dating app be sure to only connect to people in your own city whose information can be verified. Someone you met online says that they work at a particular company? Call the office and dupe the receptionist into giving you some information. Does the person claim to own property? Check the tax auditor's website for that county. Do you have any Facebook mutual friends? Contact the mutual friends and ask questions, lots of questions. And by the way - this advice stands whether you're male or female. Evil comes in every shape and flavor.

---

86 Personally, I think dating apps are liquid insanity. But there are many people who have used them successfully and have not been slaughtered in their sleep by their new love interests.

Explaining threats to children

If you are providing your children with access to devices and social media platforms you're going to have have the conversation, the only other option is to not allow your child to have access to the device. Your goal as a parent is not to scare you children to death, rather almost to death. Just as your approach to disciplining your children will vary based on the personality and character of each child, so will the content and tone of the conversation. Remember:

- Children as young as 8 years old are regularly consuming pornography online[11].
- Children as young as 3 years old are playing via device apps with little to no supervision.

Tell your K-4th grade children that there are people in the world who seek to do harm to children specifically. Beginning in the 5th grade children need to be told that there are people in the world who would do them harm "sexually". Generally you don't have to explain past that point; they will understand exactly what you're talking about without having to get into the specifics of rape. However, you should be ready for the conversation.

Remember, you either have the conversation or they don't get access to the device, it's your choice.

THE LEAST YOU SHOULD KNOW

Digital risks, like all other human risks, need to be analyzed and evaluated as a cost-benefit scenario. Otherwise, you're just floating around the ether as a potential victim without even understanding if or how you were victimized.

All digital risks are made possible either via incoming vulnerabilities or outgoing vulnerabilities.

Incoming vulnerabilities take advantage of some weakness in your defenses and do not involve an action on behalf of the victim. There are four basic categories: remote access, brain access, data exhaust, and external influences.

Outgoing vulnerabilities exist when we accidentally help the "bad guy" and requires some action on behalf of the victim. There are three basic categories: web-enabled gadgets, data sharing, and seeking connection.

Explaining threats to your child is not optional if he/she has unmonitored access to a device.

CONVERSATION STARTERS

Using an analogy of predators and prey in the animal kingdom helps to illustrate the point of digital risk with children of all ages. It's important to emphasize to your children, at every age that a lion (predator) is going to try to eat a rhinoceros (prey) because it's in his nature. However, just because the rhino can become prey doesn't mean that it will get eaten by the lion. The rhino is naturally endowed with thick skin and sharp horns for defense.

However, there are behaviors that alert the lions to the rhino's presence. When children share too much information about themselves they put themselves at risk and make it easier for the lions to attack. Even though the lions exist there are things we can do to keep ourselves safe.

The idea is to make the risks very clear while empowering the child to be his own best advocate. You can extend the analogy by illustrating where it fails. In the lion/rhino scenario, the rhino knows a lion when he sees or smells one. This is not how the digital world works. Online, during an in-game chat, or on Instagram, anyone can be a lion.

Ask your 5th grade (or older) child: Did you know that webcams connected to a wi-fi signal are potentially hackable?

With your 1st to 4th-grade child

- First go to the Facebook page of someone who is not connected to you (check the page first to make sure there's nothing obviously lecherous or sexual).
- Ask your child: Let's pretend to be detectives and see how much information we could guess just from looking at someone's Facebook page.

The goal here is to get your child to begin viewing social media from a critical point of view and to identify breadcrumbs of information accidentally left behind by its users.

With your 5th grade (and older) child

- If your child has any social media profiles (which he absolutely should NOT under COPPA Federal Guidelines), have your child log out of their account and visit a profile of someone he is not connected to.
- Ask your child: Let's see how much personal information we could figure out about this person just by what's listed publicly.
- Then go to your child's profile (as a public person) and go through the same process.

The goal here is to get your child to see just how much information is given away in a social media bio, profile pic, and publicly available posts.

For your 7th grade (and older) child: How do you think home gadgets like the Amazon Echo operate? Did you know that the device is listening all the time? How do you feel about that?

Ask your child: Did you know that when you use a phone or tablet right before bed that it's harder to fall asleep? Do you think most people know that?

ACTION ITEMS

Review all of the risks with your spouse. Make a complete list of the changes which need to be made to hardware, privacy settings, and then implement the changes. Then make a list of all of the behavioral changes which need to happen among all of the family members. Agree on the three most critical changes and present those changes to the family. Whichever behavioral changes are implemented need to be respected by all members of the family - including mom and dad. You're far more likely to see changes in your children if they see you struggling as well.

Engage the help of your 5th grade (and older) children to help you identify and cover all of the webcams in your home with a piece of electrical tape. The goal is to reinforce the message while engaging their help in helping to keep the family safer.

Set up the Do Not Disturb settings on every phone in your home - it's life changing.

SECTION II: DIRECT THREATS

Chapter 7: Cyberbullying

Chapter 8: Sexting

Chapter 9: Sexual Predation

Chapter 7

CYBERBULLYING

In September 2013, 12 year-old Rebecca Sedwick[87], committed suicide by jumping off a concrete silo in Lakeland Florida. She had been the victim of relentless IRL (in real life) and online bullying. Apparently, Rebecca was dating the wrong girl's ex-boyfriend. According to police investigations, fourteen year old Guadalupe Shaw[88] bullied and cyberbullied Rebecca relentlessly. According to the investigators, Shaw convinced fourteen other girls to harass Rebecca. If the coerced refused to comply, they would face the wrath of being bullied themselves. Nice, huh?

"Cyberbullying" becomes headline news each time the tragic death of a child results. But we never hear the less tragic stories; the millions of other cases where child victims suffer bullying in silence, from bullies known and unknown. There would be far too many stories to tell.

---

87 *"Charges in Rebecca Sedwick's suicide suggest 'tipping point' in bullying cases"*
http://www.cnn.com/2013/10/25/us/rebecca-sedwick-bullying-suicide-case/index.html
88 Eventually charges against Guadalupe Shaw were dropped for lack of evidence

Has the world gone completely mad, or is there something uniquely cruel about our global digital environment? Children are not born cyberbullies. This new generation of children is not damaged or flawed; they have not been born with less compassion or a greater propensity for cruelty. If we need someone to blame, as parents, we must look to ourselves. Unsupervised and ready access to digital tools, lack of parental engagement, and a growing societal indifference and desensitization is cultivating a new breed of super-bullies.

If we want to curb bullying in all its forms, we must begin in our own homes.

BD-ERA (BEFORE DIGITAL) BULLYING

If you were born before 1975 you probably remember the name of your school's bully since in the BD-era all bullying happened face to face. Children's movies and cartoons reflect this era of bullying in its characters: the Butch-esque Little Rascals bully with the always agreeable and dim-witted sidekick. Our BD-era Butch may not have had much of a reason to choose you as his victim. He may have just wanted your milk money. For whatever twisted reason, he decided that you were going to be another victim. Maybe it really was just about the milk money. Sometimes it was because you were too different or too smart, too quiet or too outspoken.

You either gave in or you fought back; knowing that you would probably lose either way. Since all BD-era bullying occurred face-to-face the potential risks were apparent and obvious: physical harm, property damage, and personal humiliation. The bullying may have happened in full view of a crowd or quietly in the shadows. But once you entered your home you were safe, at least until the following day.

BD-era bullying is unfortunately still alive and thriving. Victims of traditional bullying suffer physical and emotional scars for years. From getting tripped in the lunch room to getting beaten up on the school bus, these scenarios continue to play themselves out every single day in school buildings and on school buses all over the world.

AD- ERA (AFTER DIGITAL) BULLYING

Through the use of digital tools and devices, cyberbullying has become sophisticated, pervasive, and unrelenting. The process begins the same way. The AD-era bully, we'll call her "Susie", begins by picking you as her victim.

You may have absolutely no idea that Susie is your bully. She might be hiding behind the anonymity of web apps and potentially aided by mob mentality. Susie begins to stalk you wherever and whenever you are online. She creates a fake Instagram account and leaves nasty comments on the photos from your last family vacation. Susie then convinces some of her minions to also up on you online. When you block Susie on Instagram she just creates another Instagram account and continues her systematic attack.

When you decide to take a break from Instagram, Susie and her mob follow you onto Twitter. One of Susie's minions Tweets your cell phone number publicly, and you begin to get phone calls from people you don't know. It's hard to sleep when your phone vibrates and dings all night with obscene texts and cruel messages.

At school you become the singular focus of school gossip. People whisper and laugh as you walk through the hallways. Every student has heard about and seen the cyberbullying content (photos, posts, tweets, texts, etc). Pretty soon you figure out that there is nowhere to hide.

The pace is relentless. Digital applications never go to sleep and neither do the messages or the barrage of cyberbullying that you experience as Susie's victim.

———<><>———

Cyberbullying is the use of electronic or digital communication to bully or harass a person typically by sending or posting messages of an intimidating or threatening nature. Cyberbullies set out to do harm to a particular victim via some digital platform. Although different states have slightly varied legal definitions of cyberbullying for the purposes of prosecuting cases, the crux remains consistent. A cyberbully is a person who uses digital platforms to do harm to another person; essentially BD bullying with a far more efficient and longer reaching delivery system.

Cyberbullying cases can take many forms in terms of technologies and student involvement. Cyberbullying generally comes in two flavors: direct and proxy. You may see shades of direct and proxy cyberbullying as well as the appearance and disappearance of many of the perpetrators at any given moment.

Direct cyberbullying occurs when one individual bullies another individual via some digital app or platform. Remember that although this is a one-on-one scenario the victim may not know the actual identity of the bully. Direct cyberbullying merely refers to the fact that it is one person versus another.

Proxy cyberbullying occurs when one or several cyberbullies engage the help of many other individuals to cyberbully the victim. Even in the case of proxy cyberbullying, the victim may not know the actual identities of any of the cyberbullies making it very difficult to navigate their own social sphere at school. The victim feels as though she is surrounded by the enemy, and she might be right.

Self-harm cyberbullying (aka Digital Munchausen) occurs when a victim is posting cruel and negative comments about himself/herself. This behavior is similar to other self-injury behaviors. In the only study published so far on this phenomenon, Elizabeth Englander, PhD has named it "Digital Munchausen" because of its similarity to Munchausen's Syndrome where patients fake illness in order to illicit attention.

In her study: Digital Self Harm: Frequency, Type, Motivations, and Outcomes[89], she found that 9% of the high school students surveyed admitted to "falsely posting a cruel remark against themselves during high school." Also:

- 13% of boys and 8% of girls had done it at least one time
- 23% repeated the behavior once a month

Although the specific motivations were different between the boys and the girls surveyed, overall the goal was to gain some sort of attention. Students specifically mentioned engaging in this type of self-harm as a 'cry for help' and 'so others would worry about me".

CYBERBULLYING STATISTICS

Your child has probably already been at least two of the following: the perpetrator, the victim, or the bystander. Chances are that your child has

---

[89] Read the entire study here: *"Digital Self Harm: Frequency, Type, Motivations, and Outcomes"* Massachusetts Aggression Reduction Center

already been all three.

There is a very thin line between being a victim and a bully. Revenge is easily achieved on digital platforms. Today's victim is tomorrow's bully and vice versa.

- 7 out of 10 young people have been a victim of cyberbullying[90].
- 37% of young people have experienced cyberbullying on a frequent basis
- 20% of young people have experienced extreme cyberbullying on a daily basis
- 88% of teens who use social media have witnessed cyberbullying of another person while 66% of teens who witness cyberbullying also witness others joining in[91]
- 38% of girls report being cyberbullied compared with 26% of boys online
- 13% of teens report that someone has spread a rumor about them online
- 21% of all kids using technology have received a mean or threatening email
- 13% of teens who use social media say that they have had an experience on social media which made them feel nervous about going to school the next day

Of those students who had been cyberbullied relatively frequently (at least twice in the last couple of months):

- 62% said that they had been cyberbullied by another student at school, and 46% had been cyberbullied by a friend.
- 55% didn't know who had cyberbullied them.

WHAT ABOUT THE PARENTS?

Part of your job as a parent is to protect your child. It can be difficult to imagine that your child might be a victim and/or a bully. Until our generation of parents engages in a proactive campaign to educate their children, cyberbullying is going to continue to escalate in frequency and intensity. Even a basic analysis of cyberbullying statistics begins to show a significant disconnect between the realities of cyberbullying and the global lack of parental engagement.

---

90 Ditch the Label: Cyberbullying Statistics
91 PEW Internet Research Center, FOSI, Cable in the Classroom, 2011

- Only 7% of American parents are worried about cyberbullying while 33% of American teenagers have been victims[92]
- 85% of parents of children age 13-17 report that their children have at least one social media account[93]

As you can see in the statistics above, there is a large gap between the 7% of parents who say they are "worried about cyberbullying" and the 33% of children who are identifying themselves as victims. If 33% are identifying themselves as victims, there is a fair percentage who **are** victims, but do not self-identify that way. In addition, those statistics do not identify the percentage of bullies involved in the process. The cherry on the sundae is the 85% of parents who report their children having at least one social media account.

If we take these statistics as absolute facts with zero margin of statistical error and apply it to a sample of 100 children between 13 and 17 years old: 85 have at least one social media account, 33 self-identify as victims, but only 7 parents are worried.

This lack of parental awareness and engagement illustrated in these statistics reflects what I see when presenting to parents in varying: geographic, socioeconomic, and ethnic groups. Regardless of the location or the level of affluence, the single constant is this weird undercurrent of something I've named: Parental Willful Bewilderment. I suspect that it comes from knowing at some deep level that *if I acknowledge the existence of issue then as a parent I must act on it. So I'm just going to pretend like it's not happening.*

As we've seen over and over from Chapter 1 – it all begins with device ownership. And make no mistake…

Your child does not **need** a phone!!

If she needs a pickup after volleyball practice, she can call you from the phone of any teammate. You can also purchase a simple flip phone. They cost less than one dollar and come with a monthly service plan of around $5/month.

---

92 PEW Internet and American Life Survey, 2011
93 American Osteopathic Association, 2011

Cyberbullies are everywhere. They are: male and female, rich and poor, extroverted and introverted, have been victims and have never been targeted. Statistically, it is just as likely that your child will be targeted by a good friend or by an enemy. Your child's best friend, who sat at your dinner table just a week ago thanking you for "the lovely dinner" might be the very same Eddie Haskell[94] making your kid's life miserable.

In studies done to determine why children engage in cyberbullying behaviors, some patterns emerge. Cyberbullies tend to gain notoriety in their twisted attempt to be humorous at someone else expense, and do not believe that they will get caught. Additionally, cyberbullies tend to spend far more time online than their peers. How many hours per day does your child spend in unsupervised digital activities? If your answer is 'more than one' you may be brewing your own little Digital Butch or Digital Susie.

When asked why they engage in cyberbullying, cyberbullies responded[95]:

- As revenge 58%. If your child has been a victim – be extra vigilant   he/she may just end up becoming another cyberbully.
- Because the victim "deserved it" 58%
- For fun 28%
- To be mean or to show off to friends 25%
- To embarrass the victim 21%

In 2006, 14 year-old Megan Meier[96] hung herself in her closet after a cyber-relationship with a young man ended abruptly. After a brief but active online-only relationship, "Josh" (whom she had never met in person) suddenly turned on her telling her that 'the world would be better off without her.' It turns out that "Josh" never existed; an adult woman (who was also a neighbor and family friend of the Meier's) created the young man's fake online persona in order to draw Megan into a carefully planned scheme intended to hurt Megan.

Children (and adults) have a hard time believing that the person with

---

94 For you younger parents – Eddie Haskell was a character on the show "Leave It To Beaver". Do a wiki search

95 *Teen Online & Wireless Safety Survey: Cyberbullying, Sexting and Parental Controls.* Cox Communications Teen Online and Wireless Safety Survey in Partnership with the National Center for Missing and Exploited Children, 2009.

96 The Megan Meier Foundation

whom they are speaking online can literally be anyone. The person who says she is a 16 year-old teenage girl can actually be a 54 year-old man. Younger children are especially at risk for being intentionally duped by an adult who would do them harm.

—————

Since cyberbullying by definition is the abuse and harassment of a person via a digital platform – the category of victims should include celebrities and politicians. There is no end to the cruelty and harassment which public figures suffer. While it's true that public figures choose to live a public life, it is also true that when your children post content onto a digital platform, they are making themselves an open and willing target for public ridicule and harassment.

In our typical day-to-day life, cyberbullying exists and shows up on every single social platform. Don't believe me? Just visit any news site and read the comments beneath any article. The level of hatred, bigotry, and cruelty can be shocking. More than 50% of children, who are victims of cyberbullying, never report the behavior to their parents. While boys are more susceptible to physical abuse at the hands of a bully, girls are more susceptible to emotional or verbal victimization[97] (e.g., rumor-spreading or gossiping).

It is fairly likely that your child has already been a victim, even if he/she does not consider it cyberbullying.

CYBERBULLYING AND SUICIDE

I am not a mental health professional and I have no expertise in the areas of suicide or adolescent mental health. Based on my research and first-hand observations in this area, I can tell you that cyberbullying alone does not cause suicide. However, there is a significant amount of research which suggests that 'peer victimization' is an important risk factor[98] for adolescent suicide. If cyberbullying is combined with other mental health conditions and risk factors,

---

97 *"Relational and overt forms of peer victimization: a multi-informant approach,"* Journal of Consulting and Clinical Psychology, vol. 66, no. 2, pp. 337–347, 1998.

98 van Geel M, Vedder P, Tanilon J. *Relationship Between Peer Victimization, Cyberbullying, and Suicide in Children and AdolescentsA Meta-analysis.* JAMA Pediatr. 2014;168(5):435-442. doi:10.1001/jamapediatrics.2013.4143

the potential for suicide is increased.

Moreover, communities suffering the aftershocks of an adolescent suicide might accidentally contribute to suicide contagion. A child who is already at risk for suicide could perceive the outpouring of grief, candlelight vigils, and other community events as a glamorization of suicide. For children who already feel isolated and neglected, that level of family and community attention and recognition could be compelling.

Data gathered from 2,180 students (7th-12th grade) by the National Longitudinal Study of Adolescent to Adult Health[99] showed that not only do adolescents tend to overestimate their friends' suicidal behaviors, but that exposure to the suicidal behaviors exacerbates their own risk of suicidal behaviors. Respondents who accurately perceived their friends' attempted suicide were 2.54 times more likely to attempt suicide themselves while respondents who overestimated their friends' attempted suicide were 5.40 times more likely to attempt suicide themselves. The study concluded that

> *"Practically, it is important to screen at-risk youth for exposure to peer suicide and to use the social environment created by adolescent friendship networks to empower and support youth who are susceptible to suicidal thoughts and behaviors."*

Other data and studies support these findings. Children who are exposed to the actual suicide of a classmate are five times more likely to attempt suicide themselves than a child who never has; even when the surviving classmates did not have a personal relationship with the victim. According to a new study in the Canadian Medical Association Journal (CMAJ), having a classmate commit suicide significantly increases the chance that a teenager will consider or attempt suicide themselves. The risk is greatest for 12 to 13 year olds.

The overwhelming percentage of children who are bullied never attempt suicide. Please speak frankly with your children if they have been exposed to the suicide or the attempted suicide of a classmate or community member. You don't want your children to see suicide as the logically concluding action of a desperate soul who has suffered through cyberbullying. Make sure your child understands that the solution to a seemingly overwhelming problem is to get help, and never give up.

---

99 Zimmerman, Gregory M. et al. *"The Power Of (Mis)Perception: Rethinking Suicide Contagion In Youth Friendship Networks"*. Social Science & Medicine 157 (2016): 31-38. Web.

The media must be careful to avoid being reckless in their reporting of suicides. Implying suicide causality to cyberbullying in headlines such as "14 year-old Commits Suicide as a Result of Cyberbullying" implies that such causality actually exists, when it absolutely does not. Children do not have the media literacy skills to approach such news stories with a critical bias and understand that cyberbullying does NOT "cause" suicide or school shootings. If that were the case, we would be burying tens of millions of children each year.

Every time you hear such a story, explain this point to your children. Say it over and over again. Point out the ways that your child can get help even if that means speaking to someone outside of your home. In addition, be sure to refrain from contributing to the potential "glamorization" of suicide in your own community, even when motivated by the best of intentions.

PREVENTING VICTIMIZATION

When I present to parents all over the United States, the most typical questions I am asked are those related to cyberbullying. These questions are generally reactive in nature and relate to their child having already been a victim. Being proactive in your child's digital safety is far preferable to dealing with the emotional after effects of your child's experience as a victim. Attempting to ensure that your child avoids becoming a victim will require work and consistent vigilance on your part. Every second of this critical parenting work is well worth the grey hairs earned in its execution.

Your child's online "friends" Your child should only be "friends with" or "followed by" other children or family members known IRL (in real life) by mom or dad. Beware the adult who wants to be your child's follower, even if that adult is known to you. Anyone you are unsure of should be unfriended or blocked.

TMI posts. Your children talk too much[100], in case you hadn't noticed. Your child is giving cyberbullies potential ammunition to use against him/her (examples: problems at home, issues at school, illnesses, family deaths,

---

[100] TMI= Too Much Information

personally identifying data, etc). The child who posts "my mom hates me" is probably **not** going to find a sympathetic ear on a public forum and will instead get a response similar to "she hates you bc you're fat and ugly".

Your children are looking for human validation of their adolescent problems and concerns. They want to know that someone understands and is willing to be there for them. The cyberbullying victims I have met are quite willing to risk becoming a victim if it means that there is a chance that someone will care, even if that someone is a stranger.

Sharing passwords. Tween and teen girls especially have an especially horrifying habit of sharing their account passwords with their girlfriends. If you remember from earlier in this chapter, 46% of all cyberbullies are friends with the victim. Today's friend is tomorrow's enemy. In a few notable cases the stereotypical "Susie" convinces a child's true and loyal friend into sharing the victim's password. Once the bullies get their hands on your child's login credentials, they will begin posting inappropriate and humiliating content, making it seem as though your child posted it herself.

Do not feed the trolls. Cyberbullies and trolls are the same thing…if you feed the trolls they get bigger and stronger. If someone is posting negative content on your child's wall (ie Why are you so fat?) the absolutely wrong thing to do is to respond directly to the troll (ie. Why would you say that? I thought you were my friend?). Feeding trolls only makes them stronger and provides objective proof that the posting has affected the victim. The only response necessary is : 1) Report to mom/dad 2) Block that individual. Easy peasy.

Time spent online. "Hyper-networking teens" – those who spend three hours or more per school day on social networks are 110% more likely to be a victim of cyberbullying.

This is my "cookies in the pantry" theory. If you're on a strict diet and you buy cookies whose fault is it that you ate them? You're the dope who bought the cookies and placed them conveniently in the pantry. Your child's chances of being victimized online if they are not actively participating in social networking are slim. If the bullies do not have digital access to your child, they will probably get bored and pick on someone else (aka the cookies are not in the pantry).

By allowing your child unsupervised time on social platforms, you are effectively making it easier for him/her to be victimized. Don't buy the cookies, put them in the pantry, and expect them not to be eaten.

REPORTING THREATS TO THE SCHOOL AND LAW ENFORCEMENT

I'm Cuban, and we have a great expression about not "stirring a turd once it's dry." If a turd has already dried, it stops smelling. However, if you disturb its desiccation process by poking at it or stirring it, you've fluffed up its stinking potential.

The same goes for reporting cyberbullying to the school. If you discover that your child has been the victim of a tasteless/cruel/nasty bit of cyberbullying, it makes sense that you will want to march right up to that school, yank the bully out of his/her chair and personally witness the discipline taking place – preferably with a paddle. None of these things will happen, and you will be sorely disappointed.

If this is the first time your child has had a run-in with this particular bully (and the post/photo is NOT immediately threatening – see "EXCEPTION" note below) report the situation to your child's principal and ask him/her to **not act** on the information. Make it clear to the administrator that you are merely reporting the situation in order to create a paper trail. This way if something else happens, the next occurrence will be noted by the school as issue #2 rather than issue #1.

I have seen dozens of scenarios where "stirring the turd" awakened the troll, creating a much bigger issue where there might not have been one had it been ignored.

Exception: If your child has been personally or physically threatened in any way in a post, text, or photo:

- Take a screen shot of the threat (you must have proof)
- Go and report to your child's principal
- The principal will call local law enforcement. If the school refuses to call local law enforcement, do so yourself and file a police report. NOTE: Please, please, please be sure that the situation really is a threat and warrants this response. If not you've just stirred the turd and set it on fire.

Take a break from social media. This is the most important recommendation and the one which is most frequently ignored. If your child becomes a victim of cyberbullying and you don't force a break from all digital use (social media, tablets, gaming, and smartphones) outside of homework for a significant amount of time (two weeks to a month) – you are begging for it to continue. This is particularly true if you have "stirred the turd" and were forced to report to the school or law enforcement.

Is it fair that your child, the victim, should have to take a break from social media when he/she didn't do anything wrong? No, it's not fair. But by allowing your child to continue to engage in digital communication, you are effectively putting the cookies back into the pantry – and expecting them to not get eaten – again. And well, that would be stupid.

Beware your victim does not become a bully. Your child's victimization makes it far more likely that he/she will become a cyberbully by attempting to take digital revenge. Be sure to make the realities and potential consequences of this clear to your child. Also read the following section on bullies – just in case.

The cycle of victim to bully and back, is fairly consistent and common. You may need to face that fact that your child is currently a victim because someone is taking revenge on your little angel's bullying behavior. That's a hard pill to swallow. But it's highly possible and one of the first questions you should ask your victim: "Why do you think Susie would bully you in this way? Did you do anything to Susie to make her want to take revenge?"

PREVENTING BULLYING BEHAVIOR

We can't control what our children do when we aren't around, particularly when we really have tried our best as parents. We can, however, make sure that their life stops on a dime the first time they get caught, preventing the second to thirty-fifth occurrences.

This is what I like to call: **Avoiding the Likelihood of Incarceration.**

- 81% of youth say that bullying online is easier to get away with than bullying in person
- Male bullies are nearly four times as likely as non-bullies to grow up to

physically or sexually abuse their female partners[101].

- By age 24, 60% of former school bullies had been convicted of a criminal charge at least once.

GETTING THE PHONE CALL

Do not blindly defend your child when you first hear about your child's alleged behavior without having all of the information – this may prove to be embarrassing for you as you dig deeper into the details of your child's involvement. You will probably first hear about your child's alleged bullying behavior from either the school or the parent of the victim. This is a golden opportunity to set the tone in your home for how these situations will be handled.

The moment you pick up the phone and begin to hear about the alleged misdeed – just apologize. It doesn't matter if your blessed angel is not to blame. Apologize anyhow. Try something like "regardless of what occurred today, I'm sorry it happened at all. I will help you get to the bottom of it, and do whatever I can to make sure it never happens again." You aren't admitting guilt, but you are saying that you will be a willing participant in sorting out the details.

Listen to everything the caller says without interruption, unless of course there's literally no way that it could be your kid – because your kid has been locked up in juvie for the past 6 months. For efficiency's sake, feel free to offer that up right away.

Be careful not to undermine your child's teachers. This is **not** the time to undermine your child's authority figures (teachers, coaches, administrators). It's very easy to slip into Mama Bear mode and rush to defend your child. After this situation is over, your child will still be expected to go to school and football practice and to have some measure of respect for his teachers and coaches. By tearing down your child's teachers and coaches, the only thing you've succeeded in doing is creating a conflict between you and your child. Your child might feel like he is betraying you if he remains respectful of his

---

101 2011 Harvard School of Health Study

authority figures. Especially that one you just called a knuckle-dragging-mouth-breathing-near-sighted-imbecile. Nice.

Interrogate your own child like he knows who shot JFK. Once you're off the phone ask the: who, what, where, when, and why. Try to catch him in a lie, double back and ask the same question four different ways. Make sure that your child knows that you take any accusation very seriously and that you will make him feel very uncomfortable until you get the truth. If he's actually innocent and was put into a precarious situation, then the lesson is to choose your friends and actions more carefully.

This is also the perfect time to try and discover if your child's behavior was instigated by having been a victim himself. Children never want to reveal to their parents that they feel "less-than". This could be your opportunity to learn more about what's actually happening in your child's digital and school life. As parents we all think we know, but most of the time we really don't have the full story.

Make your child take responsibility for his behavior and his reputation. Children should be expected to be stewards of their own reputation and behavior. They are responsible for how outsiders view them. To take that burden away from a child, denies them an opportunity for emotional growth and maturity. Just remember the cyberbullying allegations might very well be true. If you defend your child despite his guilt, you're on your way to brewing your own little Frankenstein. Unless of course you want your 30 year-old son to live in your basement forever, or at least until he "finds himself".

Digital access, stops NOW. If it ends up being true that your child misbehaved in any way (large or small) you absolutely must bring their life to a screeching halt. Everything stops: electronics, television, music, telephones, play dates – literally everything.

Your remedy needs to be loud, long, and consistent. If you don't make it 100% clear to your child that you will not tolerate bullying behaviors in your home, the actions will be repeated. You've put those cookies back into the pantry. Just don't be surprised when it happens again.

Remember: your child's participation in the digital universe as a bully makes it far more likely that he will be victimized later on, probably soon.

Although I am a believer in the cleansing power of Karma, you probably should try to avoid a revenge induced backlash.

CONSEQUENCES OF CYBERBULLYING.

Each state has its own criminal cyberbullying or online stalking and harassment laws. In addition, most states have cyberbullying policies which regulate how school districts are expected to respond to reported occurrences of cyberbullying within the school community even when they occur off campus.

Generally speaking, a school administrator will be expected to call local law enforcement whenever there has been a threat of physical harm. The consequences for cyberbullying can include:

- School suspension or expulsion
- Criminal charges. These may include: online harassment, stalking, and cyberbullying (as a legal term). Some states (like Florida) are attempting to include parents in criminal charges when their children engage in criminal cyberbullying.
- Loss of reputation. There have been hundreds of publicized cases where accused cyberbullies have lost high school and college scholarships, college acceptances, internships, and other opportunities.
- Legal fees and court fees. If your child has been accused of cyberbullying behaviors and these accusations rise to the level of criminal charges, get your checkbook ready. You will need to hire a criminal attorney who specializes in adolescent criminal defense. It won't be cheap.
- Civil litigation. If the bullying is severe enough, the parents of the victim could seek and be granted civil damages in addition to any criminal charges pursued by the prosecutor.

A NOTE ABOUT COPPA

If your child is under 13 years old and personal information has been posted on a website or social media platform (unauthorized photos, personally identifying information) COPPA[102] (the Children's Online Privacy Protection Act) demands that the website remove the content.

When you contact the website you will probably have to prove that

---

102 COPPA is the Children's Online Privacy Protection Act, a set of guidelines created by the United States' Federal Trade Commission (FTC).

you are the legal parent/guardian of your child and that your child is under 13 years old. Once you've done that, they have no choice but to remove the content.

If you are not getting a response to your COPPA request, you can contact the FTC directly at www.ftc.gov

Bottom line

Approximately 1.5 million school-aged adolescents (i.e., ages 12 to 18) report that they have been victimized by violence while at school.[103] While student-directed anti-bullying education is valuable, there is a risk that these programs can actually increase bullying behaviors. In September 2013, a study[104] released by the University of Texas in Arlington, found that "unintended consequences may result from campaigns designed to educate students about the harms of physical and emotional harassment." According to researchers' findings, bullying prevention programs in schools generally **increase incidences[105]** of physical and emotional attacks among students by teaching kids about the ins and outs of bullying.

We are never going to completely eradicate bullying from childhood. Unfortunately, bullying is going to remain a developmental part of a child's life experience. As parents our job is to mitigate those negative outcomes in our children's lives by keeping the lines of communication open at all times.

In terms of prevention, parents should be: limiting a child's access to technology at younger ages, setting limits and consequences, and knowing how to respond when a cyberbullying situation arises.

---

103 R. Dinkes, E. F. Cataldi, G. Kena, and K. Baum, *"Indicators of School Crime and Safety"*, U.S. Department of Education, Washington, DC, USA, 2009.

104 *"A Multilevel Examination of Peer Victimization and Bullying Preventions in Schools"*; Journal of Criminology, Volume 2013 (2013)

105 When I present to students and school districts I'm very careful to not give kids any "new ideas" of how to misbehave. I prefer to just scare them straight – it's way more fun.

THE LEAST YOU SHOULD KNOW

Unsupervised and ready access to digital tools, lack of parental engagement, and a growing societal indifference and desensitization is cultivating a new breed of super-bullies.

Cyberbullying is the use of electronic or digital communication to bully or harass a person typically by sending or posting messages of an intimidating or threatening nature.

Direct cyberbullying occurs when one individual bullies another individual via some digital app or platform.

Proxy cyberbullying occurs when one or several cyberbullies engage the help of many other individuals to cyberbully the victim.

Self-harm cyberbullying (aka Digital Munchausen) occurs when a victim is posting cruel and negative comments about himself/herself.

Your child has probably already been at least two of the following: the perpetrator, the victim, or the bystander. Chances are that your child has already been all three.

Your child does NOT NEED A PHONE. No smartphones until 9th grade.

Cyberbullying alone does not cause suicide. However, 'peer victimization' is an important risk factor for adolescent suicide. Also children who are exposed to the suicide of a classmate are five times more likely to attempt suicide themselves than a child who never has.

Your child needs a two week to one month break from all devices if you're discovered that he/she has been a victim or perpetrator of cyberbullying.

CONVERSATION STARTERS

Ask your child: Have you ever noticed kids picking on other kids while on a social media platform or while playing a video game? What do you when someone says something rude or inappropriate to you online or in a game? Are you ever tempted to "get back" at that person?

Ask your child: Have you ever had to block someone online? Do you know how to block someone on all of the social platforms and games you use?

Ask your child: Do you think it should be considered cyberbullying when the victim is a public figure like a celebrity or politician? How about when the victim is a teacher or coach?

Ask your child: It turns out that very often cyberbullies end up being a victim's actual friend. Which of your friends would you suspect the most? The least?

Ask your child: Have you seen any situation where a victim of cyberbullying became a bully, out for revenge?

Ask your child: What do you think a parent should do to help protect their children? If this happened to you what would you like for me to do to help you?

Ask your child: Do you know any friends who post TMI? What do you think about that?

Ask your child: Do you know any friends who share their login information and passwords? Do you think this is a good idea?

ACTION ITEMS

Log into your child's social platforms every week (yes, you should have all of their passwords) and go through all of your child's comments and the responses received. How do they strike you? Screenshot any examples which concern you and discuss them with your child, or your school administrator.

If your child is a victim of cyberbullying, consider the possibility that your child might be engaging in some sort of self-harm campaign for attention. I would **not** have a "Digital Munchausen" conversation with your child proactively; you definitely don't want to give your child the idea that this might be a healthy way to gain attention. However, if you hear of something on the news, or experience a case in your community it would certainly be worth the discussion.

If your child is exposed to the suicide or attempted suicide of a classmate or friend, make sure that your child knows that the solution to any problem (like cyberbullying) is to never give up. Make sure that they know that the vast majority of children with problems never attempt suicide. Regardless of the depth of your grief in the face of a child suicide in your community, be careful of not accidentally over-glamorizing that child's life or death. You could be sending mixed signals to your own child.

Chapter 8

SEXTING

When Margarite and Isaiah were 8th graders and "dating", Margarite sent Isaiah a fully nude photo she had taken of herself while standing in front of a mirror. They broke up months later and one of Margarite's ex-friends convinced Isaiah to send her a copy of Margarite's photo. Within hours, the ex-friend forwarded the photo of Margarite (accompanied by a crude caption) to everyone she knew, encouraging the recipients to forward the photo to others. By the next morning students at four neighboring schools had received and forwarded the image.

Police arrived at the school later that day. They handcuffed and arrested Isaiah, the ex-friend, and another girl who helped spread the photo. The county prosecutor charged all three students with the dissemination of child pornography, a felony in the State of Washington which could result in the children being listed as registered sex offenders.

Similar scenarios are playing out in middle schools and high schools all over the United States. Like most other digital risks, sexting is not impacted by geography, socio-economic levels, ethnicity, or even age. This is not a pubescent or even pre-pubescent issue. According to the data[106] I have collected from my student audiences, sexting now begins in the 4th/5th grade.

I receive more requests for school presentations because of sexting than any other digital risk. In 2016, I noticed that the sexting data I collected were overlapping with social media risks related to human sex trafficking. This disturbing reality is making its mark on very young children. As a direct result of parsing through student data which unequivocally reflect that very young children are engaging in a wider variety and deeper level of risky digital behaviors than older children, it has now become "standard" to suggest the inclusion of 4th and 5th graders during student presentations.

WHAT IS SEXTING?

The term "sext" was the original term given to sending sexual content via a digital interface like a text. It has now come to mean any sexual exchange across any digital platform including photos, videos, and just words or text. Given the ubiquity of digital devices in the world and the vast selection of platforms and apps it should not surprise us that sexting is everywhere.

Sexting is not necessarily a criminal act. If grown-ups want to send each other photos of their bits or sexually suggestive texts they are welcome to do so. Just know that similar to taking a photo of your dinner and posting it on Facebook, sexting is nauseating and disappointing for two reasons. First of all, no one cares about what you ate for dinner - seriously, NO ONE. Secondly, just like a photo of disembodied genitals, the photo of your dinner never looks the same as it did in real life. It's sort of like an on-location joke - you had to be there to get the punch line.

In 2011, when U.S Representative Anthony Weiner sexted photos of

---

106 See Chapter 1: The Central Issue for specific data. Sexting is at the top of the list of riskiest behaviors. It is extremely naive to believe that your 10 or 11-year-olds (or their peers) would never take a photo of themselves naked or partially naked and send it to someone - even a "someone" they don't know. In fact a common post-presentation comment I hear from children (via anonymous exit survey) is some variation on the following "Because of your presentation I'm going to stop sexting with randos" (randos= random people I don't know) or "I'm going to stop sexting with ppl idk" (ppl idk = people I don't know).

his junk to women on social media it was vomitous and inappropriate, but not criminal. Why? Because he's an adult sending sexual content to another adult. However, in 2016, when Weiner once again decided to take a photo of his nether regions and got caught - again (because obviously) there was a major difference in the potential criminal consequences.

In the 2016 version of his now very public case of criminal stupidity he was caught sending the photos to a 15 year-old girl. As of January 2017 Weiner was facing charges of production of child pornography which carries a 15 year mandatory minimum sentence in the State of New York.

Sexting becomes a crime when the subject or content of a child or when any pornographic content is sent to a child - in a simpler way, if the content is OF or SENT TO a child. That definition is fairly straightforward, but if you pay close attention you will notice that the law does not exempt children as potential perpetrators of this crime. If your 12-year-old daughter sends a photo of her bare breasts to her boyfriend, she can be charged with felony creation/production of child pornography, felony possession of child pornography and felony trafficking of child pornography - potentially three felony counts for one image. It doesn't matter that she sent it willingly or that she took a photo of her own body.

Parents are surprised when they begin to understand the law and realize that their very young children could be charged with felonies. Your child can also be charged with felony possession and felony trafficking of child pornography for keeping or sharing a photo that they didn't create or ask for. This is when parents begin to panic a little and with good reason.

Complicating this issue is the fact that a photo or video does not have to be nude to be considered child pornography. Any content meant to be sexually suggestive or sex-y can be considered child pornography. I've personally seen sexting cases where children thought themselves exempt from sexting laws because their head wasn't in the photo, or they had underwear on, or the photo was sent via some supposedly anonymous app. These mythical loopholes do not exist.

Prosecutors will also take the child's intent into account when deciding how to proceed with a sexting case. For example, in the Margarite and Isaiah case, Margarite was not charged with a crime even though she took the original photo of herself. Law enforcement and the prosecutor agreed that her intent was merely to send the photo to Isaiah. There was obvious intent on the part of Isaiah and the two girls who had encouraged the malicious and ugly behavior which came after.

The decision on how to charge an alleged perpetrator belongs to the prosecutor. If your child is engaging in risky sexting behaviors, the line between an attractive photo and a sexually suggestive one can become very blurry, very quickly. Let's say that your 10-year-old son receives a bikini pic of a female classmate in a text.

If he were to forward that photo to his buddies he could potentially be charged with felony possession and felony trafficking of child pornography if the prosecutor determines that the photo is sexually suggestive. And it won't matter that he's not in the photo or that the girl in the photo isn't nude.

TYPES OF SEXTING

Love sexting. Some kids are sexting within a relationship. They send a sexy photo to their boyfriend or girlfriend because they can't imagine a day when the love will die and one of them will want to take revenge on the other. It's also possible that the new girlfriend will find photos of the old girlfriend on the boyfriend's phone. One young lady in Canada has been sentenced to 15 years in prison and will be a registered sex offender upon release for doing that very thing.

Sexting with strangers. 15% of teens who have sent or posted nude/seminude images of themselves say they have done so to someone they knew only online. Think about that for a moment. The child did not even know the person in real life, and yet decided to send sexually suggestive or explicit materials. This is the exact pattern of how sextortion begins.

Sextortion[107] *(called "Harassment Sexting" in the 1st edition)*

A predator dupes or bullies a child into sending a single sexted photo. Once the photo is received, the predator threatens to tell the child's parents or reveal the photo on social media unless…the child agrees to send the predator hundreds or thousands of additional photos and videos. Sometimes "sexting" is the tip of a much larger iceberg. As the cases of human sex trafficking increase dramatically across the United States, it has become clear that sexting can be just a clue towards a much larger issue of sextortion or human sex trafficking.

When a student asks me for help or advice on a sexting issue I immediately send up a prayer to all of the gods. My prayer is simple: *Please, please, please let this be just a sexting case.* In terms of child safety the best case sexting scenario is when: Kid A sends photo of junk to Kid B - and it ends there. Would you rather your kid NOT send a photo of his junk to anyone, ever? Yes. Particularly since he forgets to use soap when he showers? Eww, double yes. However - could this scenario be way worse? Yes. This is the reason law enforcement takes sexting so seriously and also the reason why I have disagreed with law enforcement when I think that a case was dropped too quickly.

A sexting allegation might be the one and only clue a parent ever gets that a child might be in imminent danger.

WHY ARE KIDS SEXTING?

It's not easy growing up in a completely digital society and it's not a coincidence that sexting cases involving younger children are increasing. The younger the child is, the more deeply immersed he is in the digital world. Your 9-year-old doesn't remember a world without Instagram. The concept of pulling a device out of your pocket to record your entire life doesn't seem odd or excessive to her.

To complicate matters, your child's favorite athletes, musical artists, and movie stars post photos to their Instagram accounts constantly. If the celebrity is young-ish, it's likely that she/he is posting sexually charged content.

---

107 The 1st edition included the following: "Although not typical among younger users of technology, sexting can also be used as a tool of intimidation." Since publishing the first edition, this issue of "sextortion" is significantly on the rise and involves extremely young children. In 2016 a fourth grade girl asked me to help her. because a 13 year-old male acquaintance had been sending her naked photos of himself and began attempting to coerce the 9 year-old girl into returning the favor - if she failed to comply that he would tell her mother what a "whore" she is. I've had a front row seat to hundreds of these scenarios since printing the 1st edition.

Singers like Rihanna and Lady Gaga are adults who can pose on Instagram in a thong if they like - and they do. However, exceedingly sexualized content is what now passes for attractiveness. If I'm a tween girl, I may want to pose like Lady Gaga in my underwear. If I'm a tween boy it doesn't seem strange that my female classmates try to emulate Lady Gaga. Additionally, tweens and teens feel the pressure to both ask for and collect sexted content as some sort of 21st century souvenir of conquests.

Through media sponsored hyper-sexualization and the vast and easy availability of online pornography, our children have become entirely sexually desensitized. Very young children see themselves as sexual beings, well before any hint of puberty.

According to the National Campaign to Prevent Teen and Unplanned Pregnancy

- 15% of teens who have sent or posted nude/seminude images of themselves say they have done so to someone they knew only online.
- When stating the reasons why they sent/posted suggestive messages or nude/seminude pictures/videos, 44% said it was in response to one that was sent to them.
- Sending and posting nude or seminude photos or videos starts at a young age and becomes even more frequent as teens (ages 13 to 19) become young adults (ages 20 to 26).
- 38% of teen girls and 39% of teen boys say they have had sexually suggestive text messages or e-mails—originally meant for someone else, shared with them.
- 36% of teen girls and 39% of teen boys say it is common for nude or semi-nude photos to get shared with people other than the intended recipient.

Data collected from my student presentations

At the end of the student presentations, each student completes an anonymous exit survey. Those student responses are then processed, calculated, and reported back to school administrators[108].

The graph below reflects the percentage of students who identified *sexting* as the 'biggest issue at school.' The spike in the 4th and 5th grade numbers is typical for schools all over the country.

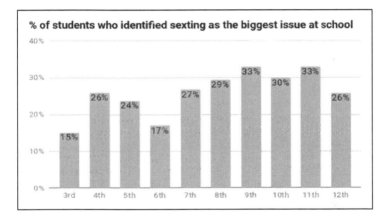

% of students who identified sexting as the biggest issue at school

"Sexting is the new flirting"

While out to dinner with another couple, my friend's husband was grilling me about statements I had made about the casual attitude young people have towards sexting. He was having a hard time wrapping his brain around my comment- that sexting has become a typical part of the lives of tweens and teens. My husband, taking the role of the magician's assistant, stopped our waitress and asked her "How do you feel about sexting?" She took a step backwards interpreting his question as an invitation rather than a request for a philosophically based opinion. I very quickly explained. She smiled sweetly and said *"Sexting? Oh sexting is the new flirting...drink refill?"*

This was not the first time I had heard similar comments from young people. I'll never forget the high school boy who, in trying to explain the

---

108 Read Chapter 12: The Children I've Met to learn more about data collection and methods.

frequency and immediacy of sexting among teens said to me *"Most of the time I've seen a pic of a girl's boobs before I've met her friends, sometimes I've seen a pic of her boobs before I've even met THE GIRL!"* I've also received thousands of anonymous survey comments from male and female elementary and middle school students reporting the "dick pics" they've received both from people they know and people they don't know - either via text, an app, or some other digital platform.

The casualness with which young people approach the subject of sexting is part of the parenting dilemma. As parents, how do we address an issue for which we have such a natural and generationally visceral aversion while our children view the same behavior as a non-issue?

When children engage in sexting behaviors

There is a fundamental disconnect of understanding related to digital safety. The myth goes like this: *my child can't be at risk when he's sitting safely in his bedroom* or *I don't have to worry about my daughter's safety because she's at her best friend's house.* At best - your child's IRL (in real life) or physical location has no positive impact on your child's safety; at worst - your child's IRL physical location has been broadcast or tagged in connection with livestreaming, a social media post, or photo tag.

Engaging in sexting behaviors makes your child vulnerable to many more consequences than he/she can ever imagine. The criminal consequences are incredibly serious. There are children who have been indicted, charged, convicted, and sentenced under felony child pornography laws. Children have become registered sex offenders. When children engage in sexting behaviors there is no silver lining. There is no upside.

Children who engage in sexting behaviors:

- are at risk of becoming sextortion victims (see Chapter 9: Sexual Predation).
- are at risk of being stalked and contacted by sexual predators who view sexting as a signal of the child's willingness to engage in real life sexual contact.
- are at risk of being cyberbullied by their peers as a result of their actions. Girls especially are cruelly victimized and 'slut shamed'.
- can be charged under felony child pornography laws, sentencing can include prison and being listed as a registered sex offender.

- are at risk of losing any hard-won gains such as college acceptances, scholarships, jobs, and much more.
- lose control of the content. Once a photo or content goes digital there is no way to re-gain control. There is no such thing as deleting digital content.
- are more likely to use apps where sexting happens frequently (SnapChat, Instagram) and/or where the evidence is subsequently hidden (vault apps, cloud drives).

WHAT TO DO IF YOUR CHILD IS CAUGHT SEXTING

Sexting scandals are often discovered on school campuses. As photos and content go viral, students very quickly become aware of what has happened. If your child is involved in a sexting scenario, it's quite likely that the building principal[109] will be the first person to contact you. Hire an attorney[110] immediately. Do not walk your child into a police station without an attorney even if you believe your child is innocent. Then, if the child's device hasn't already been confiscated by the school or police, take it away.

Despite your initial shock and your understanding of the consequences try your best to keep your cool. Just keep in mind that sexting could be a sign of being a victim of sextortion. It would be very easy to let your concern and disappointment turn into anger. It's better to allow your brain to postpone that anger - there's always time for anger later. Instead focus on gathering all of the facts and getting a clear picture of the circumstances which surrounded your child's behavior.

If your son or daughter does get caught sending out inappropriate content whether via text, photo, or video – your first step is to take away every single device within the child's reach. You absolutely must include the child's smartphone. If the he absolutely needs a telephone (he doesn't) buy a flip phone which does not include any data, web access, or texting. Either your child has shown an egregious lack of impulse control OR he is currently the victim of a sexual predator. In either case, that link to additional digital risks needs to be severed for a few months (minimum). Girls, especially, can

---

109 Understand that school administrators and educators have a legal duty to report suspected sexting and/or suspected child abuse charges to law enforcement. In almost every state, a licensed school staff member could face misdemeanor charges for failure to report.

110 You need to hire an attorney who specializes in criminal law and who has experience working with adolescent defendants.

experience torturous 'slut shaming' and other forms of cyberbullying as a result of the public exposure of their role in a sexting scandal. Regardless of actual culpability, she does not need to see and hear the running play-by-play of who said what via social media. In addition, your child needs to deactivate every account he has on every single social network. All of them.

Sexting Laws and Law Enforcement

Regardless of whether they are child porn laws or sexting laws, these statutes are a part of the larger criminal code and will vary from state to state and generally speaking take on the essence of what is explained here. Some states have made accommodations for child originated sexting. I'll be honest and say that I'm not sure how I feel about the changes. Yes, it's heartbreaking when a child is charged with a felony and is labeled a convicted felon for a stupid mistake. However, I worry about cases where a sexual predator is pulling the strings. And as you will see in the next chapter predators use every available opportunity and loophole to get their hands on child victims. In sextortion cases, predators first coerce victims into sending sexualized photos and then threaten them into sending more photos. My main concern with downgrading those felony charges to misdemeanor charges centers on the cases with adult predators. I'm concerned that a potential misdemeanor case will not be investigated as thoroughly as a potential felony case, effectively shielding the predator that is really pulling the strings and coercing the child to act on his/her behalf.

Whether or not a particular case merits investigation and/or criminal charges is completely up to the discretion of law enforcement and the prosecutors. Over the past few years I have had the privilege of working with law enforcement[111] all over the country including investigators who work in the area of sex crimes related to children. Whenever members of law enforcement attend my presentations, I always ask them the same thing: "What do you think these parents need to know?" Here are the most important responses:

1. *Law enforcement does NOT relish the idea of putting handcuffs on children* - particularly when the child has little to no malicious intent and did not intend to harm anyone. However, law enforcement's perspective is and

---

[111] Please take a moment to read Appendix 6: Thank You to Law Enforcement

must be to carry out the duties of their job description which coincidentally is right in the job title: the enforcement of laws. I have seen many cases where I believe that investigators should have gone harder in a particular case - but I have yet to see a case where I believe that investigators went too far or too hard on a child.

2. *"Appropriate" can be a legal term.* In 2016, during presentations at an upscale suburban public school district, I became friendly with the middle school's SRO[112] when he sat through all seven consecutive student sessions and still had the grace to laugh at my same dumb jokes over and over again. At the end of the day, I asked him my favorite question "What do you think these parents need to know?" I've paraphrased his answer below.

> *"I'm glad you asked me that question - because I was going to tell you anyway...every day I see kids walking into school or coming to school dances dressed completely inappropriately. This is a MIDDLE SCHOOL and we have young girls who come to school with half of their bottoms hanging out of the back of their shorts or their tops are cut way too low in the front...and I'm just thinking to myself that if that child were to post a photo of herself in that outfit on Instagram that it could end up becoming a sexting investigation. Here's what these parents are completely clueless about - PARENTS are NOT the ones who get to decide what passes for "sexually suggestive" - the detectives, and ultimately the prosecutors get to decide. It doesn't matter that mom doesn't see anything wrong with the outfit that she bought. It's up to the investigators to determine how THEY interpret the photo. Avoiding this entire problem is a parenting issue!"*

By the time he was done with his statement, he got louder and a bit red in the face - and I may just be remembering it this way but I'm pretty sure he also slammed his hand on the table when he said *parenting issue* at the very end. What can I say? I have that effect on people.

It's difficult to offer clear cut guidelines to what is and is not

---

112 A Student Resource Officer is a police officer whose job is to be physically present in a school district throughout the school day/year - not as a threatening figure of discipline but rather as someone who gets to know the students by name and provides an additional ear - kind of like a guidance counselor, but with a gun.

considered "sexually suggestive". This is much like a discussion about pornography where the casual non-legal definition is: *pornography has no definition, but you know it when you see it.* The "IT" is the crossroads of intention and sexual content. If the intention is to arouse sexual interest, meaning that the sender or subject is trying to be "sex-y" or trying to arouse that reaction and/or the content itself is sexualized (naked, barely dressed, posed) then you probably have "sexually suggestive content".

Here's a far easier litmus test. Take the photo/text/video in question and ask your child to imagine him/herself showing the content to the following individuals and asking:

1. Show it to Grandma and ask her what she thinks. (Also known as the *Grandma Rule*)

2. What would your priest/pastor, principal, police officer think? (Also known as the *Three P's*)

If you can imagine any of those individuals recoiling in horror, or beginning to pray or chant for you loudly and with gusto then perhaps that particular content should not be shared.

Remember, the only opinion which matters in deciding whether or not that content merits a criminal charge is the opinion of law enforcement and prosecutors. It would be better to stay on the more conservative side of what you think *Grandma* and the *Three P's* might think.

Prosecutors and law enforcement offices across the country are seeing an increase in juvenile sexting cases. Sometimes law enforcement is first contacted by a parent, but more often than not a school administrator is making that first phone call. In terms of actual prosecutions, the Third National Juvenile Online Victimization Study shows that over 60% of state prosecutors surveyed who worked with internet crimes against children cases had handled sexting cases involving juveniles. Of those prosecutors, almost 40% filed charges as a result of those investigations.

When prosecutors did file charges, over 60% charged juveniles with sexting felonies and the majority (over 80%) charged juveniles with child pornography creation felonies. The child pornography creation felonies were charged even in cases where the images did not show sexually explicit "conduct or exhibition of genitals".

Over 40% of the prosecutors surveyed have prosecuted 10 or more cases, 10% of the prosecutors surveyed prosecuted 40 or more cases. Children are getting criminal records including felonies as a result of sexting charges. The caseload is only going to increase as new devices and technologies are created and become popular.

Bottom Line

Allow me to help you dispel the biggest myths about sexting. If you think that your child would never engage in sexting behaviors, you're wrong. If you think that the fact that your child attends a private (or Catholic or religious or special or expensive or exclusive) school makes even the slightest bit of difference to child sexting behaviors, you're wrong. If you think that your child won't engage in sexting behaviors because your family engages deeply in a religious practice, you're wrong. If you think that your zip code, geography, or socioeconomic level makes any impact on your child's likelihood of sexting, you're wrong. If you think that it's primarily boys pressuring girls into sending nudes, you're wrong.

Being an engaged and educated parent is your best defense in safeguarding and educating your children. Limiting time on and access[113] to devices is the best approach to avoiding sexting and other digital risks. But the most important single strategy to avoiding sexting risk is to delay smartphone ownership until the 9th grade.

CASES

Viral Sexting

An 18-year-old girl sent a nude photo of herself to her boyfriend. Soon after the photo went viral in her high school. Other students actively sought to bully and harass the girl in connection with the photo. Eventually, she committed suicide.

Indiana Middle Schoolers[114]

A 13-year-old girl and a 12-year-old boy from Indiana have been charged with possession of child pornography and child exploitation after it was discovered they were using their cell phones to exchange nude pictures of themselves with each other.

---

113 reread Chapter 6: Vulnerabilities for more detail on specific vulnerabilities in your home.

[114] Boy, Girl Charged With Child Porn" NBC 5 Chicago

The Pennsylvania Eight[115]

Eight Pennsylvania high school students ranging in age from 13 to 17 have been accused of using their smartphones to take, send, and receive nude photos of each other and in one case a video of oral sex. All eight children were charged with felonies.

Virginia Sexting Ring[116]

In a small rural area of Virginia , an investigation by the county sheriff's department discovered a sexting ring involving more than 100 teenagers and 1,000 nude or sexually suggestive photos which were posted onto Instagram and shared between the teens.

---

[115] "Sexting" Leads to Child Porn Charges for Teens"
[116] "Virginia Deals With a Teen Sexting Ring by Educating Teens, Not Prosecuting Them"

THE LEAST YOU SHOULD KNOW

Sexting among adults is not criminal as long as the sender, recipient, and subject matter of the sexted content does not involve a child under 18 years old.

Sexting includes photos, videos, live streaming, and text.

If a minor child (under 18 years old) sends or receives sexualized or sexually suggestive content of any minor child (including themselves) they can potentially be charged with creation, possession, and/or trafficking of felony child pornography

"Sexually Suggestive" does not necessarily mean nude, but rather the intent to evoke a sexual response. Law enforcement and prosecutors are the ones who determine what is considered "sexually suggestive".

Remember to consider the *Three P's* and the *Grandma Rule.*

Sexting is beginning in the 4th grade and our youngest children have never known a world without SnapChat, for example. This is the new normal.

Sexting is sometimes NOT just sexting and can be an indicator of bigger dangers like sextortion, sexual predation, and human sex trafficking.

Managing sexting risks is far easier when you delay your child's smartphone ownership. No phones before 9th grade.

CONVERSATION STARTERS

Ask your child: Did you know that it is illegal for a child to take a "sexy" photo of themselves? What does sexy mean to you? Show me a photo of something you think is sexy?

Ask your child: Did you know that children are being sent to prison as a result of sexting?

Ask your child: Did you know that sexting is illegal even if the photo is not nude? Did you know that sexting is illegal even if you did not take the photo?

Ask your child: Did you know that posting sexy content can be a signal to predators that you might be interested in having sex with adults?

ACTION ITEMS

Review the content your child is posting on all social platforms. Go through his/her gallery on the phone. See what kinds of photos are being taken. Discuss any you find troubling.

If your child receives sexted content – take a screenshot, shut off the device, and call law enforcement. Force a two-week break of all electronics.

If your child is involved as a perpetrator, remove all devices. Buy him/her a flip phone. End of story.

Teach your children the *Three P's* and the *Grandma Rule.*

Chapter 9

SEXUAL PREDATION

If I told you that your child's favorite playground, library, or coffee shop is frequented by sexual predators actively seeking children as prey, would you take them there or allow them to hangout in those places without you? Probably not. Would you say "Oh, well he has to learn how to navigate the world sometime?" Probably not.

By providing your child with a device, a signal, and little-to-no supervision you have effectively invited the entire creeper playground into your child's bedroom, bathroom, and wherever else he uses his digital devices. There are approximately 806,000 registered sex offenders in the United States[117]. This number is consistently rising due to law enforcement's improvement in identifying, tracking, and prosecuting these offenders. The 806,000 who are registered are merely the ones who have been caught and have been added to the registry as part of their sentence.

---

117 2016 total as calculated by Parents for Megan's Law - www.ParentsForMegansLaw.org

As a parent, you would not want one of these individuals to move in next door to your home. The risk to your children and your peace of mind would be too high to reasonably consider. And yet as parents we are effectively allowing our children to go out and play, digitally, where sexual predators congregate. Parents ask me where sexual predators go when they're online. They look a little shocked when my answer is: wherever and whenever your children are. Sexual predators know their craft and they are willing to put the time and energy into cultivating the opportunity for real-life sexual contact with your child. They are going to go where your children go, they are going to speak in a language your children can relate to, they are going to play the games and engage in the social media sites your children express themselves through. They are everywhere your children are.

WHAT IS SEXUAL PREDATION?

Sexual predation is the act of attempting to obtain sexual contact with another person by using predatory behaviors. As mentioned in Chapter 6: Understanding the Two Major Points of Vulnerability, this concept of predator and prey is analogous to the process which sexual predators use online and offline in an attempt to make sexual contact with potential victims.

By definition, sexual predation is not limited to abuse between an adult predator and a child victim. There are sexual predators interested in obtaining sexual contact with other adults. In that way, not all sexual predators are pedophiles/child molesters. However, all pedophiles/child molesters must be considered sexual predators. If a child cannot legally or developmentally give consent to sexual contact with an adult, then all pedophiles/child molesters are considered sexual predators. Their ultimate sexual contact (whether virtual or physical) is predatory, even in a scenario where a 12-year-old girl believes herself to be in love with the 50-year-old man she met online. Children cannot legally give sexual consent.

Sexual predators stalk their prey just as animals use predatory instincts to capture their next kill. Some predators show a violent and aggressive intent to control and harm their victims. While the "nice-guy" offender is rarely violent, he is extremely predatory and often operates behind the pillar-of-society-coach-of-the-year façade. Remember that offenders will take the time to groom and coerce your children into sexual exchanges.

SEXUAL PREDATOR CHARACTERISTICS

Similar to the "where are the predators?", the question of "who are the predators?" has a similar answer: Anyone can be a predator. The single and only trait all child molesters and pedophiles share is a desire to engage in sexual acts with children. Besides that one point, predators come from literally every single walk of life. For the purpose of this digital safety discussion we will use child molester and pedophile interchangeably although they are not technically the same[118].

- Most perpetrators are acquaintances, but as many as 47% are family or extended family.
- 33% of sexual assaults occur when the victim is between the ages of 12 and 17
- Predators seek youths vulnerable to seduction, including those with histories of sexual or physical abuse, those who post sexually provocative photos/videos, and those who talk about sex with unknown people online.

Thinking about the question "who are sexual predators?" remember that anyone can be a sexual predator including your child's authority figures of trust like teachers and coaches.[119] Statistically it is far more likely that a predator will be known to the victim. Unknown predators make use of internet tools to identify potential victims while pretending to be supportive and an understanding friend. Predators will take the time and energy to cultivate a "relationship" with the child, more commonly referred to as grooming.

How to prevent becoming a victim

Your best route to protecting your child against a sexual predator is to think like a predator. Think of the games and the apps your child likes best and then review the communication tools which connect strangers. I've seen many cases among my own acquaintances where an adult is "friends" which a minor child on social media who is not their family member. Your personal adult friends don't need to be connected with your children on social media, neither does any other adult who is not related to your child.

---

118 For a complete review on this subject read the definitive work by Kenneth Lanning, Former Supervisory Special Agent, Federal Bureau of Investigation (FBI) "Child Molesters: A Behavioral Analysis for Professionals Investigating the Sexual Exploitation of Children"

119 Specific issue of sexual predation and exploitation by coaches and sport authority figures.

Protecting your child against sexual predators covers the same two vulnerabilities discussed throughout the book: incoming and outgoing threats. Incoming threats exploit the weaknesses: in your child's social account privacy settings, your home's wi-fi signal, and where you choose to let your child "hangout" online. Outgoing threats relate directly to content: the username and profile image your child uses, your child sending out sexually provocative materials.

Experts agree that the best way to protect children from online solicitations and exposure to pornography is to supervise their online activity, or at a minimum to ensure that parental controls, such as "filtering" or "blocking" software, is installed on any computer used by children.

WHAT IS SEXTORTION?

In a typical sextortion case, a predator somehow convinces a victim to willingly send a nude or sexually suggestive photo or video to the predator. Once the image is obtained by the predator, the victim is threatened with public exposure and coerced into sending the predator hundreds or thousands of additional images in order buy his silence.

On March 21 2013, Miss Teen USA, Cassidy Wolf, received a sextortion email[120] from a man whose name sounded vaguely familiar to her. The email stated that he had hacked into the webcam on her laptop and snapped hundreds of photos of Wolf while she undressed in her bedroom. Wolf had absolutely no knowledge that she was being watched, photographed, and videotaped via her own webcam. The 19-year-old man, Jared James Abrahams, had been a high school classmate of Wolf's and was ultimately arrested for allegedly taking nude images of women via their own webcams and then blackmailing them into sending more explicit materials to him– the classic sextortion scenario. Abrahams confessed to what he had done and admitted to having 30 to 40 other "slave computers", remote devices under his control. However, the investigation yielded as many as 150 slave computers recording the private residences of young women from all over the world.

Not all sextortion victims are caught unaware. In 2013, a 25-year-old California man named Brian Caputo was indicted on charges of sexual exploitation of a minor, receipt of child pornography, and distribution of child

---

120 CNN Article: *"Miss Teen USA: Screamed upon learning she was 'sextortion' victim"*

pornography. Caputo had spent the prior eight years using social media accounts on Facebook, Kik, Yahoo and others to communicate with dozens of young girls across the United States. At first, Caputo pretended to be a young girl, convincing the victims to send him photos of themselves nude or partially nude. Once in possession of incriminating content, Caputo "sex-torted" additional sexual images and content in return for his silence. The investigation later revealed that Caputo had been victimizing many young girls across the country including one young woman who eventually uploaded more than 600 sexually explicit images of herself to Caputo's Dropbox account.

In 2017, 24-year-old Bryan Asrary[121] was charged with impersonating Justin Bieber online in order to get nude photos from underage girls and he is facing child pornography and extortion charges. The National Strategy for Child Exploitation Prevention and Interdiction reports 60 percent of survey respondents reported dealing with sextortion. The report also showed that "sextortion cases tend to have more minor victims per offender than all other child sexual exploitation offenses."

WHAT IS HUMAN SEX TRAFFICKING?

According to NCMEC[122] "Child sex trafficking involves the recruitment, harboring, transportation, provision, obtaining, or advertising of a minor child for the purpose of a commercial sex act. Traffickers often prey upon a child's vulnerability and use psychological pressure and intimidation to control the child for financial benefit relating to their sexual exploitation. Purchasers of children for sex encompass all racial, socio-economic and cultural statuses. Child sex trafficking has devastating consequences for its minor victims, including long-lasting physical and psychological trauma, disease or even death." In fact, 1 in 6 of the 18,500[123] runaways reported to the National Center for Missing and Exploited Children (NCMEC) in 2016 were likely sex trafficking victims.

---

121 *"Sextortion becoming major problem with minor children"*
http://www.foxnews.com/entertainment/2017/01/24/sextortion-becoming-major-problem-with-minor-children.html
122 NCMEC is the National Center for MIssing and Exploited Children
123 NCMEC http://www.missingkids.org/1in6

DIGITAL SEXUAL PREDATION STATISTICS

It should not be a surprise that online enticement of children by sexual predators is on the rise. Digital accessibility is growing and wi-fi is ever more accessible. It is almost incomprehensible to consider that these risks exist at this massive scale. But they do. It would be far easier to continue to believe that your 9-year-old son is perfectly safe playing Minecraft on a public server. But he's not. In the end, as parents, we are complicit in the process by allowing and encouraging our children to use these devices with no education and little or no supervision.

According to the United States Department of Justice:

- 1 in 25 youths received an online sexual solicitation in which the solicitor tried to make offline contact.
- In more than one-quarter (27%) of incidents, solicitors asked youths for sexual photographs of themselves.
- 15% of cell-owning teens (12–17) say they have received sexually suggestive nude/seminude images of someone they know via text.
- State and local law enforcement agencies involved in ICAC Task Forces reported a 230% increase in the number of documented complaints of online enticement of children from 2004 to 2008.

According to the CSOM (Center for Sex Offender Management):
- 1 in 7 youths (between 10 and 17) will receive an unwanted sexual solicitation over the Internet.
- 4% of youths have experienced an "aggressive" solicitation where someone attempted to contact the child offline.

Data collected from my student presentations

At the end of the student presentations, each student completes an anonymous exit survey asking what (if anything) the student is willing to change about their digital behavior as a result having seen the presentation. Those students comments are then processed, calculated, and reported back to school administrators[124].

The graph below reflects the percentage of students who responded with a

---

124 Read Chapter 12: The Children I've Met to learn more about data collection and methods.

comment which explicitly reflected a sexual predation risk. These comments might include references to: sexting unknown people, communicating with strangers via live streaming, giving out personal details publicly, or having already had some experience or some knowledge of being at risk of sexual predation.

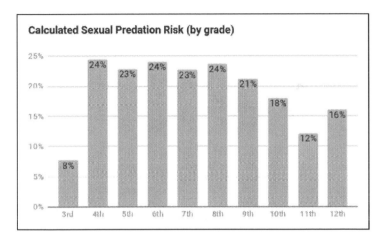

Students who consume porn and engage in sexting behaviors increase their risk of becoming victims of sexual predation.

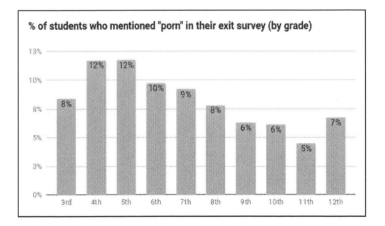

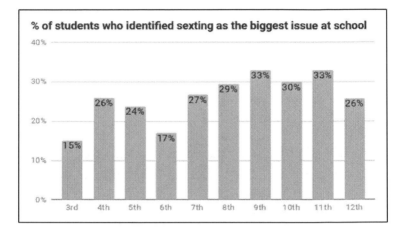

Sexual Predation Cases

Children can also be predators: Zachary Taylor

Zachary Taylor[125] was first arrested for molesting a 4-year-old when he was only 9-years-old himself. He wasn't arrested because he was so young. When Taylor turned 15 years old he broke into his neighbor's house and pulled a 4-year-old boy out of his bed and raped him. The first time Taylor offended, he was in preschool and was caught fondling a classmate behind a bookcase. Prosecutors are currently seeking life imprisonment.

Cleveland man ran a Kik group for pedophiles

A 34 year old Cleveland man ran an online chat group to share images and videos of toddlers being raped was sentenced to 26 years in federal prison. Brian Keeling[126] admitted to sharing files, preferring videos where toddlers screamed or said "no" while being sexually assaulted.

Female predator sends nudes to 13 year old boy

35-year-old, Amanda Wilson[127], sent inappropriate pictures and sexually graphic videos of herself to a 13-year-old boy. Wilson purchased a cell phone for a 13-year-old boy, where numerous conversations took place. Deputies say the investigation revealed that Wilson sent the boy inappropriate and explicit videos and pictures of herself, and that she also requested the same from the boy.

A Female Predator Case: Tanai Fortman

In a departure from the typical male-predator scenario, Fortman[128] was arrested on child pornography charges after police say her boyfriend found five sexually explicit 30-second video clips involving Fortman and a 4-year-old girl. She was indicted on 16 counts including rape, gross sexual imposition, and

125 "Prosecutor: 'Sexual predator' teen should be jailed for life"

126 "Cleveland man who ran online group with videos of toddlers being raped sentenced to 26 years",http://www.cleveland.com/courtjustice/index.ssf/2017/06/cleveland_man_who_ran_online_g.html

127 "Deputies: Lakeville woman sent explicit videos to 13-year-old boy"
http://www.whec.com/news/deputies-lakeville-woman-sent-explicit-videos-to-13-year-old-boy/4418803/

128 "Tanai Fortman, Ohio woman, blames diet pills in child porn case, report says"

pandering sexually oriented matter involving a minor.

A Pediatrician Predator Case: Christopher Pelloski, MD

Christopher Pelloski[129] was the director of the pediatric oncology program at Children's Hospital and OSU's James Cancer Hospital. A search warrant was obtained for Pelloski's home and found evidence he downloaded sexually explicit videos of children. In addition, the investigation into his personal devices yielded about 85 images of child pornography. At the time of his arrest, he was actively treating pediatric cancer patients.

A Teacher-Predator Case: John David Boyle

A middle school teacher from California named John David Boyle[130], met with an undercover agent in his classroom, allegedly to have sex and watch child pornography. Investigators say Boyle chatted online with the agent, whom he believed was also a sexual predator primarily interested in boys. His online accounts, including his Skype account, indicate he has had sexual contact with minors, including one of his own 14-year-old male students.

A Webcam-Only Predator Case: Dutchman

A Dutchman[131] identified only as "Michel S" has been accused of abusing approximately 400 boys and girls aged 12-14 who he met in online chat rooms by coercing them into committing sexual acts via webcam. Victims have been identified all over the world including the United States.

Sexual Predation by a Group: Brian Way

Brian Way[132] owned a video production company in Toronto which produced and curated child pornography materials. He then sold those materials back to predators all over the world. Canadian law enforcement combined forces with international jurisdictions and together they arrested 348 adults worldwide and rescued nearly 400 children who were being actively victimized in order to fill the international demand for these pornographic materials. Investigators

---

129 *"Ohio pediatric doctor Christopher Pelloski to plead guilty to child porn"*

130 *"Covina Teacher Indicted on Multiple Child Pornography Charges"*

131 *"Dutchman accused of filming 400 nude children"*

132 *"Hundreds held over Canada child porn"*

cataloged hundreds of thousands of images and videos of "horrific sexual acts against very young children, some of the worst they had ever viewed".

All the victims identified were pre-pubescent, with some as young as five years old. Among those arrested were 40 school teachers, nine doctors and nurses, six law enforcement personnel, nine pastors and priests and three foster parents. Citing a particularly egregious example, in the home of a retired Canadian school teacher, investigators found over 350,000 images and over 9,000 videos of child sexual abuse. Another teacher admitted to producing child pornography while teaching pre-school in Japan.

PROSECUTING CASES

In 1998, the United States Department of Justice created the ICAC (Internet Crimes Against Children) Task Force Program in order to help state and local law enforcement agencies develop internal training and programs to respond to the rising number of child pornography and child enticement cases.

ICAC divisions represent 2000 federal, state, and local prosecutorial agencies. There are almost certainly several in your immediate area. In 2011 alone, ICAC investigations contributed to the arrests of nearly 5,700 individuals. An estimated 50k people in the United States are "consistently trading illegal images" involving children at any one given moment. These images and videos include sexual torture of distraught children and infants. In 2012 alone NCMEC analysts reviewed more than 19 million child pornography images and videos.

In recovered evidence, one suspect posted a sonogram photo to a pedophile's message board with the comment: "I have a new baby about to be added to the game".

IF YOU THINK YOUR CHILD HAS BEEN VICTIMIZED

If your child has been victimized online, even if he/she has not been physically assaulted, the experience can be traumatic. By the same token, this behavior may have become so normalized that your child may remain unfazed and may consider this behavior to be business as usual on a digital platform. You need to address the situation either way.

Call local law enforcement immediately. Grab screenshots of the content in question if you are able. If your child has been the victim of sexual exploitation – you can also file a report online to the NCMEC's Cyber Tipline at www.cybertipline.com.

THE LEAST YOU SHOULD KNOW

Providing your child with a device and no supervision increases the likelihood that he/she will be exposed to sexual predators.

In 2017, there are 806k registered sex offenders in the United States.

Most perpetrators are acquainted with the child

In sextortion cases a predator, at first, convinces a victim to provide sexualized images willingly. Later, the victim is threatened into sending more images.

Child sex trafficking is a large and growing problem.

My data shows that children as young as 4th and 5th graders are engaging in extremely risky digital behaviors, increasing their likelihood of becoming victims of sexual predation.

CONVERSATION STARTERS

Make sure your child understands that if they are put into the position of sextortion victim, that you will want to know and that regardless what your child may have done wrong, the adult is still to blame. You don't want to take all responsibility away from the child, but you also don't want to scare them into silence. Where age -appropriate, share the cases in this chapter with your child.

Sexual predation is wrong regardless of how handsome or nice looking the predator might be. Celebrities, athletes, it doesn't matter. Begin this conversation in an obvious place with your child's celebrity crushes. Explain that sex between an adult and a minor is illegal and just plain creepy 100% of the time.

ACTION ITEMS

Take a sharp look at the adults who surround your child. Include everyone, especially adults who tend to be the "Pied Pipers" of your community. Adults who prefer the company of children are suspicious. Adults who are overly interested in your child's success/life and who you are not paying to be interested in your child (like a tutor) should make you suspicious.

Your child may be accidentally alerting online predators to his/her willingness to engage in virtual or actual sexual contact. If your child is using sexually aggressive or explicit language, has posted sexually suggestive photos, or has a sexually suggestive username – a sexual predator may interpret this as your child's willingness to connect.

Children who spend more than one hour of unsupervised time per day online are far more likely to be victimized.

Do not insist that your children display physical affection (hugging, kissing) a relative or family or friend who the child is uncomfortable with. Have respect for your child's instincts. They may see or feel something that you don't.

SECTION III: YOUR CHILD'S ACTUAL DIGITAL LIFE

Chapter 10: Understanding Social Media

Chapter 11: Review of the Apps Your Child Is Probably Using

Chapter 12: The Children I've Met

Chapter 10

UNDERSTANDING SOCIAL MEDIA

Social media is "an electronic platform which encourages user generated content and community engagement." It must be *electronic* and it must be a virtual/digital application or platform which facilitates the next two parts of the definition. The purpose of social media is to gather users who will *create content* with their own followers/friends, and in turn invite new followers/friends. The platform *encourages user engagement* via features such as: commenting, liking, and sharing content.

The entire social media infrastructure is a carefully developed house of smoke and mirrors, brilliantly implemented by the best of the platform developers. Simply stated, these developers are creating an empty structure. Its users do the heaviest lifting, under the guise of building personal connections.

When Mark Zuckerberg created Facebook, he created the equivalent of an empty digital apartment building. He built the first building and shouted into the ether "You can have free rent if you bring all your own furniture, artwork, and music – oh and your friends can come live here as well, but **you** have to bring them." So we all came. He built it, and we arrived by the bus load. We brought all of our furniture, friends, pets, children, art, and music. And then they brought all of their friends, and so on, and so on. Eventually, Zuckerberg had to put up more buildings to accommodate the throngs of free rent seekers.

Zuckerberg's genius is in the intrinsic and viral nature of the personal connection; each single user carries the breadth of his own personal connections. Facebook is constantly and consistently under construction and the crowds have not died down. Facebook only needs for us to connect to approximately 330 users[133] (on average) for the structure to hold. As long as that base holds, and the user growth continues, even at a modest rate, the overall growth will increase dramatically year over year. Facebook's increase of active users since its inception shows the massive growth of active daily users:

- 2004: 1 million
- 2010: 608 million
- 2017: 1.94 billion

Consider for a moment that social media platforms are free to its users. We don't pay Facebook or any other social platform for the pleasure of using their service. What's in it for them?

Anytime that you don't pay for a digital product, it means that you are the product. You and I, and all of our friends (even our cats) are the collective product of Facebook. Or rather, our eyeballs and our attention are the product. Every time Facebook constructs additional space for more people, they are able to sell even more billboard space to advertisers. Digital advertisers, if they're smart, will spend a significant amount of money to catch the eyeballs and attention of large numbers of their highly targeted intended audience.

In return, as we engage with Facebook on a regular basis, we accidentally and intentionally tell Facebook which ads we're interested in seeing. That cute photo of my cat tells Facebook that I might be interested in ads for pet supplies. The fact that I liked a particular Facebook page on extreme

---

133 "6 new facts about Facebook" – February 3, 2014

sports means that I might be interested in heli-skiing, although it's far more likely that I would personally like a Facebook page on the many uses for bacon.

This structure - of a digital platform offering free access and space in return for advertising exposure - is the foundation of social media. Adults accept the trade-offs and understand that we are being sold to, almost all of the time. As adults, we know how to tune out the advertising noise. Part of the concern of internet safety as it relates to children is this issue of rampant consumerism. Your children are constantly being courted as potential consumers and they may not realize it. They might just confuse advertising noise and click baiting for human connection.

Undercooked human brains

In the discussion of social currency and digital engagement, more=better, 100% of the time. This becomes problematic when it comes to your child's inability to balance the desire for *more* with their developmental lack of impulse control. Your child's brain is not done developing until their mid-20's and the part which develops last is the prefrontal cortex[134]. This is the area in the brain which regulates executive function and impulse control. Impulse control is that thing that tells you to not take a photo of your junk and send it to seventy-two of your friends. Interestingly, one of the portions of the brain which is completely developed by the tween years is the nucleus accumbens. This area of the brain actively seeks pleasure and reward. So, the young brain actively seeks pleasure and is unable to quickly and appropriately measure consequences or engage in effective impulse control. Yay parenting!

If you are the parent of a tween or teen, neither of these two findings will come as a terrible shock. However, it might serve to lower your expectations of what your child is developmentally capable of handling on their own. Your children do not have the neurological capability to responsibly and safely interact with unsupervised 24-7-365 digital access.

UNDERSTANDING PLATFORM STRUCTURE

Social media platforms are synchronous, asynchronous, or no-synchronous. The category type depends upon its connection reciprocity or what you need to

---

134 NPR's The Teen Brain: It's Just Not Grown Up Yet,
http://www.npr.org/templates/story/story.php?storyId=124119468

do as a user to connect to another user.

Synchronous social media platforms require agreement between the parties before they can connect or see each other's content. The best known synchronous social platforms are Facebook and Linkedin. If you want to be connected to someone on Facebook, one party sends the other a friend request. If the request is accepted, the connection is made and you become official Facebook friends. The same occurs on Linkedin; where you send a connection request. If the person receiving the request approves it, you are now considered that person's Linkedin connection[135].

Generally speaking, synchronous platforms are far safer than asynchronous platforms, but only when used appropriately. The purpose of synchronous connections is to verify a real life relationship before allowing digital connection to a potentially unknown individual. If a Facebook user "friends" a total stranger, the entire purpose for the privacy settings associated with a synchronous structure becomes moot.

Asynchronous platforms do not require agreement between two parties before they can connect. In fact, asynchronous platforms do not actually make connections between individuals in the strictest sense. Jane decides to *follow* Johnny's Twitter account. But Johnny doesn't have to return the favor by following Jane's Twitter account. You will see many scenarios of public figures having several million *followers* but only show that they are *following* a few hundred. For example, President Obama has 42.4 million Twitter followers, but he follows only 652,000. Given those numbers, at least 41.7 million users who follow Obama, are not followed **by** Obama.

Instagram and Twitter are the two most popular asynchronous social platforms used by tweens and teens. Once you create a Twitter account you are able to follow someone else's timeline. Once you have followed a fellow Twitter user, everything that person (or brand) posts will show up in your feed. By following another user, you are telling Twitter that you want to see all of this content in real time. On your timeline, you will see a running update of all of the tweets posted by all of the users you follow. You do not need permission[136]

---

135 Facebook's "friend" is synonymous with Linkedin's "connection" – they just use different language to denote a reciprocated agreement to connect.

136 Exception: Most asynchronous platforms (like Twitter and Instagram) will allow you to completely privatize and lock down your account which would require a follower to request access. The vast percentage of tweens and teens will not privatize accounts; in fact, only 12% of all Twitter users have their accounts privatized. Kids also have the habit of clicking 'PRIVATE' when parents

to follow a Twitter user, the approval is inherent in the system.

The same structure works in reverse. As a Twitter or Instagram user, other users are following your profile. Whenever you post something new they will be updated in real time on their own timeline. The important point to remember here is that these groups can be 100% mutually exclusive. It is quite possible for you to have 100 followers who you don't follow in return. This asynchronous structure is the central risk associated with these platforms.

- If you are a Twitter or Instagram user you can follow any other user without prior acceptance or approval.
- If you are a Twitter or Instagram user – you can view the feed of any other user without officially following that user, just by navigating to that person's profile.
- Posting content to Twitter, Instagram, or any other asynchronous platform should be considered the same as posting content to a public bulletin board in a coffee shop. Anyone who walks past it will see it.

Asynchronous platforms have radically higher percentages of cyberbullying, sexting, and sexual predation occurrences than synchronous platforms. It is remarkably easy to stalk, harass, and gather information about a user just by reading their publicly posted content.

Of the three connection categories for social media platforms, the no-synchronous platform is the most dangerous for its users. No-synchronous platforms don't create connections between users. In fact, some no-synchronous platforms (like YikYak) don't even provide users with profiles. One of the most egregious examples of the no-synchronous category is Ask.fm. Ask.fm has been in the news many times in connection with cyberbullying and teen suicides in the UK, Australia, and the United States. In fact, British Prime Minister David Cameron called for a national boycott of Ask.fm and other sites which allow cyberbullying to flourish.

The premise of Ask.fm[137] is simple; if you have an Ask.fm account, anyone can come onto your wall and ask you a question. The real danger in Ask.fm is in the anonymity of its structure. Users never know who is posting a question, and therein lies the problem. Tweens and teens feel free to post whatever they like, safe in the knowledge that there will never be any consequences. Or so it would seem. Similar to asynchronous platforms, you

---

are watching, unclicking 'PRIVATE' to gain new followers, and back again.

137 Your children have no business using Ask.fm regardless of how old they are.

should consider any content posted on no-synchronous platforms as completely public. In addition, any sexualized content posted by your child will alert potential predators to your child's perceived willingness to have additional sexual exchanges, both digital and in-person, increasing their risk for sexual predation.

NEW DIGITAL STRUCTURES, UNINTENDED RESULTS

The foundation of social media (electronic platform & user content & community engagement) became unintentionally weaponized the moment that younger generations were given open and unsupervised digital devices. That was the moment that brands and corporations began competing for digital eyeballs.

During the past eight to ten years, consumer brands and public relations agencies have begun to measure their digital outcomes. They need to know if their digital efforts have yielded the desired results and by how much. Even when these measurement programs are executed poorly (which is most of the time) measuring growth presupposes that growth is good. More=better. Brands measure how many, new fans, new likes, new followers, new content, new comments, instances of shared content, and what kind of content produces the most of X desired end result.

All of this quantification of online behavior has leaked down to the younger and savvier digital generation. Where our generation might have measured individual social success by where we sat for lunch in the cafeteria or whether or not we were invited to a certain party. This generation's social currency is far more scientifically devised, calculated, and compared.

Your child's real-life social currency is now measured in small digital increments with the same scale used by brands. Tweens and teens very quickly figure out that their content is capable of making an impact. If you walk into any middle school in the United States and stop a random 13-year-old and ask how many followers he/she has on Instagram, you will get the exact number as of 5 minutes ago. The number of friends/followers your child has is the new social currency for social media engaged kids.

In order of importance, here is how your child probably views their own digital value:

- **What is total number of followers?** For gamers, this number can be translated into the number of subscribers on their YouTube *Let's Play* gaming videos.

- **How many of those views/follows are from celebrities or brands?** Being followed by Lady Gaga is worth all of your real friends/followers combined.

- **How much engagement is the profile generating?** This is the raw # of likes, follows, comments, etc

You probably have never heard of YouTube sensation PewDiePie[138], but your children have. PewDiePie is the digital handle of a 25-year-old Swedish man who holds the title of The Most Popular YouTube Channel. His videos fall under the category of *Let's Play* content. PewDiePie videotapes himself as he plays video games. Users login to watch PewDiePie's facial expressions and running commentary (which can be hilarious) as he plays popular video games. Gaming, which has traditionally been a bit of a solitary endeavor, becomes more social when you can share the experience virtually. It makes sense then, that gamers can't seem to get enough of the *Let's Play* category of videos.

Social and digital marketing have changed the entire foundation of how brands and products coexist with their consumers. As of May 2017, PewDiePie had 55.7 million subscribers on YouTube and has a reported personal net worth[139] of $15 million dollars. Brands seek out individuals like PewDiePie to create content about their products. This strategy makes perfect sense for a gaming company; if you're releasing a new game, the first person you're going to call to review and promote it is PewDiePie.

In the 1970's and 1980's, wearing the Gloria Vanderbilt jeans with the label on the backside and the Nike swoosh on your sneakers was probably the extent of your publicly displayed devotion to any particular brand. At that time stickers, buttons, and other youth-focused marketing strategies were the

---

138 Real name Felix Arvid Ulf Kjellberg

139 *"The Highest-Paid YouTube Stars 2016: PewDiePie Remains No.1 With $15 Million"*, December 20, 2016, by Madeline Berg, https://www.forbes.com/sites/maddieberg/2016/12/05/the-highest-paid-youtube-stars-2016-pewdiepie-remains-no-1-with-15-million

exclusive domain of musical artists and celebrities pictured on the cover of Tiger Beat Magazine. As teens in the 1970's and early 1980's, we showed our brand loyalty by wearing the clothing and displaying the posters in our bedrooms. And that was pretty much the extent of our raving fandom.

My generation would never have put up a poster in our bedrooms of Red Bull products or NorthFace jackets. But the current generation will follow those social media accounts, share their content, and become public advocates for the products and services they love. By showing their brand devotion via social media these young people position themselves as curators and reviewers of brands and products. Like PewDiePie, there are a significant number of other young people who have made a name (and a fortune) for themselves by gaining a significant online following, and then selling access to that following.

Digital marketing has changed the entire dynamic between consumer and brand. Young consumers of content are being put in the position of decision maker, content curator, and arbiter of taste. The moment that a new movie is conceptualized and years before it ever hits the big screen, the digital marketing engine will begin to churn. If that movie is meant for teens, those marketers will actively seek the engagement of individual young people with large social networks.

If your child has enough of a following on Twitter, Instagram, or YouTube, there is a reasonable likelihood that brand executives will reach out to your child and ask him/her to become a living, breathing brand advocate. Even very young YouTube sensations have become wealthy on the strength of the millions of eyeballs following their channel and their content. If your child desires higher social digital currency and is an active and unregulated user of social tools, the moral and ethical boundaries begin to blur. The question then becomes how to build massive traffic and followers?

Large traffic is built on viral-ability. What kinds of content tend to go viral? Content which is: sexualized, entertaining, and emotionally evocative tend to be the most sought after and shared. Sexualized content sells, by the bucket load. In the realm of more=better, your children will need to fight against their underdeveloped prefrontal cortex and diminished impulse control when attempting to increase their social and actual currency.

DATA PRIVACY

Facebook will periodically get some bad press on the issue of privacy settings. When I hear these news stories it makes me want to drop kick the television. (I'm trying to limit my caffeine intake.) Here's the truth. Ready? **You have no expectation of data privacy when using any digital platform or product including wi-fi, smartphones, social media, or online software.** If you want an absolute guarantee of privacy then don't use social media. It's really quite simple. Facebook doesn't owe humanity anything. They've created a product and you can either choose to use it or not. If you don't like it, delete your account.

It's also not Facebook's job to protect your child. That's your job. Facebook's privacy settings are the most robust and finely tuned of any social media platform on the planet. Could they do more? Yeah, probably. But they're not in the business of data protection; their business is to sell your eyeballs to advertisers. And frankly, they do a hell of a good job at making that happen. If you have any designs on trying to shut down this or that social media app you can start by deleting your own account.

Every time you click within a digital structure (like a social media app) you are adding to your own digital exhaust. Imagine your digital exhaust as a giant barrel filled with every click, every like, every share you've ever clicked in your past, with space for every click you will ever click in your future. That barrel begins to form a complete image of the user as a person. Google will begin to tailor your search results based on your historical clicks and data exhaust. If you consistently read Fox News online, the next time you do a Google search, Google will place the Fox News results at the top and probably won't bother showing you any MSNBC results. In addition, Facebook will see your Google search patterns and continue to offer up Fox News-esque content items. In other words, you probably won't see any Stephen Colbert content. Which would be a shame because Stephen Colbert is a comedic genius who makes me laugh until my face hurts. It's no coincidence that after you Googled "best tequila to use for margaritas," your Facebook wall was filled with advertisements for Patron Tequila. And just for the record please don't pollute Patron Tequila by adding any disgusting juice, or fruit, or ice.

Social media platforms will never sell your personal data to third-party companies for their use. So they might not know that a woman named Jesse Weinberger only drinks Patron Tequila, as a totally random example. But

Patron might get data to show that *40-year-old women* is a growing market for them and that packaging a bottle with a pound of chocolate-covered bacon might be a really, really good idea.

Your personal data will just show up as dots on a graph in a similar data mining project. Should you be worried about your actual privacy? Well....in the first edition of the book I said -*"I wouldn't worry about it if I were you."* However, the level of invasiveness of the data mining and the depth of our collective digital usage is making this data exhaust an increasingly creepy issue to resolve.

You might already be hyper-engaged in social media on your own - checking your Facebook feed like a lab rat looking for a fix. Conversely, You may feel like you're being forced into using social media when you would really rather not. We can't ignore the fact that most of humanity is participating in digital communication. Social and digital interaction are only going to grow as time goes on and at some point, your child will need to learn how to operate in the new digital world. Please don't confuse this point with *but everyone else is doing it*. Allowing your child to use social media is not the only road to teaching effective digital communication. The fact remains that your child's digital engagement depends almost entirely on your participation in age-appropriate supervision, creating family policies, and enforcing those policies.

Don't forget that your child's participation in social media is not a right; it's a privilege which you bestow and can revoke whenever you like. They don't need social media any more than they need a phone.

Social media risks

Beyond the specific guidance in Chapter 6 on understanding vulnerabilities from a general digital perspective, there are risks specific to social media structure. These can be more readily understood within the following categories.

Who are the connections? The only social media connections allowed to your children are the people they (and you) already know IRL (in real life), without exceptions or footnotes. It goes without saying then, that your child should never communicate, arrange for offline meetings, or exchange information with anyone you don't already know. In addition, your child should **never** connect on social media with, any coach, teacher, or other adult via social media. No exceptions.

What is being shared? No TMI (too much information), no Gonna-Be content, no sharing passwords with friends, no posting of private information (address, real name), no sexualized content (including profile name, handle, avatar), no feeding the trolls, no bullying or generally nasty content, no GPS tagged photos or posts, no "checking-in" at public locations, no dating apps.

Which privacy safeguards are being used? Create strong passwords, lock-down the wi-fi signal in your home, cover up all of your webcams, use a screen lock code so that a friend can't swipe your child's phone and misbehave in his name, never log into your bank account via a public wi-fi signal, beware of Phishing scams, lock down all social media profiles to the public, and remove identifiable profile photos.

A note on hashtags

Most people don't really understand the purpose or relevance of hashtags. Think of hashtags as a method of cross referencing or organizing content, sort of like a series of labeled buckets. When you post on social media, you can use a hashtag to place your content into a bucket with other similar content or in an attempt to extend the reach of your post.

Let's assume that like me, you're a huge *Game of Thrones* fan. You decide to watch the next episode alone and away from any family members who might risk their lives by asking a stream of inane and annoying questions. Rather than being forced to illustrate what "Valar Morghulis[140]" means, you watch alone. Then in typical digital-life upside down fashion, in an attempt to connect with other fans, you hop onto Twitter and post:

Ding-Dong the #Joffrey is Dead. #ValarMorghulis #GoT[141]

The phrases or words which come after the "#" symbol are considered hashtags. Those hashtags become live links within the tweet and if you were to click on #Joffrey, you would see a list of all of the other tweets with the same hashtag.

---

140 "Valar Morghulis" means "All Men Must Die" – best when directed at those who interrupt you while watching #GoT

141 The #GoT hashtag is the semi-official hashtag for Game of Thrones, and anyone can use it.

People make up dopey hashtags to reflect the flavor of their tweet for example:

My daughter forgot her
textbook at school #IShouldHaveHadGoldfishInsteadOfChildren

In this example of nerdy sarcasm, your purpose is not to associate with others who have used the hashtag, neither is the point to extend your reach, rather the point is simply to make a point.

Digital parenting bottom-line

Software companies and app developers have no obligation to create software which is in the best interest of our children; their only aim is to make money. Similarly, television stations may have the word *family* or *learning* in their name, and yet most of the programming they produce is garbage. Video game companies produce games with highly sexualized and violent content because it sells. As parents, it is solely our job to monitor, educate, and discipline our children. We cannot and should not expect school staff, software companies, or media outlets to raise our children for us.

Should you allow your children to use social media? This is the wrong question. Similar to - *Is my child ready for a smartphone?* - the real question is - *Are **you** ready for your child to have social media?*

- If as a parent, you are not actively checking which platforms, people, games, and content your child is engaged with – you are complicit in the outcome.

- If as a parent, you do not create and deliver consequences consistently to your children – you are complicit in the outcome.

- If as a parent, you do not educate yourself in how to help your child stay safe as well as how to prevent brewing your own little Frankenstein-bully – you are complicit in the outcome.

- If you are expecting gaming, software, and media companies to do your parenting job for you – you are complicit in the outcome.

THE LEAST YOU SHOULD KNOW

A social media platform is "an electronic platform which encourages user generated content and community engagement."

Anytime that you don't pay for a digital product, it means that you are the product.

This structure - of a digital platform offering free access and space in return for advertising exposure - is the foundation of social media.

Your child's brain has not completely developed until his mid-20's - the last part to develop is the prefrontal cortex which largely controls executive function and impulse control.

Synchronous social media platforms require agreement between both parties before they can connect or see each other's content. Asynchronous platforms do not require agreement between two parties before they can connect. No-synchronous platforms don't create connections between users.

Your child's real-life social currency is now measured in small digital increments with the same scale used by brands.

Digital marketing has changed the entire dynamic between consumer and brand. Young consumers of content are being put in the position of decision maker, content curator, and arbiter of taste.

You have no expectation of data privacy when using any digital platform or product including wi-fi, smartphones, social media, or online software.

Your child's participation in social media is not a right, it's a privilege which you bestow and can revoke whenever you like. They don't <u>need</u> social media any more than they <u>need</u> a phone.

Think of social media risks in terms of these three categories. Who are the connections? What is being shared? Which privacy safeguards are being used?

Software companies and app developers have no obligation to create software which is in the best interest of our children; their only aim is to make money.

As a parent, you are complicit in your child's social media outcomes.

CONVERSATION STARTERS

Did you ever wonder why social media apps are free? How do you think they make money?

How do you think Facebook knows which advertisements to show you?

Did you know that your brain isn't done developing until you're 25 years old? Did you know that the last bits to develop are related to impulse control? What do you think about that?

Do you have any adults who have friended or followed you on social media? How did they come to connect to you?

How do you feel when get a new follow request or a comment on social media? Is there any other aspect of your life which makes you feel the same way?

Without checking, do you know how many followers you currently have?

How easy do you think it is to become a famous YouTuber? What do you think their job consists of?

Do you or anyone you know, actively try to get brands or celebrities to notice you on social media? Who are the most typical celebrities to pursue?

Do you ever use hashtags? Which are the most popular hashtags among your friends?

ACTION ITEMS

Many school districts are now using social media tools as a method of communication within their communities. Sports teams might ask athletes to follow the Twitter timeline for last minute game or practice changes. Following the news on Twitter implies that your child or your family are already engaged with social media. The best solution is to create a Gmail account specifically for this purpose. Call it something like jonesfamilysocial@gmail.com and use this new email to sign up for social profiles as a family.

First go through your child's friends and followers without your child present. Make note of individual followers you don't personally know. Then ask your child to take you through the same list and see how they respond to the questions of particular connections.

Ask your child to tell you the names of their favorite YouTubers. Make a note of their favorites and watch those YouTube channels without your child present. You'll need to watch four or five videos of each channel to get a sense of the content your child is consuming.

Chapter 11

APPS REVIEW

By this point you understand the need for parental surveillance and monitoring your child's digital experience. The next step is to identify specific risks with the ultimate goal of implementing an overall plan. The purpose of this chapter is to give you a brief explanation and outline of the apps, platforms, and devices most children are using.

HOW TO USE THIS CHAPTER

This chapter is broken up into the most typically used social apps, gaming sites, and devices. Each one will include:

- **How it works.** A basic summary of how the app operates. Think of this as the "least you need to know"

- **Connection agreement.** Is the site synchronous, asynchronous, or no-synchronous

- **Privacy settings & blocking recourse**. What are your privacy setting options, and what recourse is available to you if you choose to block another user or report misbehavior?

- **Relative popularity**. How popular is the app really? Is it likely that your child is engaging on this platform?

- **Cases and current events**. There are criminal and other cases related to all of these apps. These are the stories which you can share with your children (where appropriate).

- **Specific areas of concern**. What to watch out for specifically in that particular app, device, or game

It would be best to read this entire chapter even if you are fairly certain that your child is not using some of these games or apps. Learning about the threats related to these specific apps will extend your education on what to look for going forward with some new app or game which hasn't even been developed yet.

GLOBAL TRENDS

In the United States, Facebook is not as popular among teens as it is in the UK and Europe. In terms of global usage and risks the sites which experience the highest percentages of cyberbullying are: Facebook, Twitter, and Ask.fm[142].

In the United States the cyberbullying numbers are very similar with: Twitter, Ask.fm, and Instagram as the usual suspects. Photographic and video enabled apps are consistently a draw for sexting and sexual predation. Instagram, Snapchat, and Twitter are typical places to find sexting and vast amounts of pornographic content.

Apps like Snapchat and Kik give kids the tools to engage in sexting behaviors as well as a false sense of security. As a result, children as young as 11 years old are being charged[143] with felony child pornography in the United

---

142 Report: "The Annual Cyberbullying Survey" by Ditch the Label
143 See Chapter 8: Sexting for more on children charged with criminal sexting charges.

States.

Sexual predation can be found across all apps and sites where children congregate including otherwise benign games like Clash of Clans and Minecraft. Sexual predators go where the children are. The United States Department of Justice has estimated that there are 750,000 sexual predators online world-wide at any given moment. Where are your children hanging out in the digital world?

STRICTLY SOCIAL APPS

This first group covers the most popular social apps. The relative popularity of these apps varies slightly when you move from one area of the world to another, but in general we are looking at: Twitter, Instagram, Snapchat, and Ask.fm. Facebook remains very popular among teens in some parts of the United States and is the "first-stop" for teens in Europe and the UK.

Facebook

Introduction

Think of Facebook as the "community" within the digital world. If the digital sphere imitates the real world, then Facebook is your neighborhood.

It's where you live and return to each day; a physical location in which you gather your friends and family and share your life in all of its digital forms: text, video, audio, photographic, and more.

Facebook is undoubtedly the poster-child for all social apps; and as such sometimes becomes the punch-line or the punching bag for all that is wrong with digital engagement. Ironically, Facebook offers its users the strongest options for privacy settings.

Facebook: How it works

Your participation in Facebook begins by creating an account (this is true for most social platforms). Essentially you are creating your own profile on their website called a "wall".

In order to create a Facebook account you need:

- To be at least 13 years old. Children under 13 years old who have accounts have lied about their dates of birth in order to gain access. This is the same in every other platform which conforms to COPPA[144].
- A valid email address

Once you create the account you are given empty "wall" space and your own web location upon which to build your profile. You have the opportunity to decorate your wall with a cover photo (the large horizontal photo across the top of the profile) and your profile photo (the smaller square photo) which represents your profile every time you post any content.

Note: the word "profile" refers to a personal Facebook page. As an individual, your Facebook *profile* collects *friends*. Corporate or organizational *Pages* have *fans* rather than friends. As an individual you ask other users to

---

144 COPPA is the Children's Online Privacy Protection Act, a set of guidelines created by the United States' Federal Trade Commission (FTC).

friend you. As a company you ask individuals to *like your page*, making them your *fans.* Phew! Did you get all of that?

Facebook: Types of content allowable

Facebook is the most versatile of all of the social networks and has become the de facto "homepage" for millions of users. If you "like" the Facebook pages of news agencies, you will get immediate news alerts. When this content is mixed in with your local friends and neighbors and rounded out with extended family and old friends from college and high school, it's no wonder that so many people choose to begin their day on their Facebook page.

In terms of content, Facebook is the most robust of all of the social platforms. The Facebook timeline can accommodate any kind of content including: text, photos, videos, and audio. In fact most videos will play right in the timeline without a user having to leave Facebook to go watch the video on an external website. In 2016, Facebook released *Facebook Live* the ability to live stream to your Facebook audience. The intention was to give Facebook users live and immediate access to communicate with their connections. Within the first year, Facebook Live has become the outlet for live streamed suicides[145], gang rapes[146], and police shootings[147].

In addition, developers have created third party apps which work within the Facebook structure. Think of these as accessories for your Facebook home. A "third party" developer creates software which extends the operation of the core app. For example, I'm a compulsive reader and have a Goodreads account. Goodreads brilliantly created a third-party app for Facebook. So now my Facebook friends can keep up with what I've been reading right from my Facebook wall. On Facebook, as fellow users of Goodreads, we can recommend books and share book reviews with each other.

By choosing different third party apps, you can show your personality

---

145 *Facebook takes steps to stop suicides on Live,* Jessica Guyunn, March 1, 2017, https://www.usatoday.com/story/tech/news/2017/03/01/facebook-live-suicide-prevention/98546584/

146 *Police: At least 40 people watched teen's sexual assault on Facebook Live,* Emanuella Grinberg and Samira Said, March 22, 2017, http://www.cnn.com/2017/03/21/us/facebook-live-gang-rape-chicago

147 For Philando Castile, Social Media Was The Only 911, Issie Lapowsky, July 7, 2016, https://www.wired.com/2016/07/philando-castile-social-media-911/

and your interests, right from your Facebook wall. There are third party apps which represent almost every possible hobby and interest imaginable.

Facebook: Connection agreement

Facebook is one of the very few synchronous social platforms. In order to *friend* someone on Facebook, both parties must agree. This is the beginning of where it goes all wrong for children. Remember that kids are follower-whores and will *friend* literally anyone just for the sake of increasing their numbers.

My definition of friend is someone I would stop to talk to if I bumped into them at the grocery store. If I would zip right past the person on my way to grabbing broccoli, that's not a friend. Come up with an equivalent definition for your family. And at a minimum, mom and dad **must** physically know every single person on that friends list. If not, the person should be removed from the friend's list, and blocked.

Facebook uses another term: **friends of friends.** This is a shortcut term to mean the friends of my direct friends. These are the people who I have not chosen to friend directly but we do have at least one friend in common.

The Facebook privacy settings are defaulted to allow *friends of friends* to see all of your content. This means that you are potentially exposing all of your content to thousands (or tens of thousands) of people you've never met.

Facebook: Privacy settings & blocking recourse

Just recently Facebook made a significant change to its privacy settings. Users can no longer hide within the Facebook universe by removing themselves from the search feature. This means that anyone can search for you by name and potentially find you in the results list. This change has made it even more critical to be mindful of the other available privacy settings.

If you have recently received many more friend requests, this is probably the reason why. If you had the box ticked for remaining invisible to searches for your name, that feature no longer exists. Your profile and name will now show up in all Facebook searches.

In January 2103, Facebook rolled out its "Graph Search". This new searching feature harnesses the power of Facebook's bank of Big Data. Hundreds of billions of points of data are compiled into Graph Search which should not be confused with a search engine search. When you search on Google for example, the engine returns links which may or may not contain an answer to your original question. Instead, when you use Graph Search, the database responds with an actual answer to your questions.

In addition Graph Search is semantic, which means that you aren't searching for keywords in a caveman or Boolean method. Instead in Graph Search you type a normally phrased question, and receive the answer.

For example you could ask:

- Friends who like Hunger Games
- Single women who live in Tampa
- Photos of my friends of friends taken in Europe
- Restaurants my friends like

If you type into the search bar: "Find all friends of friends who live in Boston Massachusetts," Graph Search will show you all of the friends **of your** friends who currently live in Boston. This search can be manipulated to isolate almost any piece of demographic or consumer data: age, current city, hometown, employer, job description, which restaurants frequented, etc.

Facebook Graph is a great feature for adults, especially for predators searching for information on our children.

Facebook: Specific Privacy Settings

The Facebook privacy settings are the best of any other social platform. But if you don't **use them**, then there's not much of a point. The privacy settings restrict who can see your posts, photos, and any other content you post. You can even create lists of friends and post specific content to just one or more lists. You can also put up a post to everyone **except:** mom or dad or *family.* Tricky, no?

Go to the top right hand side of the Facebook screen and click on the small gear icon, and then choose PRIVACY settings

- All of your child's privacy settings should be set to FRIENDS only, never FRIENDS OF FRIENDS. You will have to make this choice in multiple locations.
- Review the "tagging" settings. Change them all so that anytime your child is tagged in a post, she has to approve before it goes live.
- Remove the ability to tag in photos completely.

- Pay close attention to the privacy settings of specific photos. Each photo can be assigned a different privacy setting ranging from "hidden" to "public" and including removal of specific users (like mom or dad) or limiting exposure to just a specifically created distribution list.

Facebook: How to Block

It's very easy to block someone on Facebook. Just navigate to their wall and click where it says FRIENDS, and choose the option to block that person. If you block that person completely you will become completely invisible to that person. They will not even see any of your comments on the posts of mutual friends.

Facebook: Relative popularity

In some parts of the United States, tween and teen use of Facebook is waning. Facebook tends to be in one of two camps with very little grey area: either it's used constantly or it's hardly used by teens.

One thing seems to be consistent, regardless of use in middle school or high school, most kids come back to Facebook in the college years to keep tabs on old friends and connect with alumni groups. In Western Europe, Facebook is still extremely popular among tweens and teens. It's not surprising then, that Facebook experiences a very high percentage of cyberbullying in these areas.

Facebook: Cases and current events

Case: Nicole Cable[148]

Nichole Cable was a lovely 15 year old from Maine. The night before she was abducted and murdered, Nichole complained to her boyfriend that a man named Kyle Dube groped and physically assaulted her. But she was able to get away and chose not to press the issue.

But here's what she didn't know. Kyle Dube created a fake Facebook account and had been communicating with Nichole under a different name. Nichole did NOT know that the man she thought she was communicating on

---

148 *Nichole Cable, 15-Year-Old Missing Maine Girl, Died From Asphyxiation,* https://www.usatoday.com/story/news/nation/2013/06/13/missing-maine-girl-asphyxiation/2421117/

Facebook was actually Kyle Dube.

Nichole unwittingly set a date and time to meet Dube's alter ego at the end of the driveway of her own home. Apparently this "other person" promised Nichole free marijuana. Nichole walked down to the end of the driveway where Dube jumped out of the woods wearing a mask. Nichole was found dead days later.

Case: Ashleigh Hall[149]

In 2010, half way across the world in England, in an area called Teeside, a similar situation unfolded for seventeen year old Ashleigh Hall. She met a young man on Facebook and began a short cyber relationship with him.

She found "Pete Cartwright" handsome in his bare chested photos and agreed to meet him in person. In reality "Pete Cartwright" was a sickly-looking, toothless 33 year old convicted double rapist living in his car. Peter Chapman (his real name) had already served seven years for a prior rape conviction.

The night before the police found her body, Ashleigh told her mother she was going over to a friend's house. She had actually made plans with that handsome young man she had met from Facebook. Peter Chapman texted Ashleigh and told her that his "father" was going to pick her up. Expecting to be transported to go meet "Pete", once she was in the car Chapman attacked Ashleigh; ultimately kidnapping, raping, and murdering her.

Both of these worst-case scenario stories illustrate a few of the typical and terrifying pitfalls. The first is the "friending anyone" trend among children. The second is the disconnect between virtual and reality: in all of these types of cases, the child has been duped into thinking they are going to meet a friend or at least a friendly person. Although both of these victims were teen girls, make no mistake; young men are just as much at risk. In other cases the "young girl" they go to meet ends up being a man or the situation turns into an ambush by school bullies.

Case: Portland Ambush[150]

---

149 *Facebook murderer who posed as teenager to lure victim jailed for life*,
https://www.theguardian.com/uk/2010/mar/08/peter-chapman-facebook-ashleigh-hall

150 *Portland Teens Allegedly Carve Swastika In Boy's Forehead Over Facebook Comment*,
http://www.huffingtonpost.com/2014/02/18/portland-teens-carve-swastika_n_4807902.html

In 2014, three Portland, Oregon teens were charged as adults for luring, kidnapping, and torturing a classmate. The young lady who was charged in the case acted as "bait" and lured the victim behind a shed with the promise of sex and drugs.

The victim was then ambushed by the other teens. The victim was hit with a crowbar in the back of the head after which a swastikawas carved into the victim's forehead with a box cutter. The motive? Apparently the victim had made a comment on Facebook about one of the perpetrators being "gay".

Case: Gag Order[151]

Under the category of "stupid things kids do" : in 2014, Boston College student Dana Snay couldn't help posting a snarky celebratory post on Facebook after her father, the headmaster of Gulliver Preparatory School, won his age discrimination suit against his employer. Understandably pleased, if completely misdirected, Ms. Snay posted the following:

> "Gulliver is now officially paying for my vacation to
> Europe this summer. SUCK IT."

In the end, it only sucked for the Snays who lost the entire $80K settlement. Part of the settlement required a gag order. Ms. Snay's post lost her family the entire settlement, and presumably her planned summer in Europe.

Facebook: Specific areas of concern

- Children must be 13 years old to start a Facebook account. You can report your too young children and Facebook will revoke their account.

- You can report offensive posts provided the report-er has access to the profile of the perpetrator

- Friend-whore behavior is pervasive on Facebook. You will need to review who your child has friended at least once a week.

- *Friending* your child is not enough. They can easily create lists to hide content from family members. You must have their username and

---

151 Read the entire story here: *Daughter's Facebook Brag Costs Her Family $80,000*, http://www.cnn.com/2014/03/02/us/facebook-post-costs-father/index.html

password in order to see their complete profile. You will also need to log into their account to review privacy settings.

- Private Facebook video chats and text chats can be initiated among *friends* – this is where some of that Friend Whore behavior becomes particularly scary. Check your child's Facebook inbox.

- There are a host of inappropriate third party apps for Facebook. For example the Facebook app called "Bang with Friends" will match you up with one of your friends or friends of friends who are interested in scheduling an evening of casual sex.

- You are accidentally/on-purpose releasing your privacy by using check-in apps like FourSquare which alerts your Facebook audience of where you are at any given moment. The same applies to any GPS tagged content.

There is no such thing as "online privacy". Once your content goes out into the ether – it can be changed, edited, manipulated, shared, promoted, and seen anywhere and everywhere.

Instagram

Introduction

If Facebook is the "community" within your digital world, then Instagram is the photo album you keep in your digital apartment. This is the place where you share the photographic memories of your daily life. Facebook purchased Instagram in 2012 for $1 billion (US); so this virtual photo album quite literally lives within the Facebook community.

Instagram: How it works

Instagram is an online photo-sharing and social networking service that enables its users to take photos, apply a variety of digital filters to them, and share them on a variety of social services including[152] Facebook, Twitter, Foursquare, Tumblr, Flickr, and VKontakte.

Instagram is essentially a photo app. A user creates a profile which is ridiculously easy to do. All you need is an email, a username, and password. You have to be 13 years old to create an account. Once the profile is created, the user can then begin taking photos. Unlike the more popular 16:9 aspect ratio typical among mobile devices and cameras, Instagram photos are oriented as a perfect square giving the photos an old-fashioned Polaroid feel. Users can apply a variety of filters to the photo in addition to a text caption and hashtags.

Once the photo is posted it gets distributed to everyone who *follows* that account via the followers feed screen. So if I officially follow **your** Instagram, everything you post shows up in my feed. If I don't officially follow Instagram but I have an account, I can still lurk on your wall without you know that I'm there.

You also have the option of geotagging each individual photo with the precise location where the photo was taken.

---

152 Foursquare is an app which allows its users to check in at a public location like a restaurant or airport. Tumblr is a blogging platform popular among teens – think of this as a giant stream of consciousness brain dump. Flickr is a photo and video hosting site which is used by photographers and bloggers. Vkontakte is the East European and Russian version of Facebook partially known as the place where American men can find mail order brides.

Instagram: Connection agreement

Users create a profile on this asynchronous platform which if you remember means that there is no "following agreement". Anyone can follow your profile and see everything that you post. Unless you keep your account private, which the overwhelming majority (over 80% of tweens and teens) refuse to do.

Instagram: Privacy settings & blocking recourse

There is only one true "privacy setting" on Instagram: setting your account to private which forces users to ask for follow approval. This means that your child will have to approve anyone who wants to follow them, and all of their content will be private and closed down to the public. Just know that your child will be very reluctant to do this. Plus the "private" setting is a toggle "on or off" and can be switched ten times a day from private to open. Your child can and probably will switch the privacy when mom isn't looking.

Users have the ability to block offensive posts individually and can block users from seeing their profile at all. However, once predators know your child's Instagram handle[153] – they can just create a new account themselves under a new handle and continue to harass your child. Users also have the opportunity via "Instagram Direct" to send a photo or video directly to up to 15 other users. Whether or not you see this content (on the receiving end) depends entirely on your privacy settings. You can choose to see direct messages from only the users you follow or anyone at all. Even if you keep your account private, you will still have an inbox waiting for you filled with photos and videos from anyone and everyone in the world.

Instagram: Relative popularity

Instagram users upload 40 million photos to the site each day, and 17% of teens say that Instagram is the most important social network which is up from 12% in 2012. Although the focus is photography, teens consistently count this platform among the top three most important social networks for American teens.

---

153 The terms "username" and "handle" are almost always synonymous and refer to the method by which a user is identified and location on any social networking platform. If you know a user's handle or username, you can find where their account lives online

The description of Instagram can be a bit misleading. Instagram use transcends its photographic foundation and has become as much about communication. Within Instagram there is a literal "popularity" feature. Your child's photo will be deemed officially popular by the platform if it receives 7-10 likes per minute when the photo is first posted. This surge has to continue until you get the notice that it went popular which can be anywhere from 8 to 25 minutes after posting. For kids, to have an Instagram photo "go popular" is a **huge** ego boost and carries serious social currency.

Take a guess which type of photographic content becomes "popular". Yes, cat photos make the list, but sexualized content trumps all other content. Your children know this.

Instagram: Cases and current events

Virginia Teens[154]
In 2013, three Virginia teens were arrested for posting more than 50 explicit photos of their classmates in Instagram. The teens (15 year old girl and two boys: 13 and 14 years old) just asked their classmates for the explicit photos. Their classmates willingly sent the photos.

Eladio Ramirez[155]
Also in 2013, a 22 year old man was arrested after he sexually assaulted a 14 year old girl he contacted through Instagram. Officials have identified the suspect as 22 year old Eladio Ramirez of Modesto California. He is facing: two counts of sodomy, two counts of lewd and lascivious behavior, penetration with a foreign object and unlawful sexual intercourse.

Digital Burn Book[156]
Cyberbullying is also alive and well on Instagram. In 2013 a 15 year old boy from Colorado has been charged with five counts of third-degree harassment as a result of his creating a so-called "burn book" on Instagram used to bully

---

154 *Prince William teens charged in connection with explicit Instagram postings*
https://www.washingtonpost.com/local/crime/prince-william teens-charged-in-connection-with-explicit-instagram-postings/2014/03/08/17760fe0-a6e7-11e3-9cff-b1406de784f0_story.html

155 *Sexual Assault Arrest Stemmed From Instagram Encounter,*
http://www.centralvalleytv.net/shop-local/item/1328-27sexual-assault-arrest-stemmed-from-instagram-encounter

156 *Instagram tool of alleged teen cyber-bully arrested in Colorado,*
http://www.cbsnews.com/news/instagram-tool-of-alleged-teen-cyber-bully-arrested-in-colorado/

classmates via the photographic posts.

Peter Kiever[157]

In 2014, 18 year old, North Carolina resident Peter Kieverhas been charged with 14 felony sex crimes after posting naked photos of young girls on several Instagram profiles. Months earlier a 12 year old girl filed charges against Kiever for harassing her and repeatedly asking her for nude photos. The photos that Kiever was able to post were offered willingly by the victims.

Nicholas Hinton[158]

Also in 2014, 19 year old, Ohio resident Nicholas Hintonposted a threat on Instagram claiming that he was contemplating "shooting up" his alma mater, North Ridgeville High School. Police were alerted to the Instagram and Hinton was arrested without incident.

Instagram: Specific areas of concern

There is a significant amount of cyberbullying, sexting, and sexual predation on Instagram. If you choose to allow your older than 13 year-old child to use this app it will need to be monitored weekly.

- Asynchronous nature of the platform. Anyone can follow your profile using the official "following" feature. Other people can just lurk on your site and never actually follow. Kids do **not** like to privatize their profile, and if they do are likely to switch it back and forth from private to open and back again.

- Many kids use the "bio" section of the profile page to cross-promote their handles on other social platforms. For example: your child might promote his Twitter handle on his Instagram bio and then promote his Kik on his Twitter bio, etc. This just gives perpetrators of all kinds the ability to gather even more information about your child.

- Listing phone numbers as part of an image has been popular on Instagram

---

157 *Officials: Son of sheriff candidate arrested in Instagram photo case,*
http://www.wsoctv.com/news/suspect-charged-nude-photos-young-girls-instagram/113091939
158 *North Ridgeville teen Nicholas Hinton accused of posting threat on shooting up school on Instagram,* http://fox8.com/2014/03/21/teen-charged-for-threats-against-school-on-instagram/

– which is stupid obviously.

- Instagram has a "Photo Map" feature which places all of a user's photos onto a map if those photos have been geotagged with the location where the photo was taken.

- The use of hashtags extends the reach of a specific post and can imply sexual interest.

- Be sure to review every follower your child has, even if your child's account is set to PRIVATE. The privacy setting won't matter if your child is accepting anyone who applies for approval, and don't forget your child might be switching the privacy toggle on and off when he thinks you aren't paying attention.

- Also review who **your child** follows. What types of photos are those account posting? Is your child consuming hyper-sexualized content?

- Beware the direct messaging option with Instagram; this is a sexting or sexual predation scenario just waiting to happen.

Twitter

Introduction

If Facebook is the community, then Twitter is the conversation. Whether you're having that conversation at work, at a cocktail party, or after a one-night-stand determines the content and the context. Like the real world, millions of conversations are all happening at once. Your interests determine your Twitter experience.

There is a significant amount of cyberbullying,[159] pornography, and sexual predation on Twitter. In fact a study found that 100,000 cyberbullying tweets are sent each week. Frankly, I think that number is too low by half.

Twitter: How it works

Officially, Twitter is considered a micro-blog because you can only post 140 total characters at a time including spaces. In action, Twitter is a rapid fire conversation among hundreds of millions of people at once.

Sometimes those people (or users) talk/tweet with each other in a back and forth texting type of a format. Because of the limited text length Twitter is used particularly well by news agencies. The format supports their rapid fire news alerts with links back to their websites. Twitter has also become a favorite among school districts and extracurricular activities and sports leagues. Getting the message out about a field change during a Sunday morning soccer tournament has never been easier, but is still really annoying.

In order to create a Twitter "timeline" all you need is a unique username and an email address. You must also be at least 13 years old.

Once you create an account you can tweet as often as you like. Eventually you will see other users will begin following you. You can also view another user's followers list to potentially gather more information or just out of curiosity.

Twitter is also the home to a significant amount of pornography and sexted material. The use of sexualized hashtags can be used to vet the viability of a child's willingness to engage in sexual conversations. In addition specific Tweets can be geotagged for the exact location where the user was standing

---

159 Read the entire story: *"Twitter Is Turning Into a Cyberbullying Playground"*
https://www.yahoo.com/news/twitter-turning-cyberbullying-playground-053413648.html

when the Tweet was sent.

On the dark side (or rather the idiot side) of Twitter, we're hearing more and more about tweens, teens, and even young adults who treat Twitter as they would a private journal and tweet a daily stream of consciousness: to their own detriment. Making hostile, bigoted, or otherwise socially unacceptable comments on an open forum like Twitter can trigger: school expulsion, job termination, withdrawal of scholarship offers, personal humiliation, embarrassment, and of course imprisonment.

Twitter: Types of content allowable

If you consider Twitter to be a conversation, the content on the timeline are considered the examples to support or illustrate your statement. If you're tweeting about your baby's first experience with an ice cream cone, the attached content might be a video or a photo.

In addition to the 140 character text post, other features have been added to Twitter including the ability to watch videos directly in the timeline when that link is part of the Tweet – most commonly seen in conjunction with YouTube videos.

In January 2013, Twitter launched another app called Vine[160], which is also quite popular among teens. Vine enables users to create super short 6 second videos which automatically loop.

Twitter: Connection agreement

Users create a profile on this asynchronous platform which means, that there is no "following agreement". Anyone can follow your profile and see everything that you post, unless you keep your account private, which the overwhelming majority of users refuse to do. Less than 12% of Twitter profiles are kept private.

Twitter: Privacy settings & blocking recourse

Just like Instagram, there is only one actual "privacy setting" on Twitter: setting your account to private, forcing users to ask for follow approval. This means that your child will have to approve anyone who wants to follow them, and all

---

160 In an effort to increase his Twitter followers a young man created a Vine of himself having sex with a microwaved Hot Pocket.

of their content will be private and closed down to the public.

Tweens and teens who are forced to lock-down their asynchronous accounts are also smart enough to flip that switch from on to off and back again while mom isn't watching. Twitter users can easily block a user or report inappropriate content by going to the offending user's profile and going to settings.

Twitter: Relative popularity

Twitter is consistently listed in the top 3 most important social networks for teens. As such, it is also the home for: cyberbullying, sexting, and sexual predation.

If I were a sexual predator and I wanted to find out as much information as possible about your child I would start with Twitter. The rapid fire nature and Twitter's excellent searching features make it quite easy to triangulate data. For example: If I am trying to abduct your child and I'm not sure where she goes to school, first I can check to see if she follows any official school accounts, then I will verify that other students at that school follow your child, and lastly I will check the latest sports schedule via her soccer league's Twitter timeline. It's very easy to obtain outside verification of data, especially on Twitter.

Be aware that many middle school and high school students are also posting and hashtagging their need for a ride home on their public Twitter timelines.

Twitter: Cases and current events

Case: Lost Cisco Job Offer[161]

Recent college graduate and 22 year old Connor Rileywas offered a great job by tech giant Cisco. But she wasn't sure what to do with the offer so she tweeted the following:

"Cisco just offered me a job! Now I have to weigh the utility of a fatty paycheck against the daily commute to San Jose and hating the work."

---

161 *"Woman's "Fatty Paycheck" Tweet Catches Attention of Cisco"*,
http://www.dailytech.com/Womans+Fatty+Paycheck+Tweet+Catches+Attention+of+Cisco/articl
e14690.htm

A Cisco staffer saw the Tweet and her job offer was revoked. Ouch!

Case: British Juror
A British woman serving on an active jury tweeted details of the case she was on. Claiming she didn't know which way to vote in the case, she was asking for input from the Twitter-verse. She was promptly removed from the jury.

Case: Lost Athletic Scholarship[162]
In 2012 Yuri Wright was a highly recruited New Jersey high school football star. He had a full scholarship offer from several schools including the University of Michigan. During this same time he was tweeting profane and racist comments. As a result, his Catholic high school expelled him. University of Michigan also revoked their full football scholarship offer.

Case: Lost College Scholarship[163]
Freshman football player, Jay Harris was attending Michigan State on a full scholarship. That is, until he tweeted a video of himself singing an explicit rap song while holding a marijuana cigarette in his hand. His scholarship was revoked and Harris decided to drop out of Michigan State and pursue his career as a rapper.

Case: Twitter and sexting
A 16 year old boy was arrested and a 14 year old girl was detained in connection with a Twitter based sexting scandal. Police were alerted to several tweeted nude photos of girls who attend the same school as the young man. Apparently the female students willingly texted nude photos of themselves to the young man who then posted them on Twitter. All of the children involved can now be charged with felony: creation, distribution, and/or trafficking of child pornography.

Twitter: Specific areas of concern
Many of these areas of concern are almost identical to Instagram because they are both asynchronous platforms.

- Asynchronous nature of the platform. Anyone can follow your profile using

---

162 "Yuri Wright's tweets are why Michigan stopped recruiting him"
163 "Michigan State pulls scholarship after recruit Jay Harris creates explicit rap video"

the official "following" feature. Other people can just lurk on your site and never actually follow. Kids do NOT like to privatize their profile, and if they do are likely to switch it back and forth from private to open and back again.

- Many kids use the "bio" section of the profile page to cross-promote their handles on other social platforms. For example: your child might promote his Twitter handle on his Instagram bio and then promote his Kik on his Twitter bio, etc. This just gives perpetrators of all kinds the ability to gather even more information about your child.

- Many Twitter users tend to use their bios to list their real names, the name of their schools, and their actual locations.

- Geotagging a specific Tweet or photo gives a would-be predator an exact location from which the user posted.

- The use of sexual hashtags extends the reach of a specific post and can imply sexual interest.

- Be sure to review every follower your child has, even if your child's account is set to PRIVATE. The privacy setting won't matter if your child is accepting anyone who applies for approval, and don't forget that your child might be switching the privacy toggle on and off when he thinks you aren't paying attention.

- Also review who **your child** follows. What types of photos are those accounts posting? Is your child consuming hyper-sexualized content?

- Beware the direct messaging option with Twitter. A user can only direct message a follower which makes it even more important to check who your children are following on Twitter. Every one of those users can turn around and private message your child.

- Watch out for Twitter hitchhiking[164]. Kids are posting and hashtagging their need for a ride home right on their public Twitter timeline. You can imagine how convenient this is for a sexual predator.

---

164 NPR: *"Teens Use Twitter To Thumb Rides"*,
http://www.npr.org/sections/alltechconsidered/2013/08/15/209530590/teens-use-twitter-to-thumb-rides

Snapchat

Introduction

Within our digital community, Snapchat is the secret conversation. It's the note passed in the classroom not meant for public consumption. If users wanted their content to be public, they could easily share in the community (via Facebook), in a conversation (on Twitter), or by sharing a photo (on Instagram). The platform's purported secrecy is both its greatest draw and its greatest risk.

Snapchat sells their users on its core "disappearing content" feature. One Snapchat user sends another a funny or sexual photo, or "snap", and the photo will supposedly automatically disappear from the receiver's device within a predetermined number of seconds.

The truth is that Snapchat has no control of whether or not your "snaps" actually disappear from the recipient's device. There are multiple ways to capture and save photos from Snapchat and most Snapchat users don't realize that little fun fact.

Snapchat: How it works

Snapchat is a smartphone and tablet app available on all major appstore systems including Android and iOS. It does not have a web version or platform, meaning that you can only engage with this application via the app.

In terms of connection agreement, Snapchat is synchronous only if the user keeps their profile locked down, forcing approval of each friend, otherwise it is asynchronous.

In order to communicate via Snapchat, both the sender and the receiver must have accounts in the system. Like most other apps, in order to create an account you need an email address and you have to be at least 13 years old.

Unlike other social networks, Snapchat has created another version of their app (called Snapkidz) which automatically installs if the user enters a date of birth which makes them less than 13 years old. Snapkidz allows children to edit photos on their device and disables all sharing and communication features. Beware that kids under 13 years old may not like the Snapkidz option; watch out for a deletion and re-installation with an "older" date of birth.

Using the Snapchat interface you take a photo and select one or multiple Snapchat recipients for the snap. The sender will determine for how many seconds the photo will be available to view (from 1 to 10 seconds). The recipient views the snap by pressing and holding to view the photo. After the time runs out the snap is no longer available on the screen.

Presumably the snap or communication is deleted and irrecoverable after the allotted time interval expires. In reality those snaps and communications are viewable: there are free and readily available third party apps which circumvent the Snapchat programming and automatically keep a copy of every snap the user sends or receives.

- The recipient could potentially take a screenshot of the image on the screen or even take a photo of the screen with a secondary device or phone.

- All law enforcement forensics divisions will have the tools available to connect the device via cable to a mobile extraction tool. These pieces of software will do a complete dump of any device regardless of screen blocks or platform logins. It's actually a fairly simple process.

This scenario is where it pays to remind your children that regardless of privacy settings or features, digital content never disappears and can never be completely deleted.

Snapchat: Types of content allowable

When Snapchat first launched, the focus was strictly on photos which

were meant to "disappear" within the sender's predefined number of seconds. Now the platform has expanded to include videos and private chat, as well as photos and videos which a user can designate as semi-permanent by assigning them to the "stories" section of the app.

If Instagram is focused on the community aspect of sharing photos, Snapchat up until now has focused on the "hidden" aspect of sharing privately. However, Snapchat's move towards adding more features shows its attempt to become more of a communication destination.

In Snapchat's 2014 addition of the 'Here' feature, users can share a two-way live video and audio communication with a single other user, similar to FaceTime or Skype.

Snapchat: Connection agreement

In order to add friends to your Snapchat profile you have to either already have them listed in your contacts or you need to know their username or handle. Once you create an account and a username for yourself, you have the option of linking yourself to all of your friends in your own device's contact list. Snapchat can view your phone's contact list and will make adding friends much easier by linking to a user's mobile number.

Snapchat: Privacy settings & blocking recourse

There is really only one privacy setting: either you accept snaps from just friends or you accept snaps from everyone. While it's very easy to block another user on Snapchat, it is just as easy to "unblock" them with the tap of a key. If you have banned certain friends from being able to communicate with your child on Snapchat, you might want to pay close attention to their active list of Snapchat friends. Children know how easy it is to temporarily open communication and then close it down again with an easy tap.

Snapchat: Relative popularity

Along with Instagram, Twitter, and Facebook – Snapchat is consistently on the short list of most important apps for teens all over the world:

- As of 2013 there were 26 million Snapchat users and 400 million snaps are uploaded through the platform each day
- 70% of users are women
- 32% of US teens and 25% of UK teens use Snapchat
- 77% of college students use Snapchat daily

As a result of their increasing popularity, Facebook attempted to buy Snapchat for $3 billion (US) in 2013. Snapchat refused and has since added many community-type features to its base photo-sharing application.

Snapchat: Cases and current events

Case: Jared Honea[165]

A 26 year old Louisiana high school teacher named Jared Honea was arrested on various sexting charges after engaging in sexting behaviors via Snapchat. Honea had exchanged several Snapchat messages with a 15 year old student, including asking the minor for nude photographs.

Case: Alexander Taylor[166]

An Oregon high school teacher named Alexander Taylor was sentenced to ten days in jail and 18 months of probation. In addition, his teaching certificate was revoked and he lost his job after he admitted to sexting one of his students via Snapchat.

Case: Canadian Porn[167]

In Quebec, Canada ten boys (ages 13 to 15) were charged with possession and distribution of child pornography as a result of trading explicit photos of each other's girlfriends. The photos were allegedly taken on Snapchat and then shared among the perpetrators.

Case: Brett Lewis[168]

A 19 year old man in Arizona named Brett Lewis was arrested for sexting with a 14 year old girl he met on Snapchat. Lewis received the girl's Snapchat username from one of her friends. After meeting virtually, the two began swapping explicit photos back and forth. The girl then arranged for Lewis to pick her up at her home. After police responded to a call for a missing 14 year old girl, she was found in Lewis' apartment. The girl later admitted to engaging in sexual acts with Lewis.

---

165 *"Shreveport Teacher Arrested, Accused of Sexting with Student"*,
https://www.ktbs.com/news/shreveport-teacher-arrested-accused-of-sexting-with-student/article_02d61fcf-c30d-5189-a0e2-2d72bafa18e3.html

166 *"Oregon City HS teacher admits 'sexting' and will go to jail"*,
http://katu.com/news/local/oregon-city-hs-teacher-admits-sexting-and-will-go-to-jail-11-20-2015

167 *"Child porn charges laid against 10 Laval teens"*,
http://www.cbc.ca/news/canada/montreal/child-porn-charges-laid-against-10-laval-teens-1.2426599

168 "Scottsdale police arrest man in 'Snapchat' encounter with minor "

Snapchat: Specific areas of concern

For many tweens and teens, Snapchat feels like a safe way to send sexually provocative photos because they believe that the images they have shared will magically self-destruct. Many perpetrators of sexting and sexual predation are under the same impression. Given this misplaced sense of security, Snapchat may be your child's first experience with cyberbullying, sexting, and sexual predation.

- The very nature of Snapchat creates a false sense of security. Once digital images and content are released into the websphere, they can never be completely controlled or deleted. This is the nature of digital communication. Snapchat is not the exception.

- The amount of sexting and sexual predation on Snapchat cannot be overstated. There is no question that your child will be exposed to hyper-sexualized content, and might even contribute to its growth.

- If your children advertise or promote their Snapchat usernames on their other social profiles or anywhere publicly, they are inviting unwelcome contact by sexual predators. A predator only needs your child's username or cell phone number in order to initiate contact via Snapchat.

- Be sure to review your child's friends list every week. Unless you know who each person is in real life, the friend must be deleted.

- When you "block" a user, the "un-block" is just a tap. Be sure that your child hasn't un-blocked someone you just blocked.

- Third party apps have been developed specifically with the purpose of capturing and saving every snap your child sends. This is an obvious sexting risk in addition to a cyberbullying risk. If today's friend is tomorrow's enemy, you may not want photos of yourself to go public.

- The new 'Here' feature by Snapchat enables two-way live video chatting similar to Facetime or Skype. Anyone on the friends list can use this feature to have a live video conversation with your child.

Ask.fm

Introduction

Where does Ask.fm live within our virtual community? Ask.fm is the passive-aggressive note left in the office kitchen, the person who vandalizes your car in the parking lot, and the heavy breather who calls your house late at night.

It is a haven for those who would prefer to lurk in the shadows. Although a significant proportion of the lurkers are aggressive, many of these young Ask.fm users are merely seeking emotional validation and engagement, from anyone. Unfortunately, the well-intentioned will not find a soft place to land on Ask.fm.

Since 2013, Ask.fm has come under fire for the massive number of cyberbullying and teen suicides connected to the platform. Any digital platform which promotes and harbors anonymous communication among its users will have a similar outcome. Combining anonymity with a lack of parental oversight is a recipe for disaster.

Ask.fm: How it works

Ask.fm is built on the very simple premise of answering anonymous questions. That's basically it. As a user, you create a profile and other users come to your profile and ask you questions. Users will probably not know the identity of the person who is posing the question.

Here's how it works:

- A user creates a profile
  Most kids use their real names and location – which is completely unsafe.
  For example: Sally Smith from Topeka Kansas
- Another user can ask the first user a question, anonymously
  We'll call her Anonymous
- Anonymous goes onto Sally's Ask.Fm page and posts a question –
  questions like the following are extremely common on Ask.fm
  * Why are you such a whore?
  * Why don't you kill yourself?
  * Do your parents hate you because you suck at soccer?
- Sally sees the question on her profile but does not know the real identity of

the person who posted it

Users can access their profile via a device app as well as via the Ask.fm web platform. Once logged in, Ask.fm users will see a screen with pending questions. You can choose to answer or ignore any of those questions, but as soon as you answer a question your response is posted on your profile.

Ask.fm: Types of content allowable
Users have the option to respond to questions with: plain text, by uploading a photo, or by recording a video response.

Ask.fm: Connection agreement
Ask.fm is no-synchronous, which means that there is no connection agreement between you and the users who ask you questions. What's more, your profile is completely open to the public. The only guarantee is that the individual posting the question is a registered user.

Ask.fm: Privacy settings & blocking recourse
Your only privacy setting is to either allow anonymous questions or only allow questions from users who choose to show their identity. In the latter case, this does not mean that you "know" who they are but merely that they are choosing to reveal their username. There have been a number of cyberbullying and sexual predation cases where the perpetrator managed multiple Ask.fm accounts with the goal of causing harm and/or shielding their true identity.

Ask.fm profiles are completely open to the public and you do not even need an Ask.fm user account to access the data. As long as you know the person's username, you can access all of the posted content. Asking questions requires an account.

Ask.fm: Relative popularity
Ask.fm is popular globally, reporting 114 million registered users (about half of which are children) in 150 countries, and consistently ranks in the top sites where children are cyberbullied mercilessly. As of 2013, Ask.fm was the 10th largest social network in the world and reported 30 million questions per day.

Ask.fm: Cases and current events

There is no other social network which has been so closely tied to a rash of child suicides than Ask.fm. Here is just a partial list of the victims.

- Rebecca Sedwick, 12, jumped from a cement silo in Florida
- Jessica Laney, 16, of Florida, who hanged herself
- Hannah Smith, 14, of England, hanged herself
- Joshua Unsworth, 15, of England, hanged himself
- Anthony Stubbs, 16, of England, was found dead in the woods
- Daniel Perry, 17, hanged himself in July 2013 after being encouraged to do so by Ask.fm users
- Ciara Pugsley, 15, of Ireland, found dead in the woods near her home
- Erin Gallagher, 13, of Ireland named Ask.fm in her suicide note
- Shannon Gallagher, 15, of Ireland Erin Gallagher's sister

Ask.fm: Specific areas of concern

This social network's lack of connection agreement and anonymity are both the reason why children like the site and the reason why they should never be allowed to use it. There is zero benefit for children in using this platform. The risks of using Ask.fm are enormous including: incredibly cruel cyberbullying, sexting, sexual predation, exposure to graphic sexual content, and identity theft.

- Any member of the public can see anyone's wall on Ask.fm without even having an account, all you need is the individual's username.

- Users tend to answer very personal identifying questions, publicly on Ask.fm. Young users routinely post their: full name, school name, age and date of birth, phone number, home address, and much more on a completely public forum.

- As in all other social networking scenarios, children tend to cross-promote their usernames making it incredibly easy for potential sexual predators to amass information about your child.

- Inappropriate content. You can fully expect your child to be asked sexual questions including very specific questions related to: oral sex, anal sex, bestiality, sexual preferences, drug use, self-harming behaviors, and suicide lists (where children ask for input from other users on whether or not they have considered suicide).

- Digital Munchausen is alive and well on Ask.fm. Engaging in these sorts of self-harming behaviors is quite easy to do on Ask.fm. If you find that your child is being cyberbullied on Ask.fm (or elsewhere) consider the possibility that it might be self-directed.

YouTube

YouTube is not a social networking site, but it has become a foundational piece of our collective digital experience. Very often, digital users are accessing YouTube without even realizing it. As the most popular video server on the planet, YouTube is used by individuals, brands, organizations, and artists all over the world.

So what's the big deal? The issue is not with YouTube as a platform, rather with the video content which is easily accessible to anyone with access to a web browser (anyone) or appstore.

When you create and upload a video to YouTube it is accessible and viewable within seconds by hundreds of millions of users worldwide. YouTube has no internal content vetting or censorship process and it relies on users to report inappropriate content for removal. The moment that an offending video is pulled off the YouTube servers, five more crop up in its place. There is very little that YouTube can do about policing its content169.

YouTube is simultaneously one of the web's greatest assets and one of its greatest risks for children. Proceed with extreme caution. Young kids love YouTube for its funny and entertaining content. Hilarious cat and dog videos, music videos, and the all-important Minecraft videos are popular among very young YouTube fans. However, children under 14 years old should absolutely not be allowed unsupervised access to YouTube. Remember the site is accessible via any web browser and via a device app.

RELATIVE POPULARITY

700 YouTube video links are shared on Twitter every minute

500 years of YouTube videos are watched on Facebook every day

YouTube has 6 billion hours of video watched each month

72 hours of new video are uploaded to YouTube every 60 seconds

---

[169] "Boob Tube: Why YouTube can't stop porn", https://www.dailydot.com/upstream/boobtube-why-youtube-cant-stop-porn/

SPECIFIC AREAS OF CONCERN

Sexual content including pornography. There is a massive amount of pornography available on YouTube; much of which is being consumed by children. This content ranges from merely sexually suggestive and mild nudity to rape fantasy and extremely violent and graphic sexual content.

Extremely graphic violent content. YouTube does not allow graphic and grisly content, but this has not stopped the onslaught of videos of live beheadings and mass executions.

Drug and alcohol content. If your child has any desire to learn how to hide his drugs, build a soda-can-beer-can wrapper, construct an anal alcohol funnel (called butt chugging), or figure out how to insert a vodka soaked tampon, YouTube is the place to go.

Self-injury instructional videos. Bulimia, anorexia, cutting, and other self-injury "how to" videos are widely available. In addition, these videos act as a sort of community for children who engage in these behaviors. Users offer each other support in living a self-injury lifestyle and share tricks for evading discovery by parents and teachers.

Other criminal behaviors. What do you want to learn about? Tune into YouTube to learn more about: lock picking, building a pipe bomb, sneaking into or out of a home undetected, and much more.

There is no way to filter or limit YouTube content outside of its internal filtering system. Your children know that by just logging you out of YouTube, all of its content is once again open and available.

Gaming

Gaming Consoles & Online/App Gaming

Video games and gaming are a multi-billion dollar global industry covering every age group and every digital device. The subcategory of "edutainment" has blurred the lines between educational and gaming content for very young children. In terms of digital risks and gaming, any particular video game may not be considered risky by virtue of its content but rather by the platform through which it operates and the methods of communication it may make possible among players.

Gaming Consoles

When you buy a gaming system for your home, regardless of the manufacturer, there are common risk themes across systems and platforms. There are three major console systems in the US:

Playstation (owned by Sony)

Xbox (owned by Microsoft)

and to a smaller degree: Wii (owned by Nintendo)

GAMING CONSOLES: HOW IT WORKS

All of these consoles operate via a television connection as well as an internet signal to facilitate automatic system updates. An internet signal is also required for group and community live gaming which allows players to meet inside of a game even though they are physically located in separate places.

Xbox and Playstation both have "eyes" or webcams which are used during gaming. These webcam-like devices can see and hear you. These features are used both during games and as a mode of communication with the console and with other players. They also present a hacking risk.

Gaming Consoles: Gaming Content

Purchasing a gaming console means that you will also need to purchase games which operate on that particular system. You will need to decide which types of gaming content are appropriate for your children. Games carry a general parental rating, similar to movies. However, you should take a close look at online reviews and ratings. Start with the fantastic user curated database of reviews on Common Sense Media.

Your personal rules might be slightly more or less strict than the consensus. Video games can contain hypersexualized and exceedingly violent scenarios where your child takes the role of the perpetrator.

Gaming Consoles: Parental Controls

All of these systems have associated parental controls which can limit how and if your child is able to connect to her friends via the community gaming feature. There are also extensive blocking features available. I have found that parents tend to forget about gaming consoles as a potential digital risk. Review the parental controls for your particular console, and then use them!

Online/App Gaming

Online/App Gaming: How it works

In order for your child to participate in online or app gaming, he must have access to a specific game and a device. Games might also have many different modes. For example Minecraft can be played in several different ways with differing levels of risk.

- Minecraft can be played in "stand-alone mode" which means that the child is creating and building a Minecraft world on her own via a smartphone or tablet. Risk: None
- Minecrafters can play on Xbox Live with other friends in their network; this increases the level of play to include collaboration with other players. In this scenario the players can communicate with each other through audio chat. Risk: sexual predation via other players. You can restrict play with strangers via console parental controls.
- Minecraft can also be played on a computer while connected to a public or private server. Your child can hop onto a server run by an individual. Those so-called "public" servers have open chat and many of the players utilize third party communication tools in order to engage in video and audio chat. Risk: High for sexual predation. There are no parental controls or blocking recourse.

Online/App Gaming: Gaming Content

Online gaming and gaming apps range from extremely violent to fun and silly games for young children. Even a simple and straightforward game like Words with Friends, which I love, has a random player generating feature. The system can find you a random opponent. Once you begin playing, you can chat freely with that stranger.

Children and adults also love the addictive Clash of Clans game, which is a fun and harmless game in terms of content. However, if you keep your clan "open", any stranger in your clan can chat with you. This is a sexual predation scenario waiting to happen (see cases below).

Online/App Gaming: Parental Controls

Most gaming apps and platforms don't have parental controls per se. As a general rule, any game which allows open chat or communication with unknown teammates should be avoided completely. Sexual predators go where the children are; including very young and otherwise benign gaming environments.

Cases and current events

Case: Minecraft Predator

Arthur Hartung[170], 34, of Seattle, was arrested for sexually exploiting a 12-year-old boy in Colorado while playing video games including Minecraft and League of Legends. Hartung pretended to be another child playing these games. Further investigation of his devices showed that Hartung was planning on meeting the victims in person for sexual purposes. Hartung had previously been convicted on child pornography charges in 2002.

Case: Xbox Live Predator[171,]

Washington police arrested a 20 year old man from New York, named Joshua Stetar who drove 40 hours cross country to harass and stalk a 15 year old girl he met while playing Halo 2 on Xbox Live. Before his arrival, he had allegedly been sending flowers and gifts to the girl's home in addition to thousands of text

---

170 *"Seattle-area online gamer busted for alleged child porn, exploitation after 2002 conviction"*, http://www.seattletimes.com/seattle-news/crime/kirkland-man-arrested-child-pornography/

171 *"Police Arrest Man Over Alleged Stalking Via Xbox Live"*, https://www.wired.com/2008/01/halo-stalker-ar/

messages. Once he arrived he texted: "Tell the cops that I'm gonna rape you and your sister".

Case: Xbox Live Sexting[172]

A judged sentenced 21 year old Scott Gibbons to 14 years in prison after Gibbons enticed and sent an 11 year old Tampa boy graphic sexual images. Their first contact was during an Xbox Live game, and then the communication moved first to Facebook and then to the child's cell phone. When arrested, Gibbons was already on probation for inappropriate contact with a different child.

Case: Xbox Live Sexual Abuse[173]

A 20 year old New York man named Richard Kretovic was sentenced to six months in jail and ten years probation for admitting he sexually abused a child under the age of 13 who he met while playing Xbox Live. Kretovic spoke to the boy over the gaming console and the two of them engaged in sexual acts more than once at Kretovic's home.

Case: Playstation Predator[174]

A 21 year old man named Ryan Freeman from Tennessee is facing charges after police said he attempted to entice a 13 year old boy to take a bus to Chattanooga to have sex with him. The boy thought that the person he met via his Playstation console was 16 years old. Freeman then friended the child on Facebook and offered him gifts and money in exchange for sexual photos. Freeman was ultimately arrested when the police met him at a train station where Freeman thought he was meeting the child for sex.

Specific areas of concern

Beware any webcam device including the Kinect with Xbox 360 and the new

---

172 "INVESTIGATORS: Child predators lurk on gaming systems",
http://hillsboroughcounty.wtsp.com/news/news/517462-investigators-child-predators-lurk-gaming-systems

173 "Richard Kretovic Sentenced on Sex Abuse Charges",
http://archive.seattleweekly.com/home/937595-129/crimepunishment

174 "Tenn. man accused of trying to entice Clermont Co. boy", http://www.wlwt.com/article/tenn-man-accused-of-trying-to-entice-clermont-co-boy/3536298

Xbox One175 which ships with the Kinect standard. The Xbox One never turns off unless it's unplugged; it is always watching and always listening – even in the dark. The easiest fix is to cover all of the webcams in your home with a Post-it-Note.

The standard directive to check who your children's friends are in the digital sphere is critical when gaming. Your children might be gaming with other "children" for hours at a time and over a span of months. When this gaming occurs with audio or video, predators are able to gather a great deal of information from your child. In addition, your child might really believe that they are communicating with another child rather than a sexual predator. That gaming contact might then transfer over to social media and phone contact and ultimately with in-person and presumably sexual contact.

Sexual predators are patient and are willing to engage in the "grooming" process required in making your child comfortable with an in-person meeting

---

175 "Kinect for Xbox One: An always-on, works-in-the-dark camera and microphone. What could possibly go wrong?"

Chapter 12

THE CHILDREN I'VE MET

(*Originally appeared on my Facebook page on October 22, 2014*)

Dear Parents,

I love your children. They are hilarious, and honest, and heartbreakingly raw. They are trying to feel "recognition" from anyone, even if the methods they use to gain that recognition are dangerous or potentially humiliating to themselves.

Your children are living in a social, academic, and digital environment which is overwhelmingly pressured. Regardless of where you live or how much money you have the story is the same. Your children (whether they realize or not, and whether they will admit it or not) are attempting to navigate a gauntlet of pressures and risks - both IRL and virtually. Academic pressures are way, way tougher than when we were children. Social pressure has become a numbers game. This generation of children equates their social value with the literal number of friends/followers/likes they have received on their last Instagram post - literally.

My eye has just started twitching because I know what I want to say to you, and I know that it will break your heart. But you need to hear it, and I wouldn't be doing my job or trying to help your children if I attempted to shield you from the truth.

Regardless of where I go geographically or socioeconomically - the following is true:

I am seeing moderate to extreme sexual precocity at very young ages. Children are having digital sexual conversations and are consuming online porn as young as 8 years old. Children as young as 11 years old are being treated for pornography addiction.

Smartphone ownership is beginning in the 3rd grade. These children do not have the emotional or cognitive maturity to handle an always-on device.

Social media engagement is beginning in the 4th grade. That means that 4th graders routinely have Facebook, Instagram, SnapChat, and Kik accounts (among others). The Federal COPPA guideline says NO accounts for children under 13 years old. NOTE: Your under 13 year old children have no business engaging in social media. Trust me, I have seen the underside of that rock.

Here are just a handful of conversations I've had with your children in the past two months:

During a classroom presentation to 5th graders, a sweet little girl raised her hand and said "So you're saying that it's not a good idea that my step-father is sending me naked photos of himself, right?"

After a presentation to 7th graders, a boy waited for me (I knew this was not going to end well) - he said "Big Mama, you see that girl over there with the pink shirt? She keeps sending me photos of her boobs, can you please make her stop? It makes me feel bad"

A 6th grade boy asked to speak with me alone after a presentation and asked me to help him with his pornography addiction. He said that he was trying to deal with it alone - using tricks like putting his devices in another room so that he would have to physically get up to use them. Then he said "My tricks are not working. I want to stop and I don't know how."

While teaching at a middle school - which in this particular district/city encompassed 5th-7th grades, a 6th grade girl came out to the hallway to see me. We were on a break and I happened to be chatting with some law enforcement officers. In larger school districts I prefer to have an SRO (School Resource Officer - police officer) or ICAC detectives (Internet Crimes Against Children division of the local prosecutor's office) present.

Larger school districts, just given the larger population of students will undoubtedly have situations which pop up requiring the intervention of law enforcement. So, I was standing in the hallway chatting with an ICAC detective when this 6th grade girl (that's 11 or 12 years old) came up to me and asked to speak with me privately.

She told me that a few months prior she had met a 13yo boy online via social media platforms. They had communicated hundreds of times via Instagram and Kik. She didn't know who he was IRL (in real life), only online. He claimed to live a few towns over from where she lived. He urged her to send him topless and other naked photos. Even though she considered him her "boyfriend", to her credit she refused. However in the course of the exchanges, she had given out way too much personal information about herself. Eventually (and two weeks before the point which found us in the hallway), the 13yo boy revealed himself to be a 42 year old man.

He told her that now that he knew where she lived, went to school etc - that he was going to come to her home regularly to have sex with her. If she refused, he would only rape her repeatedly anyway, and murder her family.

Okay, so if you're reading this, I want you to take a breath. Here are the big issues related to this story. #1: An 11-year-old having unrestricted and unsupervised access to a device and the web is bonkers   #2: The only reason she told ME is because I am the only one having these conversations with your children and #3: This poor child was carrying around this enormous load for two weeks before she had the coincidental opportunity to share it with me. (NOTE: Law enforcement is helping the child and she is now safe.)

I love technology - I was a programmer for more than 20 years and a digital and web strategist after that. My own children have technology. I am an advocate of 1:1 programs in school districts (when executed correctly). Please don't misunderstand what I'm saying. There is enormous value in the technology. Law enforcement, school administrators, and educators want to tell you (but can't) that very young device ownership is disrupting your child's ability to remain a child. It is disrupting their cognitive development -and some studies even show that the physical structure of the brain is being changed by too many hours of digital use, and becoming more common - digital addiction.

Parents: this is your job. If you don't want to stalk your children online and remain hyper-engaged and educated - I understand. Believe me, I understand it's an exhausting job. But here's the thing. Either you engage 100% or your children can't own the device. And either way no child under 14 years old should own a smartphone - categorically. No child under 13yo should be using social media – at all.

As for me, I will keep going. And I will continue to carry those faces in my heart. The high school girl who is mercilessly bullied online and melted into hacking sobs when I asked her how she was coping, the high school boy who lost a full academic scholarship because of photos found on his phone, the 3rd grade girl who cried because she didn't understand why her friend would call her ugly on Instagram, and all of the other stories large and small.

It makes me want to smash their phones. But instead, I wrote this.

Student Presentations Data

During the presentations, I ask student by show of hands how many are using certain apps, own a phone, etc. They raise their hands and I count them. There are over 30 questions asked – only a few of the data points are shared here.

In addition, at the end of my student presentations, each student completes an anonymous exit survey. The survey asks two questions:

1. After hearing the presentation, what (if anything) will you change about your digital behavior?
2. Which of the following do you think is the biggest issue at your school? Choose one of the following: Cyberbullying, Sexting, TMI (giving out too much information which could ruin reputations), Addicted Overuse of Devices, or None.

The student comments are then processed, calculated, and reported back to school administrators. A few of those data points are shared below.

The data shown here were gathered from a random sample of student presentations during the 2016-2017 school year.

Data Sources

The school and data used here were chosen as a cross section of schools and the data results are typical for the behaviors and data I collect at individual schools everywhere I go.

Total students surveyed in this sample: 8, 844

Total schools surveyed: 16

Geographic spread of school locations

Four states: Illinois, New York, Ohio, and Pennsylvania

School types in the data sample

6 private religious schools (5 Catholic, 1 Jewish)

8 public schools

2 private secular schools.

Location type of schools in the data sample

21% Urban schools

59% Suburban schools

20% Rural schools

Income level of student communities at the schools

This was determined based on the percentage of students receiving free & reduced lunch at public schools. Private schools were segmented by their annual tuition and put into categories listed below.

Income Level	% of respondents in data sample	% of free & reduced lunch
Wealthy	31%	0 to 10%
High-middle to middle	59%	11 to 30%
Middle to low	20%	31% to 60%
Low to poor	0%	61 to 90%
Poor	0%	91 to 100%

Cell phone ownership

This is one of the first questions asked because it gives me an idea of the depth of engagement of a particular group of students just based on a single data point. Cell phone ownership is getting younger and younger. Here are the results for the sample group of 8,844 students described above.

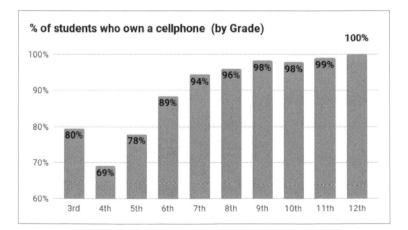

Sexting 'is the biggest issue at my school'

These responses come from the anonymous exit survey. Students are asked to choose which of the following is the biggest issue at their school - Cyberbullying, Sexting, TMI (giving out too much information which could ruin reputations), Addicted Overuse of Devices, or None.

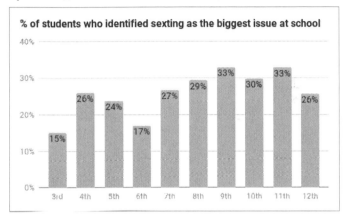

Calculated sexual predation risk

The graph below reflects the percentage of students who responded with a comment which explicitly reflected a sexual predation risk. These comments might include references to: sexting unknown people, communicating with strangers via live streaming, or having already had some experience or some knowledge of being at risk of sexual predation.

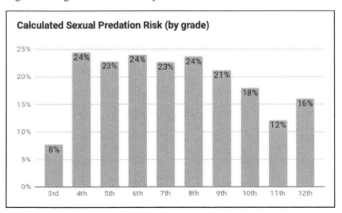

Students who consume porn and engage in sexting behaviors increase their risk of becoming victims of sexual predation.

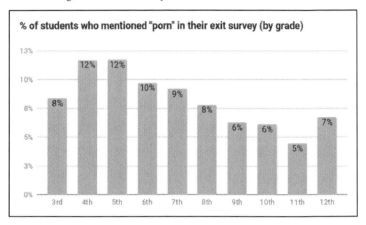

SECTION IV: PARENTAL ENGAGEMENT

Chapter 13: What You Can Do Today

Chapter 14: Big Mama's Guide to Additional Resources

Chapter 13
WHAT YOU CAN DO TODAY

This chapter is positioned as the last in this book for a reason. You cannot act until you are educated in the risks, apps, and structure of your child's digital world. If you are beginning with this chapter, consider this a virtual slap on your hand. GO BACK to the beginning and run through it all properly. There are no shortcuts. I'll meet you back here.

Acting without being educated is just as stupid as becoming educated and not acting. What are you going to do with everything we've just reviewed together? It isn't nearly enough to be horrified and tsk-tsk with your friends about the end of civilized society.

This is the last step in the journey we've taken together; it is also the most difficult. This is where you put on the waders and get into the muck hip-deep, to start sorting through devices, settings, and consequences. You can do this. Ready, set, go.

IS YOUR CHILD READY FOR A DEVICE?

If you have been wondering whether or not your child is ready for a smartphone, tablet, or other digital device – you're probably asking the wrong question. The correct question is:

"Are YOU as a parent, prepared for your child to own a digital device?"

Your child's level of digital preparedness depends entirely on your own willingness to become the digital police in your family. If your child has open and unsupervised access to the family iPad, mom's laptop, or dad's smartphone - all of this still applies.

Your under 14 year old child has absolutely no business owning an open and unrestricted smartphone or tablet. So the real question is: Mom and Dad, are YOU ready? In addition, your children over 14 years old also need to be actively monitored, supervised, and disciplined. If you have recently spent any time around a 14 or 15 year old child, you will quickly come to the conclusion that they are taller, hairier, (and smellier) 4-year-olds. They bounce from topic to topic and app to app looking to engage, or hide, or whatever their current impulse dictates. This general lack of focus and impulse control is developmentally appropriate. They are supposed to act like taller, hairier 4 year-olds.

Children are still children until they are well into their high school years. They do not have the physical, cognitive, emotional, or social maturity which 24-7 unrestricted digital connectivity demands. Those skills can only develop appropriately with experience and under adult supervision and guidance. I recognize that it's hard to be a parent in the 21st Century. And there's a lot to learn – all of the time. I teach Internet Safety for a living and I am constantly learning the new and nauseating ways our children get themselves into trouble. But you have no choice as a parent.

Well, that's not true, you actually have two choices:
1. Don't give your child a digital device or
2. Give the digital device and commit to engaging in the: educational, monitoring, and continuous policing process.

There is no third choice. Sorry.

Before you even consider giving your child his/her own device there are several conversations which you must have with the child.

If any of these conversation topics make you uncomfortable, what are you going if that situation becomes a reality in your child's life? If you have a hard time having a frank and candid conversation with your child about sexting, how comfortable will you feel if you find sexted content on your child's device?

If you can't have the conversation, the child cannot have the device.

HOW TO PLAN FOR THESE CONVERSATIONS

When you sit down to speak with your children about digital risks you should plan for a formal meeting with the specific child and both parents (or guardians). Showing a united front is absolutely critical to effectively implementing a plan and its consequences.

Your goal as a parent is to educate your child as to the risks of having a particular device. You should also encourage input from your child as to how they intend to use the device, how they feel about specific risks, and what their real-world digital experience has been thus far.

Leave the lines of communication with your children open so that they always feel comfortable in being honest with you. However, do not confuse this conversation with a "negotiation" of digital terms with your child.

Make it clear to your children that part of your job as a parent is to keep them safe and to ensure that they are interacting with the world in a way that you find appropriate according to your own family's values. These safeguards are every bit as important to their healthy development as eating vegetables and getting enough sleep.

There are four specific conversations. You can choose to have them all at once, or spread them out over time. There are only two actual "rules":

1. You need to have all of these conversations before your child gets access to a device, and certainly ASAP if they already own a device.

2. Having the "formal" conversation once needs to be followed by constant reminders on the same four topics. As you hear of relevant news stories or

learn more about specific apps, share your education with your child, where appropriate.

HOW TO HAVE THE "DIGITAL CONTENT CONVERSATION"

Children at all ages have a hard time understanding the difference between digital and virtual content as a part of reality. Most children believe that what they've posted online isn't "real" or doesn't really exist. Part of the issue here is that our children consider themselves invincible, which is developmentally appropriate, and they find it difficult to believe that digital content lives forever.

The purpose of this "digital content" conversation is to make it absolutely clear that nothing ever dies in the digital sphere. We use technical words like "delete" and "remove", but those terms are not literal. There is no global-digital DELETE button.

Discussion points:

Digital content can never be deleted - ever. Even when you delete it on your profile, it's not really ever gone. Anyone can take a screenshot, or copy and forward any digital content.

There is no such thing as "online privacy". It doesn't exist. Potentially, every person in the world can see every: post, photo, text, and video you've ever posted. This is another version of the "Grandma Filter" – if your Grandma, teacher, coach, or principal would be disappointed by looking at what you've posted, then you probably shouldn't post it anywhere.

Anyone can make a mistake and part of maturing into adulthood is learning from those mistakes. Ask your child: Have you ever posted something and realized that you probably shouldn't have? How did you feel after you saw it on the screen? Where you able to take it down? Have you seen any of your classmates or friends make a similar mistake?

HOW TO HAVE THE "SEXUAL PREDATION CONVERSATION"

Remember that in most cases sexual predators are already acquainted with their child victims and in 47% of the cases the predator is a family member or extended family member.

Generally speaking children beginning in the 5th grade can understand what you mean by "sexual harm". When you have this sexual conversation with your children it will make you both feel uncomfortable. This "yuck factor" is both inevitable and useful.

Point out that the sick feeling they have in their stomach just by virtue of having the conversation is their body's way of alerting them to danger. If they should ever have that feeling again, under any circumstances, they should tell you or another trusted adult. Be sure to make it clear to your children that they have the power to protect themselves from the people who would try to harm them, and you will help them to learn how.

If you find that you are unable or unwilling to have this conversation with your child, your child must not be given unsupervised access to a digital device.

Sexual predators who prey on the youngest of our children know just where to go to "hang out" virtually with them. The next time you see your 8-year-old playing Clash of Clans, think about who he might actually be playing with.

Discussion points:

For children in the 4th grade and younger: "There are people in the world who want to hurt children"

For children in the 5th grade and older: "There are people in the world who actively seek out children to do them harm - sexually".

Explain to children that adults who are interested in having sex with children are not "cute" regardless of their physical appearance or how famous they might be. Sex with children is wrong and it's against the law.

Sexual predators use your child's digital content to determine if he/she might make a "good target". If your child has a "sexy" profile name, photo, or posts, this is a sign to a potential predator that the child is willing to have these kinds of digital and real-world exchanges. What is your child's profile handle? Which photo is he using as his profile's avatar?

There is no way of being 100% sure of whom you are actually communicating with across a digital platform. The person who says she's a 14 year old girl might actually be a 54 year old man. Predators have even been known to use digital voice modulators to make themselves sound young while playing live video games (on Xbox Live for example).

Explain why your child should never meet someone IRL who they only know on a digital platform. Teenagers in particular have a hard time believing that they can be abducted; they feel too old and strong to become a victim. Explain that grown men and women are being abducted as unwilling participants in international human sex trafficking rings.

HOW TO HAVE THE "CYBERBULLYING CONVERSATION"

If your child has access to a digital device, it is likely that he has already been a perpetrator and/or victim of cyberbullying. It comes down to probability really; professional truck drivers have a far higher likelihood of getting into a car accident than the average driver just by virtue of the number of hours spent on the road. The same is true for your child's likelihood of becoming a perpetrator or victim of cyberbullying. If your child is spending more than one hour per day engaged in non-homework related digital pursuits this might be your first sign of potential trouble.

Discussion points:

Tell your child: You cannot trust anyone with your username and password (not even siblings). The only person who should have your login credentials are mom and dad. As unlikely as it might seem, today's BFF could be tomorrow's enemy. Armed with your login credentials, your supposed best friend can do you a world of harm.

Rude and cruel comments, even when meant as a joke, can be considered 'cyberbullying' or 'digital harassment' in some states, and are considered crimes. And yes, children are being sent to prison.

There is very little context in written content. Use this example with your children. Read the following sentence 5 times, each time placing the emphasis on the bolded word. Ask your child: How does the emphasis change the possible meaning of each phrase?

I	like	your	red	dress
I	**like**	your	red	dress
I	like	**your**	red	dress
I	like	your	**red**	dress
I	like	your	red	**dress**

Ask your child: Have you ever had a situation where you posted something that was taken the wrong way by someone else? Have you ever read something more than once to try to understand the person's real meaning?

How to have the "Sexting Conversation"

Digital misbehavior can follow trends just like fashion; even blue eye shadow is making a horrifying comeback. Within the first few months of 2014 the bulk of my school bookings have come as a result of sexting among middle school students.

It sounds ridiculous to consider that 5th through 8th graders would be engaging in sexting behaviors; some completely naked, some very sexually suggestive. Sexting among elementary and middle schools students is rising quickly. I have no doubt that this trend will continue. (Since the 1st edition in 2013, the prevalence of sexting among elementary school children has skyrocketed.)

If you think your child is too young for a sexting conversation you would be wrong. Although the conversation should be adapted to the age of the child, and you never want to give your child the "big idea" to take a photo of his junk if he hadn't already thought of it, this conversation is absolutely critical.

Discussion points:

If you take a sexually suggestive photo of yourself and send it to someone, you are committing a crime (usually called felony creation of child pornography). And no, it does not have to be naked to be considered sexting.

If you receive, then re-send or re-post a sexually suggestive photo of another child you are committing a crime (usually called felony trafficking of child pornography).

Children are going to actual prisons (not juvie) and as a result of their convictions may also be listed on the national Child Sexual Predator Registry for a pre-determined amount of time.

Children who are serious students, athletes, musicians, and artists need to know that young people are losing college scholarships, acceptances, internship opportunities, and job offers as a result of sexting. In addition, children who engaged in sexting behaviors are placing themselves at risk of then being victimized by sexual predators.

Tell your high school students: "You will never even know why you didn't get the acceptance, job, or internship. Your potential college or employer can review your social profiles and judge you based on what you have posted. Are you willing to take that risk?"

MANAGING YOUR DIGITAL WORLD

Here's a step-by-step list of how to set your own customized plan in motion by managing your digital devices and signal(s). No plan is completely bullet-proof. A tech-savvy child can find loopholes in the following plan just like a child who is determined to drink under age no matter the cost. The steps below are the best case scenario in being proactive.

Consistency in both parent education and implementation is far more important than the specifics of the plan; as you continue to learn you will know how to tweak your plan to fit your family.

The development of new social platforms and new devices will render some of these steps either more critical or obsolete as time goes on. Don't forget to follow my Facebook[176] page where I share new and emerging threats.

STEP ONE: MAKE A LIST, CHECK IT TWICE

Make a list of all of the web-enabled devices your child has access to. Be sure to include: laptops, tablets, smartphones, flip phones,   e-readers, cameras,

---

176 http://www.Facebook.com/OvernightGeekUniversity

handheld gaming systems, television based gaming consoles, televisions, watches, mp3 players, etc. Don't forget to add new devices as they are purchased:

- in your home
- the babysitter's home
- grandma's house
- any other place officially tasked with the care and safety of your child

STEP TWO: SEPARATE THAT LIST INTO TWO LISTS

List one: Devices which depend on a wi-fi connection

List two: Devices which have their own 3G/4G connection, like a smartphone and some tablets. These devices make a data/web connection via a local cellular tower and have access wherever cell service is available (in other words: everywhere).

STEP THREE: UNDERSTANDING WI-FI[177] DEVICE LOCK DOWN

Wi-fi enabled and dependent devices need to be locked down in two separate ways: first by using device settings, and secondly via your available home wi-fi signal. If this important step is handled correctly, your child's wi-fi enabled device will be doubly locked down while in your own home.

Lock down the wi-fi signal in the residence. This solution locks down the signal itself, for example the signal in your home or the grandparents' home and effects any device connecting to the web via that wi-fi signal

Lock down the device itself. This solution puts controls on the device itself, so that it's locked down regardless of where the device is taken.

STEP FOUR: HOW TO LOCK DOWN YOUR WI-FI SIGNAL

The purpose of locking down your home's wi-fi signal is to control which websites are allowable into the device when using a web browser or web-based

---

177 NOTE: 3G/4G devices do NOT depend on wi-fi and therefore cannot be restricted by any wi-fi restrictions you put into place. Your only method for restricting a 3G/4G device is at the device-settings level.

apps. For example: navigating directly to YouTube's website (via a browser) and using YouTube's tablet app (via the appstore – Apple or Android) would both be blocked if the site is blocked at the wi-fi signal level.

Make sure that your wi-fi signal is password protected with a strong password. Most hackers know to begin with "admin" as a password, since this is the default password on most wireless routers when they ship from the factory. Living in a rural area does not protect you from placing your wi-fi signal at risk. Wi-fi enabled devices can be hacked and controlled remotely from anywhere in the world.

Once you set the password, do not give it to your younger children who might then share the password with his/her friends in the neighborhood.

Download OpenDNS   - http://www.opendns.com

OpenDNS is free software which you download onto your home computer. It provides you with wi-fi-wide control of the websites which are allowed into your home. This is a completely on or completely off switch (also called a toggle). You are essentially banning or allowing websites via a browser or application house-wide. This is an excellent tool which is also used by school districts and corporations for the same purpose. As a bonus, it will also make websites load much faster.

You can choose to use the blanket category bans offered as a default by the OpenDNS software. These are put into categories of relative sketchyness including: pornography, gambling, narcotics, and much more. The sites within those categories are already pre-loaded by OpenDNS.

You can also whitelist (allow) or blacklist (ban) any site you choose. For example, Victoria's Secret is already auto-banned under the "lingerie" category. However, you can choose to either allow all "lingerie" sites, or to just whitelist: www.victoriassecret.com

---

STEP FIVE: LOW-TECH, LATE NIGHT SOLUTION

A super easy and low-tech solution to the wi-fi issue is to just unplug your router at a certain time every evening, perhaps just before you go to bed. Remember: this will not affect any 3G/4G devices, only those dependent on a wi-fi signal.

This is a great solution for sleepovers. If you must have a sleepover (BLECH), then I would suggest that in addition to making sure that all devices are plugged into a central area of the home, your child's guests should only touch those devices in the case of an emergency. Make sure that the parents of your child's guests understand your policy before they agree to sleep over. With any luck your guest list will become exceedingly short.

STEP SIX: CONTROLLING 3G/4G DEVICES

When the device belongs to your child. You can install software to control usage of 3G devices including smartphones and tablets via 3rd party apps. These will allow you to just shut down usage at a scheduled time. These apps will also allow you to cherry-pick how your child can interact with the device.

When the device belongs to a child visiting your home. As the host, it is your privilege and responsibility to make your digital rules perfectly clear to guests.

STEP SEVEN: CREATE A FAMILY CONTRACT (SEE APPENDIX 2)

STEP EIGHT: PRESENT THE FAMILY CONTRACT

Arrange for a family meeting to present the new digital contract which your children will sign. During this meeting agree on standard consequences for any infraction. I've found that a standard "two week loss of all devices" tends to work very well. The beauty of a standard consequence is that everyone is clear on the accepted behavior and the resulting discipline.

You can choose to have all of the required conversations during this meeting. However, I prefer to speak to the children one-on-one since each child will generally respond to a different approach.

Where one child responds best to fear, the child who actively seeks parental approval might focus more on the contractual expectations and consequences. Separate conversations also give you the opportunity to customize your emphasis on age-appropriate content.

STEP NINE: OUTSIDE YOUR HOME

Unfortunately, you will be at the mercy of other authority figures when your child consumes digital content outside of your home. Whether you're dealing with an indulgent ex-spouse, a clueless grandparent, or lazy caregiver; their behavior might be a willful disregard or just ignorant negligence.

Make your plan and your goals clear to those other adults who are ultimately in charge of your child in your absence.

- Share a copy of your Family Contract.

- Make the approved hours of usage clear. For example: explain to grandma that your child is only allowed one half-hour of screen time before bed.

- Tell your babysitter that your child is only allowed to use his own device with the restrictions on it, rather than surfing Google Images on her smartphone.

- When your child goes to play at a friend's house, make your rules clear. For example: your child is not allowed to surf YouTube videos, and he is not allowed to play any "M" video games. If there is any resistance or "willful bewilderment" invite the children to come and play at your home instead. Oh, and make a mental note about that house. Sheesh!

STEP TEN: SNOOP, SNOOP, SNOOP!!!

You need to snoop through all of your child's devices at irregular but consistent intervals and most critically, the moment you see him/her post or send something. This is my definition for "irregular but consistent": Check devices every week but never at the same time. On one day grab the phone as soon as your child walks in from school, on another day right before bed, on another – as soon as she's texted something.

This approach serves two purposes: to teach your kids that you're capable of anything at any time and to give yourself the chance of grabbing a situation before it gets more complicated.

Take the opportunity of watching your child tapping away on their device to say "show me what you just posted". Don't make the mistake of going this far and failing to snoop appropriately or often enough. This is a very common mistake and similar to companies spending millions of dollars on security cameras which go largely ignored after their installation. The camera itself is not a magical solution; it's just a tool for intervention. Likewise, the Family Contract and all of your efforts thus far go completely wasted if you don't investigate and enforce on a regular basis.

If your child refuses to hand you his/her device, invoke your standard consequence for the loss of all devices for X amount of time. Two weeks seems to work very well. If your child has programmed a screen password without telling you what it is, the same consequence applies.

Once you have access to the device:
Check all incoming and outgoing texts. Think: who, what, where, when, why, and how.

Check the browser history which your child should not be allowed to delete. Some kids are smart enough to cherry pick the bits of their history they want to delete. This is especially common on Google Chrome.

Log into every single social account on the device and scroll through the posts from and to your child. Pay close attention to how your child responds. Don't forget to check internal messaging systems within social apps like Facebook and Twitter.

Review who is following your child on asynchronous platforms (like Twitter and Instagram). Anyone that you don't personally know in real life needs to be blocked immediately. It's not enough to hear that one of the followers is "Susie's cousin's neighbor". If you don't personally know that child, block the follow.

Check the accounts that your child is following. Ask your child: "Why are you following someone called 'SexyTeenz'"? Take a look at the types of content that profile publishes.

Check the photos and videos in your child's photo gallery. Who are the people in those photos? Do you recognize all of the children and adults? If not, find out why.

Check to be sure that your child has not utilized the geotagging feature which adds a specific location to individual Twitter or Instagram posts.

Does your child have Location Services activated on his camera? This tags every photo with the latitude and longitude of the exact location where the photo was taken. This should be set to OFF for the camera.

Check your child's Twitter 'retweets' and all of the content reflected on his timeline. You should also check his feed which shows the content for everyone he follows. What types of content is he interested in receiving?

If you are allowing your child to install and delete apps without your permission, take a close look at all of the icons on the screen. Are there any new ones? What are they for?

Google your child's email address by using quotes around the email. For example: Go to Google.com and in the search box you would search for "susiesoccer@gmail.com", replace susiesoccer@gmail.com with your child's email address. Be sure to begin and end the email address with quotation marks, forcing Google to search for the complete email address. You might find platforms and websites where your child has made a comment or posted a forum question. Once you find a reference, check what your child's chosen "handle" or nickname is on that site. Use that data to run another search. Remember your child may have multiple email addresses.

Follow the instructions above for your child's preferred "handle" or nickname. You may find a second (or third) Twitter or Instagram account. NOTE: Do not jump to conclusions! There are hundreds of millions of app users globally. It is very possible that there are many "Susiesoccer" users. Unless you see a photo of your child, or can confirm that the profile is being followed by your child's friends, you cannot be positively sure that the profile belongs to your child. Before confronting your child, you need to be positive. Otherwise you're going to look like an idiot.

STEP ELEVEN: BEWARE OF 'VAULT APPS'

Thousands of vault apps exist with the express purpose of giving the user the opportunity to hide photos, videos, phone calls, and texts from prying eyes.

Some vault apps will physically appear on the device, disguised as something else: like a calculator for example. When the correct combination of numbers is punched into the calculator face, the vault opens revealing any files the user has decided to hide.

Other vault apps do not appear on any screen as an app. These high-tech vaults depend upon entering a specific series of numbers into the phone dialer. Once the "pin" is entered, the vault opens.

These higher tech vaults also give the user the opportunity to hide all of the content received from a particular user. Although these apps have been created with cheating spouses in mind, a great many children have caught on.

HOW TO GET A COMPLETE LIST OF THE APPS DOWNLOADED TO YOUR CHILD'S DEVICE OR SMARTPHONE:

Android devices

Go to http://play.google.com/apps and log into the Google

account associated with that device. Navigate to the MY APPS tab.

This will show you a list of all of the apps installed on the device in question. You can review the descriptions of each of the installed apps.

iOS devices

Log into the iTunes account associated with the device. Review all of the apps installed, and cross reference with the descriptions of each app.

HAMMER-ABLE OFFENSES

There are scenarios which merit smashing your child's device(s) with a hammer. I like the sound of crashing glass, if you prefer a less dramatic outcome; you can always flush the phone. Same-same.

Hammer-able on the first offense

- getting caught with irrefutable cyberbullying evidence. Use your own judgment here, but if you see some serious nastiness, smash away!!! Please don't fall for the "my account got hacked" nonsense.

- photographic sexting in any, way, shape or form; even when the photo is not of your child, and is merely a photo of a classmate or friend.

- text based sexting or sexual harassment. This is the same as finding that your son or daughter has sexually propositioned a classmate or has responded in a sexual way to someone else's content.

- planning or actually going to meet someone in person who your child does not know in real life.

Hammer-able on the second offense

- giving out personally identifying information (phone, address, date of birth, city, school, etc)

BOTTOM LINE

For whatever reason, the issue of digital safety has made itself known to you. You cannot un-ring that bell once you've heard it. So you've purchased this book and you've committed to put in the time and energy it takes to make this work.

Now it's 8:00pm at night on a Monday and you're supposed to grab the devices from your children and place them in the central charging station (and out of their bedrooms). You've had a rough day, your spouse is out of town, and you're flying solo. You can either listen to 20 minutes of whining from the 14-year-old about how it's not fair that she has to give you her phone at night, or you can say 'screw it' and let her keep the phone in her bedroom. And really all you want is a tiny bit of quiet. After all, what difference is one night going to make?

Your 10 year old son has worn you down to a teeny tiny nub and he's fully expecting you to give in. Meanwhile your 14 year old daughter is still whining and she's just waiting for you to lose steam.

These are the moments where it counts to hang tough. These are the very moments that your child is expecting. But you aren't going to do that, because you know better. Besides, now you and I are friends and I'm not letting you give up. Follow me on Facebook, throw up an SOS sign and I'll do my best to back you up.

I'll bring my hammer.

Facebook: http://www.facebook.com/OvernightGeekUniversity

234

Chapter 14

BIG MAMA'S GUIDE TO ADDITIONAL RESOURCES

NPR's *The Teen Brain*
http://www.npr.org/templates/story/story.php?storyId=124119468

Librarian's Guide to Online Searching, 3rd edition by Suzanne Bell

Read this great primer to online research put together by Sidwell Friend's
School in Washington D.C. called *Research in 8 Steps*
http://www.sidwell.edu/middle-school/library/research-in-8-steps/index.aspx

TED Talks (free, web, Android, iOS, Roku)

http://www.ted.com

All humans should be forced to watch TED. Essentially TED is a big giant
bucket of super smart people speaking from a new or amazing perspective.
TED will make you think, really think. I love TED! TED Talks you must watch:

"The key to success? Grit" by Angela Duckworth, PhD[178]
http://www.ted.com/talks/angela_lee_duckworth_the_key_to_success_grit

"Let's Teach Kids to Code" by Mitch Resnick
http://www.ted.com/talks/mitch_resnick_let_s_teach_kids_to_code

"Teach teachers how to create magic" by Christopher Emdin
http://www.ted.com/talks/christopher_emdin_teach_teachers_how_to_create_magic

"How schools kill creativity" by Ken Robinson
http://www.ted.com/talks/ken_robinson_says_schools_kill_creativity

"Every kid needs a champion" by Rita Pierson
http://www.ted.com/talks/rita_pierson_every_kid_needs_a_champion

"Our failing schools. Enough is enough!" by Geoffrey Canada
http://www.ted.com/talks/geoffrey_canada_our_failing_schools_enough_is_enough

Academic Resources

Although this book has little to do with academic issues, many parents ask me for suggestions of websites and apps to help their children with homework, research, and studying. Each app or website is listed with an associated cost, and whether the app is for iOS/Apple devices or Android devices. These are the ones I love:

Anti-Social ($15, Windows, Mac, Ubuntu)
http://anti-social.cc/
Before you sit down to study, learn, or practice those math facts download this brilliant tool which will forcibly remove all of your distractions. Do you get distracted by Facebook or cute cat videos on YouTube? You can block websites, apps, and schedule when these blocks should be active. I could never have finished this book without it!

---

178 I had the opportunity and honor of presenting to Dr. Duckworth and her students at University of Pennsylvania. Dr. Duckworth is an amazing human being! If you *live* GRIT, so will your children.

Memrise (free, Web, Android, iOS)

http://www.memrise.com

This is an online learning community where members create lessons on almost every subject under the sun: languages, literature, math, and science. You can even prepare for standardized tests like the SATs.

Khan Academy (free, web, iOS & Android)

http://www.khanacademy.org

Khan Academy is my first stop when my children begin a new math or science unit. A massive repository of educational videos are available to help your child break down a new process or concept. Our rule is that you have to watch a video three times before you ask mom for help. The site has the largest collection of videos on math and science topics, but it continues to grow. You can also create a parent account and assign videos and activities on the back end, with amazing feedback and reporting once your children complete assignments. We could not live without Khan Academy!

Tap To Learn (iOS only)

http://www.taptolearn.com/

Tap To Learn has too many fantastic iOS apps to list them each individually. Help your younger children (PreK to 7th) master: math, grammar, spelling, geography, and much more. The only HUGE bummer is that they haven't begun developing for Android OS yet. Come on people!!!

Brainfeed (free, iOS only)

http://www.brainfeed.org

Another must-have for your Apple device. This one is a giant repository of educational videos on a wide range of topics: science, technology, English, social studies, math, and much more!

OpenStudy (free)

http://www.openstudy.com/

Open study is the equivalent of a giant meeting room where hundreds of other students are studying the same exact subject. Users can ask a question and the community will provide live feedback or an answer. OpenStudy makes studying alone far less lonely.

Quizlet (free, web, Android & iOS)
http://www.quizlet.com/
This is far-and-away the best flash card app I have come across. You can create your own set of cards, load up a set created by a teacher, or view card sets created by other users on the same topic.

Math & Science

Grades: PreK-6th

Montessori: Learn 123 numbers ($2.99 Android, iOS)
Great way for the little ones to learn their numbers. Includes tracing the shape of a written number.

Math Practice Flash Cards PRO ($1.99; Android)
Math Fact Master ($.99; iOS)

Tiny Fractions ($4.99, iOS)
Another great app from Tap To Learn – this one explains fractions to younger children.

Math Vs Zombies ($4.99, iOS)
Another great app for kids from Tap To Learn. Kids have to convert the zombies back by quickly solving math problems.

Celeste SE ($1.99, Android)
Amazingly cool app which allows you to aim your Android camera view towards the sky for instant feedback

Kid Weather ($1.99, Android and iOS)
Your budding meteorologist will love this app. Tons of educational content plus kids have the ability to plot and chart their own data.

Grades: 7-12

Wolfram Alpha ($2.99, web, Android & iOS)

http://www.wolframalpha.com/

Wolfram Alpha is a super cool app which answers any computational or statistical question like: "unemployment rate: Chicago, NYC" or "tides in Key West, Florida". All of the data is reported beautifully within seconds. It also computes answers to mathematical and scientific formulas. This is a tool which has to be explored to be appreciated.

Mathway (Android & iOS)

Perfect for breaking down complicated formulas, Mathway provides free instant answers to your math problems, or subscribe to include step-by-step work and explanations.

RealCalc Scientific Calculator (Android) or **iMathPac** (iOS)

Turns your device into a real scientific calculator

RocketScience (free, iOS and Android)

Rocket Science 101 teaches kids about spacecraft, rocket science and way more. Plus the app is gorgeously designed!

English & Language Arts

Grades PreK-5th

Kids Learn Academy: Learn ABC Alphabet Tracing ($2.99 Android & iOS)
SentenceBuilder for iPad ($5.99 iPad only)
Awesome app for elementary school children to build grammatically correct sentences
Grammar Games by Tap To Learn ($1.99 iOS)
Teaches parts of speech through games
A+ Spelling by Alligator Apps (free, iOS)
We use this app weekly in our house for spelling words. You can create your own custom lists and mom or dad can record themselves saying the word so that the child can test himself.

Grades: 6th -12th

CliffsNotes (free, web & iOS)

http://www.cliffsnotes.com/

The same Cliffs Notes you remember from high school, except delivered in a digital format. Free for a limited selection of works with in-app purchases of specific works of literature

SparkNotes (free, Android)

http://www.sparknotes.com

Similar to CliffsNotes. Free with in-app purchases of specific works of literature

EasyBib (free, iOS and Android)

http://www.easybib.com

Helps automatically create an MLA standard bibliography by scanning the barcode on a book, or typing in the title of the work to be cited. Very cool app

Kids and Coding

I'm a huge fan of kids learning how to "code" which is short-hand for learning programming. Beyond the obvious benefits of preparing children specifically for a Computer Science career, coding combines: logic, math, analytical reasoning, and perhaps my favorite – error resolution. There's something beautiful about a kid trying to figure out where he went wrong and why the square on the screen is shaking instead of bouncing.

There is no other environment which provides this cause-and-effect analysis. "You did X and you expected Y but you got Z – what went wrong?" We never ask kids to breakdown their mistakes in this highly specific structure. Encourage your children to code! The industry is wide open and exceptionally well compensated.

Code.org

http://learn.code.org/

Code.org has been actively advocating for coding education for young children via their nonprofit organization and website. In 2013 they launched the "Hour of Code 2013" challenge nationwide to promote computer science. Elementary and middle schools all over the world participated in exposing younger children to the inner working of programming.

Their website contains both a "one hour of code" set of activities as well as a 15-25 hour course: "Intro to Computer Science" meant for children from Kindergarten to 8th grade. All of their materials are excellent and free to use. In addition, teachers can sign up and track the progress of their entire class.

Scratch (free, web-based)

http://scratch.mit.edu/

Created at MIT (Massachusetts Institute of Technology), Scratch was designed specifically to teach coding to children from 8 to 16 years old. "As children create with Scratch, they learn to think creatively, work collaboratively, and reason systematically."

Tynker

($50 per web course, iOS app: free with in-app purchases)

http://www.tynker.com/

Tynker offers two self-paced courses for children. The beginner's course is called "Introduction to Programming" and costs $50.

However, you can download the iPad app (also called Tynker) for free. The app might be the best way to trick your child into learning coding via a game interface. Watch out for those in-app purchases!

Cargo-Bot (free, iOS app)

This app is really a game that teaches children the basics of programming. Children learn by solving logic-based puzzles.

Coding Resources

7 Apps for Teaching Children Coding Skills

http://www.edutopia.org/blog/7-apps-teaching-children-coding-anna-adam

Teaching Kids to Code

http://www.edsurge.com/guide/teaching-kids-to-code

The Kapor Center Coding Landscape Database

This incredible organization reports on coding programs and they maintain a list containing more than 300 ways programs and software to learn how to code.

Read their 2013 Report here:

http://kaporcenter.org/wp-content/uploads/2013/10/Kapor_CodingLandscape_R3.pdf

Check out their database of resources here:

https://docs.google.com/spreadsheet/ccc?key=0AiGBf5Kfb8TedFp0VDdfbGM2VHByaGtmbnBwc mdmUkE&usp=sharing#gid=0

Additional Reading & References

National Campaign to Prevent Teen and Unplanned Pregnancy

http://www.thenationalcampaign.org

This organization is dedicated to teaching teens how to avoid unplanned pregnancy. Although the rates of teen pregnancy have reached an all-time low in this country, this is still a critical conversation to have with your sons and daughters. Their website is extremely well done and contains all of the data and resources you will need to begin having this conversation at home.

Additional teen relationship resources:

StayTeen.org - A website directed to teens which encourages them to "stay teen."

LoveIsRespect.org - Another website directed to teens which provides education and resources related to relationship abuse.

Digital Deception: The Online Behaviour of Teens
UK's Anti-Bullying Alliance teamed up with McAfee to produce this report which polled just over one thousand children in the UK.

http://www.anti-bullyingalliance.org.uk/media/6621/mcafee_digital-deception_the-online-behaviour-of-teens.pdf

The Nature and Dynamics of Internet Pornography Exposure for Youth
by the University of New Hampshire www.unh.edu/ccrc/pdf/CV169.pdf

Trends in Extreme Binge Drinking Among US High School Seniors
http://archpedi.jamanetwork.com/article.aspx?articleID=1738763

Reuters article analyzing the JAMA study above - *'Extreme' binge drinking common among teens: study* by Genevra Pittman, September 16, 2013
http://www.reuters.com/article/2013/09/16/us-teens-drinking-idUSBRE98F0W120130916

Teen Binge Drinking: All Too Common, Psychology Today January 26, 2013
http://www.psychologytoday.com/blog/teen-angst/201301/teen-binge-drinking-all-too-common

Teen health: Depression, anxiety and social phobias rising in kids, educators say – San Jose Mercury News, by Sharon Noguchi, February 5, 2014
http://www.mercurynews.com/health/ci_25074044/teen-health-depression-anxiety-and-social-phobias-rising

Chapter 2: Parenting in Transition

"How to Lock Down Your Privacy on the Amazon Echo and Google Home",
http://fieldguide.gizmodo.com/how-to-lock-down-your-privacy-on-the-amazon-echo-and-go-1794697554

Lee, Hae In et al. *"Understanding When Parental Praise Leads To Optimal Child Outcomes"*. Social Psychological and Personality Science (2016): 194855061668302. Web.

Recommended Reading: Dr. Angela Duckworth has done an immense amount work in studying what she calls "GRIT" . Read her book, it's fantastic

Grit: The Power of Passion and Perseverance

"In this instant New York Times bestseller, pioneering psychologist Angela Duckworth shows anyone striving to succeed—be it parents, students, educators, athletes, or business people—that the secret to outstanding achievement is not talent but a special blend of passion and persistence she calls "grit." In Grit, she takes readers into the field to visit cadets struggling through their first days at West Point, teachers working in some of the toughest schools, and young finalists in the National Spelling Bee. She also mines fascinating insights from history and shows what can be gleaned from modern experiments in peak performance.

https://www.amazon.com/Grit-Passion-Perseverance-Angela-Duckworth/dp/1501111108

Recommended reading: The Road to Character by David Brooks. "In The Road to Character, he focuses on the deeper values that should inform our lives. Responding to what he calls the culture of the Big Me, which emphasizes external success, Brooks challenges us, and himself, to rebalance the scales between our "résumé virtues"—achieving wealth, fame, and status—and our "eulogy virtues," those that exist at the core of our being: kindness, bravery, honesty, or faithfulness, focusing on what kind of relationships we have formed."

https://www.amazon.com/Road-Character-David-Brooks/dp/0812983416

Chapter 3: Be Proactive

Why You Should Support Your Local Library

I am a staunch and quasi-militant supporter of public libraries. There is almost no life issue which cannot be improved by research and a visit to your local public library. If you're not convinced about just how much we should treasure our public libraries – check out this site: http://www.GeekTheLibrary.org

The Bill & Melinda Gates Foundation is engaging in global Library advocacy. Check out their "Global Libraries Campaign" which aims to equip the planet with library access.

http://www.gatesfoundation.org/What-We-Do/Global-Development/Global-Libraries

Standardized Testing

As parents you need to become educated on the evolution and expansion of standardized testing in the United States. Part of that evolution now includes digital online testing. Chances are your children do NOT currently have the basic tech literacy to excel at these online tests.

Are new online standardized tests revolutionary? Decide for yourself., HechingerEd Blog, by Sarah Garland, October 9, 2012.

http://hechingered.org/content/are-new-online-standardized-tests-revolutionary-decide-for-yourself_5655/

College Applications

Common Application Fact Sheet

http://www.commonapp.org/PDF/CommonApplicationFactSheet.pdf

Online Application Woes Make Students Anxious and Put Colleges Behind Schedule; New York Times, by: By Richard PÉREZ-PEÑA October 12, 2013

http://www.nytimes.com/2013/10/13/education/online-application-woes-make-students-anxious-and-put-colleges-behind-schedule.html

Read more from Marc Prensky's work: *Digital Natives Digital Immigrants* this one is quite dated (2001), however it does a nice job of laying the groundwork for the web and tech boom which would come just after it was written.

http://www.marcprensky.com/writing/Prensky%20-%20Digital%20Natives,%20Digital%20Immigrants%20-%20Part1.pdf

"Pencils Down: The Shift to Online & Computer Based Testing" Ed Tech Strategies November 5, 2015.

"PARCC Scores Lower for Students Who Took Exams on Computers" by Benjamin Herold, Education Week, Feb 3, 2016.

"The Pen is Mightier Than the Keyboard: Advantages of Longhand Over Laptop Note Taking", Pam A Mueller, Daniel M. Oppenheimer, 2014, Psychological Science

Telzer, Eva H., Andrew J. Fuligni, Matthew D. Lieberman, and Adriana Galván. *"The effects of poor quality sleep on brain function and risk taking in adolescence."* NeuroImage 71 (2013): 275-283.

Meldrum, Ryan C., J. C. Barnes, and Carter Hay. *"Sleep Deprivation, Low Self-Control, and Delinquency: A Test of the Strength Model of Self-Control."* Journal of Youth and Adolescence 44.2 (2013): 465-77.

Tarokh, Leila, Jared M. Saletin, and Mary A. Carskadon. *"Sleep in adolescence:*

Physiology, cognition and mental health." Neuroscience & Biobehavioral Reviews 70 (2016): 182-88.

Microsoft HoloLens: Mixed Reality Blends Holograms with the Real World, YouTube video https://www.youtube.com/watch?v=Ic_M6WoRZ7k

Learn more about SnapChat Spectacles here
https://www.spectacles.com/

Chapter 4: Media Literacy

Daily Media Use Among Children and Teens Up Dramatically From Five Years Ago by the Henry J Kaiser Family Foundation. www.kff.org

Common Sense Media

- Check out this great guide for discussion with your children about gender stereotyping. http://www.commonsensemedia.org/educators/gender
- Fantastic online tool which offers reviews of all types of media. http://www.commonsensemedia.org/reviews

Dove film on extreme Photoshopping:
https://www.youtube.com/watch?v=hibyAJOSW8U

Vallone, Robert P., Lee Ross, and Mark R. Lepper. *"The hostile media phenomenon: Biased perception and perceptions of media bias in coverage of the Beirut massacre."* Journal of Personality and Social Psychology 49.3 (1985): 577-85.

Every parent should watch the films made by The Representation Project including Miss Representation
http://therepresentationproject.org/film/miss-representation/

Abercrombie's sexy undies 'slip'
http://money.cnn.com/2002/05/22/news/companies/abercrombie/

Seventeen Magazine Media Kit: www.seventeenmediakit.com

Chapter 5: How Do Your Children Connect?

For a better and more complete understanding of how the internet works
http://computer.howstuffworks.com/internet/basics/internet.htm

For more information on search engines
http://www.google.com/intl/en-US/insidesearch/howsearchworks/thestory

Learn more about how email works here
http://www.dummies.com/how-to/content/how-email-works.html

Just remember that in 100% of the time:

- An email address cannot include spaces
- An email address never begins with "www"
- An email address must contain an "@" symbol, a period referred to as a "dot" and followed most commonly by "com", "net", "edu" or "org"
- An email address is NOT case sensitive – capital letters and lower case letters are treated the same

"Samsung smart TV policy allows company to listen in on users", by Andrew Griffin, 9 February 2015, Independent, http://www.independent.co.uk/life-style/gadgets-and-tech/news/samsungs-new-smart-tv-policy-allows-company-to-listen-in-on-users-10033012.html

Samsung's SmartTV privacy policy. http://www.samsung.com/sg/info/privacy/smarttv/

"VIZIO to Pay $2.2 Million to FTC, State of New Jersey to Settle Charges It Collected Viewing Histories on 11 Million Smart Televisions without Users' Consent" https://www.ftc.gov/news-events/press-releases/2017/02/vizio-pay-22-million-ftc-state-new-jersey-settle-charges-it

Consumer Reports *"How to Turn Off Smart TV Snooping Features"*
http://www.consumerreports.org/privacy/how-to-turn-off-smart-tv-snooping-features/

Child-safe Tablets

If a so-called "child-safe" tablet has unrestricted browser access and/or open access to the Google Play, Apple, or other app stores, it is not child-safe. I have been impressed with only a few of the so-called "kid-friendly" tablets actively marketed for younger children (ages 3 to 10). The common thread is their lock-down capability: locked down browser, white-listing of websites, time limit usage, closed down app stores, and pre-approved child content. There are even adaptive learning environments and learning dashboards for parents to follow their child's educational progress.

When you consider buying your younger child a tablet, focus on: parental controls, locking down the browser to just pre-approved websites, and locking down app installation and deletion. You can begin your search with the following tablets:

LeapPad Ultra - Pre-vetted content via the Zui network

InnoTab VTech - Particularly cool feature: parents and child can text each other via the device in a completely safe and locked down environment. Also has a closed learning environment.

Nabi Tablets - Although there are mixed reviews on the value of the pre-loaded apps (Android OS) the Nabi has one very cool feature: a parent can assign real-life chores for their child in the Chores app. As the child completes those chores he/she earn virtual coins which can then be spent in the app store.

Kindle vs Nook? - People often ask me which I prefer. I'm a HUGE Kindle and Amazon fan. There are massive benefits to becoming a Prime Member via your Kindle ownership. Did you know that you can stream all of those Amazon streamed movies and shows on your television via a Roku or Amazon TV device? Yes! Yes you can.

If you are an avid consumer of digital content via: books, websites, music, movies, television shows, and magazines in addition to ordering products from Amazon at least a few times a year, then you will love Prime

Membership. Learn more about the benefits of Prime Membership here: http://www.digitaltrends.com/web/is-amazon-prime-worth-it

iTouch Parental Controls

Parents commonly overlook the iTouch which has been lying around the house for several years and might have been handed down to another sibling. Don't forget that an iTouch does everything an iPhone does minus the ability to dial out.

The iTouch has pretty solid parent controls. If you have younger children using the device (3-11 years old), go to Settings-General-Restrictions-Enable Restrictions (which allows you to set up a password) and lock down: browser access, no installation or deletion of apps, no YouTube, no FaceTime

Chapter 6: Understand the Two Major Points of Vulnerability

Webcam Hacking

Baby Monitor Hacking Alarms Houston Parents
http://abcnews.go.com/blogs/headlines/2013/08/baby-monitor-hacking-alarms-houston-parents/

Your TV might be watching you
http://money.cnn.com/2013/08/01/technology/security/tv-hack/index.html

Miss Teen USA: Screamed upon learning she was 'sextortion' victim
http://www.cnn.com/2013/09/27/us/miss-teen-usa-sextortion/

Smile! Hackers Can Silently Access Your Webcam Right Through The Browser (Again)
http://techcrunch.com/2013/06/13/smile-hackers-can-silently-access-your-webcam-right-through-the-browser-again/

Are Hackers Using Your Webcam to Watch You?
http://us.norton.com/yoursecurityresource/detail.jsp

Security Issues

How Burglars Are Using Social Media

http://www.distinctivedoors.co.uk/attachments/617347/original/how-burglars-are-using-social-media.png

Facebook Stalking Fears: 6 Geotagging Facts

http://www.informationweek.com/mobile/facebook-stalking-fears-6-geotagging-facts/d/d-id/1111161

Fugitive John McAfee's location revealed by photo meta-data screw-up

http://nakedsecurity.sophos.com/2012/12/03/john-mcafee-location-exif/

Teens Use Twitter To Thumb Rides

http://www.npr.org/blogs/alltechconsidered/2013/08/15/209530590/teens-use-twitter-to-thumb-rides

Web Usage and Trends Research

Pew Research Center

Excellent source for raw data and studies related to tech

http://www.pewresearch.org/

Teens, Social Media, and Privacy

http://www.pewinternet.org/2013/05/21/teens-social-media-and-privacy/

Internet Use Over Time

http://www.pewinternet.org/data-trend/teens/internet-use/

Device Ownership Over Time

http://www.pewinternet.org/data-trend/teens/devices/

Social Media Use Over Time

http://www.pewinternet.org/data-trend/teens/social-media/

Technology Addiction: Concern, Controversy, and Finding Balance, Common Sense Media, May 3, 2016. https://www.commonsensemedia.org/technology-addiction-concern-controversy-and-finding-balance-infographic

Pew Research Center's 2017 report called *"The Internet of Things Connectivity Binge: What Are the Implications"* http://www.pewinternet.org/2017/06/06/the-internet-of-things-connectivity-binge-what-are-the-implications/

Chapter 7: Cyberbullying

Resource: Cyberbullying Research Center

http://www.cyberbullying.us

According to their website: "The Cyberbullying Research Center" is dedicated to providing up-to-date information about the nature, extent, causes, and consequences of cyberbullying among adolescents."

The Annual Cyberbullying Survey

http://www.ditchthelabel.org/downloads/the-annual-cyberbullying-survey-2013.pdf

Digital Munchausen (aka self-cyberbullying)

Frequency, Type, Motivations, and Outcomes
http://webhost.bridgew.edu/marc/DIGITAL%20SELF%20HARM%20report.pdf

"Digital Self Harm: Frequency, Type, Motivations, and Outcomes"
Massachusetts Aggression Reduction Center

Cyber self-harm: Why do people troll themselves online?
http://www.bbc.com/news/magazine-25120783

Hidden hatred: What makes people assassinate their own character online, sometimes driving themselves to suicide?
http://www.independent.co.uk/life-style/gadgets-and-tech/features/hidden-hatred-what-makes-people-assassinate-their-own-character-online-sometimes-driving-themselves-to-suicide-9142490.html

Woman becomes first person to be jailed for 'trolling herself'
http://www.independent.co.uk/news/uk/crime/woman-becomes-first-person-to-be-jailed-for-trolling-herself-9110128.html

---

Rebecca Sedwick case

Charges in Rebecca Sedwick's suicide suggest 'tipping point' in bullying cases
http://www.cnn.com/2013/10/25/us/rebecca-sedwick-bullying-suicide-case/index.html

Rebecca Sedwick Case: Bullied girl and her tormentor both grew up in "disturbing" family situations, says sheriff
http://www.cbsnews.com/news/rebecca-sedwick-case-bullied-girl-and-her-tormentor-both-grew-up-in-disturbing-family-situations-says-sheriff/

Charges Dropped Against 'Cyberbullies' in Rebecca Sedwick Suicide
http://abcnews.go.com/US/charges-dropped-cyberbullies-rebecca-sedwick-suicide/story

---

Megan Meier Case

Megan Meier Foundation
http://www.meganmeierfoundation.org/megans-story.html

A Hoax Turned Fatal Draws Anger but No Charges
http://www.nytimes.com/2007/11/28/us/28hoax.html

Proposed Bill: Megan Meier Cyberbullying Prevention Act
https://www.govtrack.us/congress/bills/111/hr1966/text

Megan Meier's mom is still fighting bullying
http://www.stltoday.com/news/local/metro/megan-meier-s-mom-is-still-fighting-bullying/article_f901d3e0-b6b8-5302-ac0c-80b83c9703a9.html

Studies

Relational and overt forms of peer victimization: a multi-informant approach, Journal of Consulting and Clinical Psychology, vol. 66, no. 2, pp. 337–347, 1998. http://psycnet.apa.org/journals/ccp/66/2/337/

Association between exposure to suicide and suicidality outcomes in youth Canadian Medical Association Journal, July 9, 2013 vol. 185 no. 10 http://www.cmaj.ca/site/misc/pr/21may13_pr.xhtml

According to this study, having a classmate commit suicide significantly increases the chance that a teenager will consider or attempt suicide themselves. The risk is greatest for 12 to 13 year olds.

A Multilevel Examination of Peer Victimization and Bullying Preventions in Schools U.S. Department of Education, Washington, DC, USA, 2009. Journal of Criminology, Volume 2013 (2013), Article ID 735397 http://www.hindawi.com/journals/jcrim/2013/735397/ref/

Teen Online & Wireless Safety Survey: Cyberbullying, Sexting and Parental Controls. Cox Communications Teen Online and Wireless Safety Survey in Partnership with the National Center for Missing and Exploited Children, 2009.

van Geel M, Vedder P, Tanilon J. *Relationship Between Peer Victimization, Cyberbullying, and Suicide in Children and AdolescentsA Meta-analysis.* JAMA Pediatr. 2014;168(5):435-442. doi:10.1001/jamapediatrics.2013.4143

Zimmerman, Gregory M. et al. *"The Power Of (Mis)Perception: Rethinking Suicide Contagion In Youth Friendship Networks".* Social Science & Medicine 157 (2016): 31-38. Web.

R. Dinkes, E. F. Cataldi, G. Kena, and K. Baum, *"Indicators of School Crime and Safety"*, U.S. Department of Education, Washington, DC, USA, 2009.

The Nature and Dynamics of Internet Pornography Exposure for Youth www.unh.edu/ccrc/pdf/CV169.pdf

Chapter 8: Sexting

National Campaign to Prevent Teen and Unplanned Pregnancy
http://thenationalcampaign.org/

Third National Juvenile Online Victimization Study
http://www.unh.edu/ccrc/pdf/The%20Third%20National%20Juvenile%20Online%20Victimizatio
n%20Study_web%20doc.pdf

Boy, Girl Charged With Child Porn
http://www.nbcchicago.com/news/local/Middle-School-Students-Charged-with-Child-
Pornography-Following-Sexting-Scandal-257551921.html

Sexting Leads to Child Porn Charges for Teens
http://www.cbsnews.com/news/sexting-leads-to-child-porn-charges-for-teens/

*Virginia Deals With a Teen Sexting Ring by Educating Teens, Not Prosecuting
Them*
http://www.slate.com/blogs/xx_factor/2014/04/14/virginia_sexting_ring_louisa_county_deals_wit
h_teen_sexting_in_the_schools.html

Chapter 9: Sexual Predation

Center for Sex Offender Management
http://csom.org/

Fact Sheet: What You Need to Know About Sex Offenders
http://www.csom.org/pubs/needtoknow_fs.pdf

National Sex Offender Public Website
www.nsopw.gov

Resources on child sexual exploitation– the National Center for Missing and Exploited Children

http://www.missingkids.com/Publications/Exploitation

"Sextortion becoming major problem with minor children"

http://www.foxnews.com/entertainment/2017/01/24/sextortion-becoming-major-problem-with-minor-children.html

"Cleveland man who ran online group with videos of toddlers being raped sentenced to 26 years",

http://www.cleveland.com/courtjustice/index.ssf/2017/06/cleveland_man_who_ran_online_g.html

"Deputies: Lakeville woman sent explicit videos to 13-year-old boy"

http://www.whec.com/news/deputies-lakeville-woman-sent-explicit-videos-to-13-year-old boy/4418803/

Child Molesters: A Behavioral Analysis For Professionals Investigating the Sexual Exploitation of Children by Kenneth V. Lanning, Former Supervisory Special Agent

http://www.missingkids.com/en_US/publications/NC70.pdf

What You Need to Know About Sex Offenders in Your Community

http://ric-doj.zai-inc.com/Publications/cops-p220-pub.pdf

Miss Teen USA: Screamed upon learning she was 'sextortion' victim

http://www.cnn.com/2013/09/27/us/miss-teen-usa-sextortion/

Prosecutor: 'Sexual predator' teen should be jailed for life

http://www.komonews.com/news/local/124523094.html

Tanai Fortman, Ohio woman, blames diet pills in child porn case, report says

http://www.cbsnews.com/news/tanai-fortman-ohio-woman-blames-diet-pills-in-child-porn-case-report-says/

Ohio pediatric doctor Christopher Pelloski to plead guilty to child porn
http://www.newsnet5.com/news/state/ohio-pediatric-doctor-christopher-pelloski-to-plead-guilty-to-child-porn

Covina Teacher Indicted On Multiple Child Pornography Charges
http://losangeles.cbslocal.com/2013/07/02/covina-teacher-indicted-on-multiple-child-pornography-charges/

Dutchman accused of filming 400 nude children
http://www.utsandiego.com/news/2014/Jan/10/dutchman-accused-of-filming-400-nude-children/

Hundreds held over Canada child porn
http://www.bbc.com/news/world-us-canada-24944358

Specific issue of sexual predation and exploitation by coaches and sports authority figures   http://www.missingkids.com/CyberTipline

Chapter 10: Understanding Social Media

6 new facts about Facebook
http://www.pewresearch.org/fact-tank/2014/02/03/6-new-facts-about-facebook/

Cyberbullying websites should be boycotted, says Cameron
http://www.theguardian.com/society/2013/aug/08/cyberbullying-websites-boycotted-david-cameron

'Boycott these vile websites': Cameron urges youngsters to boycott Ask.fm in wake of girl, 14, who hanged herself after being 'trolled to death'
http://www.dailymail.co.uk/news/article-2386604/David-Cameron-tells-Ask-fm-clean-act-Hannah-Smith-suicide.html

UK advertisers abandon Ask.fm amid government calls for boycott
http://www.theverge.com/2013/8/8/4601880/ask-fm-boycott-uk-advertisers

NPR's The Teen Brain: It's Just Not Grown Up Yet,
http://www.npr.org/templates/story/story.php?storyId=124119468

"The Highest-Paid YouTube Stars 2016: PewDiePie Remains No.1 With $15 Million", December 20, 2016, by Madeline Berg,
https://www.forbes.com/sites/maddieberg/2016/12/05/the-highest-paid-youtube-stars-2016-pewdiepie-remains-no-1-with-15-million

Chapter 11: Apps Review

Facebook takes steps to stop suicides on Live, Jessica Guyunn, March 1, 2017,
https://www.usatoday.com/story/tech/news/2017/03/01/facebook-live-suicide-prevention/98546584/

Police: At least 40 people watched teen's sexual assault on Facebook Live, Emanuella Grinberg and Samira Said, March 22, 2017,
http://www.cnn.com/2017/03/21/us/facebook-live-gang-rape-chicago

For Philando Castile, Social Media Was The Only 911, Issie Lapowsky, July 7, 2016, https://www.wired.com/2016/07/philando-castile-social-media-911/

Nichole Cable, 15-Year-Old Missing Maine Girl, Died From Asphyxiation,
https://www.usatoday.com/story/news/nation/2013/06/13/missing-maine-girl-asphyxiation/2421117/

Facebook murderer who posed as teenager to lure victim jailed for life,
https://www.theguardian.com/uk/2010/mar/08/peter-chapman-facebook-ashleigh-hall

Portland Teens Allegedly Carve Swastika In Boy's Forehead Over Facebook Comment, http://www.huffingtonpost.com/2014/02/18/portland-teens-carve-swastika_n_4807902.html

Read the entire story here: Daughter's Facebook Brag Costs Her Family $80,000,
http://www.cnn.com/2014/03/02/us/facebook-post-costs-father/index.html

Prince William teens charged in connection with explicit Instagram postings
https://www.washingtonpost.com/local/crime/prince-william-teens-charged-in-connection-with-explicit-instagram-postings/2014/03/08/17760fe0-a6e7-11e3-9cff-b1406de784f0_story.html

Sexual Assault Arrest Stemmed From Instagram Encounter,
http://www.centralvalleytv.net/shop-local/item/1328-27sexual-assault-arrest-stemmed-from-instagram-encounter

Instagram tool of alleged teen cyber-bully arrested in Colorado,
http://www.cbsnews.com/news/instagram-tool-of-alleged-teen-cyber-bully-arrested-in-colorado/

Officials: Son of sheriff candidate arrested in Instagram photo case,
http://www.wsoctv.com/news/suspect-charged-nude-photos-young-girls-instagram/113091939

North Ridgeville teen Nicholas Hinton accused of posting threat on shooting up school on Instagram, http://fox8.com/2014/03/21/teen-charged-for-threats-against-school-on-instagram/

"Twitter Is Turning Into a Cyberbullying Playground"
https://www.yahoo.com/news/twitter-turning-cyberbullying-playground-053413648.html

"Woman's "Fatty Paycheck" Tweet Catches Attention of Cisco",
http://www.dailytech.com/Womans+Fatty+Paycheck+Tweet+Catches+Attention+of+Cisco/article14690.htm

NPR: "Teens Use Twitter To Thumb Rides",
http://www.npr.org/sections/alltechconsidered/2013/08/15/209530590/teens-use-twitter-to-thumb-rides

"Shreveport Teacher Arrested, Accused of Sexting with Student",
https://www.ktbs.com/news/shreveport-teacher-arrested-accused-of-sexting-with-student/article_02d61fcf-c30d-5189-a0e2-2d72bafa18e3.html

"Oregon City HS teacher admits 'sexting' and will go to jail",
http://katu.com/news/local/oregon-city-hs-teacher-admits-sexting-and-will-go-to-jail-11-20-2015

"Child porn charges laid against 10 Laval teens",
http://www.cbc.ca/news/canada/montreal/child-porn-charges-laid-against-10-laval-teens-1.2426599

"Boob Tube: Why YouTube can't stop porn",
https://www.dailydot.com/upstream/boobtube-why-youtube-cant-stop-porn/

"Seattle-area online gamer busted for alleged child porn, exploitation after 2002 conviction", http://www.seattletimes.com/seattle-news/crime/kirkland-man-arrested-child-pornography/

"Police Arrest Man Over Alleged Stalking Via Xbox Live",
https://www.wired.com/2008/01/halo-stalker-ar/

"INVESTIGATORS: Child predators lurk on gaming systems",
http://hillsboroughcounty.wtsp.com/news/news/517462-investigators-child-predators-lurk-gaming-systems

"Richard Kretovic Sentenced on Sex Abuse Charges",
http://archive.seattleweekly.com/home/937595-129/crimepunishment

"Tenn. man accused of trying to entice Clermont Co. boy",
http://www.wlwt.com/article/tenn-man-accused-of-trying-to-entice-clermont-co-boy/3536298

Appendix 1

BIG MAMA'S FAMILY RULES

Like all of you, my family is held closer to my heart than anything else. It's because I adore my children that sometimes I have to be really quite mean to them. Here's the perfect place to start. Take these family rules – use and apply liberally as needed:

If you have a complaint, I will assume that you are volunteering to do it yourself the next time. Choose your words very carefully.

If you are over 10 years old, I will no longer: open, clean, fill up, put away, empty out, or replace any item for you. Someday you will leave our house and will be expected to do these things. A trained Howler Monkey can put away laundry, or change batteries – they have opposable thumbs, so do you.

You should not have to be reminded to shower **and** scrub your undercarriage (with soap). I will not remind you again. I **WILL** however take off all of my clothes and climb into the shower with you where we will discuss all of the cool changes your body is going through. Wow, is that a hair?

I will no longer clean your toilet since you have decided that you don't want to flush it. I'm going to let the mold grow on the edges until it sprouts eyes and a tail. Then we will name your new little brother and claim him as a tax deduction. You will have to split your end of the college savings with him.

Any decision which begins with taking off your pants should give you pause. If you're stupid enough to take a photo of your junk for public consumption, I will take said-photo of your junk and frame it as a photo for grandma to be presented at Thanksgiving Dinner. Don't believe me? Please, please, please, dare me.

Children don't "own" anything. Whatever I paid for belongs to me and you are allowed to use, strictly at my pleasure.

Life is not now, nor will it ever be: fair. Better to get used to it now before you meet your future boss or in-laws. Consider living with me as "experiential learning".

I adore you and I refuse to allow any person in this world to put you into harm's way – including you. If placing restrictions on your life and behavior results in your hating me, that will make me sad, but I'll get over it. And so will you.

Appendix 2

FAMILY CONTRACT

Use this outline of a family contract as a starting point. Reword the points into your own language and for age appropriateness. At the bottom add-in whatever your standard consequence is going to be; two weeks of complete device lockdown (including phones) is a good solid place to start. It makes discipline easier later if everyone already knows what the consequence is going to be ahead of time.

Each child should get their own version of the contract, and then it should be signed by the child and both parents.

My personal online safety is my first priority.

I understand that my safety is also my parent's first priority and that sometimes my parents will limit: the time I spend online, the places I go online, and who I communicate with online.

I understand that my parents may choose to take my devices away whenever they feel it is appropriate.

I understand that this contract applies to all electronics including computers, tablets, smartphones, iTouch, gaming consoles, PC gaming, handheld games, and any other device I might have access to – even those that don't belong to me.

I understand that these rules apply to me even when I'm using someone else's device or I am in someone else's home.

I understand that mom and dad are going to be placing limits on how often I can use my devices and that we will have a time in the evening when all devices are turned in and shut off. I understand that this rule will be applied to all of my friends during a sleepover.

I know that there are people online who use fake accounts in order to hurt children. Because of this you can never really be 100% sure who anyone is online.

I understand that once you post something it is impossible to take back. I understand that Snapchat cannot delete my snaps or communications.

I will always use an appropriate username or handle which contains NO self-identifying or sexualized content.

I will not cross-promote my usernames in my social networking bios

I will provide and maintain a list of my username and passwords for my parents at all times, this includes the screen lock on devices. If I change a username or password without updating the list, I understand that I will receive the standard consequence listed below.

I will never share my login information with any of my friends or anyone besides my parents because I understand that someone might be a friend today, and not be a friend tomorrow.

I will never post any personal information onto a social profile including: phone number, city, school name, team name, age, date of birth, etc.

I will treat others the way I want to be treated because I understand that it's the right thing to do. I also understand that cyberbullying can be considered a crime. I will use the "Grandma Filter" at all times.

I will not share TMI content online because I understand that cyberbullies and strangers may want to use it against me.

I will never friend, follow, or connect to anyone that my parents have not met in real life because I understand that this can be a security risk.

I will ask my parents before I install any new app or social networking platform. If they decide to not allow it, I will understand. And if I have a hard time understanding, I know that the standard consequence listed below can be used to help me understand.

I will tell my parents if I receive photos, videos, links, texts, or emails which scare me or make me feel uncomfortable. I understand that adults are never supposed to share this content with me.

I will never take a nude or sexually suggestive photo of myself because I understand that this is a crime. In addition, I will never take a nude or sexually suggestive photo of anyone else - for the same reason.

I will never ever attempt to meet someone in real life who I have only known online because this is a huge security risk. I understand that there are people in the world who want to harm children.

I know that I can always speak with my parents if I need someone to talk to, and that even if they don't always completely understand – that they love me, and that's more important than anything else.

I understand that if I break any of the rules listed above whether purposely or accidentally, that I will be given the standard consequence (listed below).

STANDARD CONSEQUENCE

_____

_____

CHILD'S
*SIGNATURE*_____

PARENT'S SIGNATURE _____

PARENT'S SIGNATURE _____

DATE
*SIGNED*_____

Appendix 3

WEB STATISTICS

As you review the following quick history of computing and the Internet, pay especially close attention to the 2008 to 2010 time frame. This is where the largest jump in social usage comes into play.

A QUICK HISTORY OF COMPUTING AND THE INTERNET

1890: a punch card system is created to calculate the 1880 census. Not unlike the punch cards still used today for voting in many states. Yikes!

1941: a computer stores information in its memory for the first time

1953: the first computer language, COBOL was developed.
COBOL was developed by a woman named Grace Hopper[179] who was also a

---

[179] She's an amazing lady and the perfect subject for a K-6 biography report.

Navy Rear Admiral.

1954: another language FORTRAN is developed

1958: the computer chip is created

1964: the first prototype of a modern PC is developed which features a mouse

1969: Compuserve becomes the 1st company to offer Internet access to consumers

1971: the first email is delivered and the first floppy disks make it easy to share data across computers

mid to late 1970s: personal computers become available for purchase

1976: Apple Computers releases the first Apple I: the first computer with a single circuit board

1978: the first computerized spreadsheet program is released

1979: the first word processing program called "WordStar" becomes available

1981: the first IBM personal computer is introduced. It's called Acorn and runs MS-DOS

1984: Apple releases its first PC with a GUI (graphic user interface) using menus and icons eventually becoming the Macintosh.

1985: Microsoft answers the "Mac's" graphical interface with Microsoft Windows. The first dot-com domain is registered

1990: HTML (Hyper-Text Markup Language) is developed which makes the World Wide Web possible

1998: Google opens its doors as a major search engine

1999: "Wi-Fi" becomes a term

2001: Wikipedia launches

2003: Linkedin launches

2004: Facebook launches, initially just for Harvard students

2005: YouTube launches

2006: Apple releases the MacBook Pro. Twitter launches. Google indexes more than 25 billion web pages.

2007: the iPhone is released

2008: Facebook tried unsuccessfully to buy Twitter

2009: Facebook ranked as the most-used social network worldwide

2010

- 400 million users on Facebook.
- Global Internet users reached 1.97 billion.
- The Internet surpasses print newspapers as a primary way for Americans to get news.
- Apple releases the iPad

2011

- 550 million people on Facebook
- 65 million tweets sent through Twitter each day
- 2 billion video views every day on YouTube
- LinkedIn has 90 million professional users

2012

- 2 billion people around the world use the Internet and social media
- 213 million Americans use the Internet via computers
- 52 million use the Web via smartphone
- 55 million use it via tablets
- Facebook reached a billion users in 2012
- YouTube has more than 800 million users each month with more than 1 trillion views per year or around 140 views for every person on Earth.

IN 60 SECONDS

How many things can happen in just sixty seconds online? There seems to be some digital vortex that sucks you into Facebook or Twitter, making sixty seconds go by in half of one second. Suddenly you look up and it's dinner time **again**, and the people you live with expect to be fed **again**.

So what did you miss in all of those 60 second intervals strung together back-to-back? Think: massive scale which builds upon itself, well, every sixty seconds.

In 2013, in sixty seconds online:

- 72 hours of video are uploaded to YouTube.
  (Did you understand that? Reread it)
- 2,000,000 searches are completed on Google
- 2,460,000 posts are uploaded to Facebook
- 1,800,000 likes on Facebook
- 104,000 photos on Snapchat are shared (barf)
- 216,000 photos taken on Instagram
- 278,000 Tweets on Twitter
- 571 new websites are created
- 204,000,000 emails sent

Other than the obvious fact that as a species we spend a considerable amount of time in front of a glowing screen, what is the relevance of this data? The relevance is the massive foundation upon which the digital world rests and feeds upon itself. Tech companies create enticing new digital platforms which attract users. Those users create new content in the new platform, attracting **their** friends and family.

Those new arrivals will also become new users of the platform, creating more content and attracting additional users. All the while the tech company has reached critical mass and is selling your participation and your data to advertisers.

Appendix 4
FREQUENTLY ASKED QUESTIONS

Frequently Asked Questions/Comments

During my travels around the United States presenting to school auditoriums and church halls filled with parents, I tend to hear the same comments and questions over and over. Here are the comments and questions I hear the most often along with my typical responses.

I KNOW EVERYTHING MY DAUGHTER DOES BECAUSE I FRIENDED HER

"Friending" or "following" your child on social media is not nearly enough surveillance to tell you what you need to know. Many apps provide the opportunity to shield posts or messages from just certain individuals (like mom or dad). In addition some apps (like Snapchat) provide the user the opportunity to send a photo, video, or written message to just one or a few other users – similar to a private messaging system.

The only way to really see what your child is doing or has done is to keep a list of your child's login credentials. As a parent you reserve the right to log into their accounts at any time. Be sure to invoke your "standard consequence" if your child changes their password without your permission.

I ASKED MY SON IF HE USES SNAPCHAT AND HE SAID 'NO'

Always know the answer to any question before you ask; their answer will verify their willingness/ability to lie to you. If her answer doesn't perfectly match the intelligence you gathered, we have a problem. Trust, but verify[180]!

First, take the device out of his hand (randomly works best) and flip through the icons on the device. Only then should you ask if he uses Snapchat – right after you saw the Snapchat icon on his device.

Note: If you're not sure what the icons look like for any social media platform, just go to Google Images and type in "Facebook icon" or "Snapchat icon". You will see a small square color image – look for the corresponding images on your child's phone or device.

I HAVE A GOOD KID. SERIOUSLY, HE WOULD NEVER LIE TO ME

Oy, if I had a nickel for every time I heard this one! Please spare me the "I have a good kid" speech. I'm sure you do. Congratulations. You must be very proud. In the meantime, assume she's guilty and cross-examine her like she knows where Jimmy Hoffa is buried. They all lie. They will all look up at you with those pretty big eyes and lie right to your face. It's a normal part of their development, just expect it. Given the right circumstances your darling child is not beyond taking a picture of her junk and texting it to her little boyfriend. Seriously.

QUESTIONS RELATED TO A BYOD OR 1:1 DEVICE PROGRAM AT SCHOOL

Technology use during the academic day is becoming very popular in school districts all over the world, and with good reason. When developed

---

180 This is a translation of a Russian saying which became popular when President Ronald Reagan used it frequently during the thawing of the Cold War with Russia. In Russian the saying rhymes: "doveryai, no proveryai"

appropriately using technology can aid in the creation of a customizable framework for education. There will be some point in the (hopefully) near future when each child will create their own customized education by using collaborative, creative, and adaptive educational tools.

In order to begin working towards this eventuality, many school districts are implementing technology plans which can be BYOD (Bring Your Own Device) or 1:1 (one-to-one) where each child is given a device by the school for academic use. While there are many reasons why schools will prefer a BYOD program (cost being a major reason) I always prefer a 1:1 program especially when a Google Chromebook is the device of choice.

There are many points along the technology integration continuum. On one end, specific teachers may offer the opportunity for children to bring their own devices to be used in a specific class or

for a specific project. On the other end of the continuum, there is complete tech integration where textbooks go digital and all homework is submitted electronically.

Any school district attempting any variation of tech integration must provide: staff, parents, and students with proactive internet safety instruction. Educators especially, need to be trained in both edtech skills (cool tools and apps used during instruction) and in proactive safety standards and implementation.

Pay attention to the contract that your child has probably already signed with their school district. Generally called an AUP (Acceptable Use Policy) this document goes over acceptable and unacceptable student use of school district digital networks and hardware. Generally speaking, students can be disciplined for disregarding or breaking their AUP agreement with the school, up to and including a ban from all digital systems and expulsion.

Your child's Student Handbook may also have a section related to digital behavior. If you turn in the "I read the student handbook" signature page, you and your child are agreeing to every portion of the handbook including the language on digital expectations. It would be useful to review these school policies together with your Family Contract during your family meeting.

Your child's school is probably already spending a significant amount of resource time on web filtering the campus wi-fi signal. But in the end, it is not the school's job to filter each child's behavior while on that signal. It still remains your job as parent to teach your children how to be good digital citizens.

MY 11-YEAR-OLD SIGNED UP FOR A FACEBOOK ACCOUNT WITHOUT MY KNOWLEDGE, NOW WHAT?

The only way that your 11-year-old is able to sign up for a Facebook (Twitter, Instagram, etc) account is by lying about his/her age. The minimum age for most social platforms is thirteen years old. Your child would have to lie about their age in order to create a profile. Facebook and Instagram (and most other social platforms) give parents the opportunity to report their under-age children and have those accounts revoked.

Remember that your child also needs an email address to create a social account. If you were unaware that your child had an email now would be the time to have that conversation as well.

Perhaps the bigger issue here is that your child knew you would disapprove and then did it anyway. This is definitely a hammer-able offense, and definitely merits a "higher-level consequence", perhaps a month with no digital access including loss of cell phone.

IF I FIND A BRAND NEW APP/GAME ON MY CHILD'S DEVICE WHAT SHOULD I DO? (AKA HOW TO VET GAMES AND APPS)

First: check my Facebook[181] page and website to see if I've covered it yet. Feel free to email[182] me with questions. I will look into it, and post my findings.

Second: Check out the ratings given by Common Sense Media[183]. On this site you will find parent and kid ratings on everything from apps to videogames to movies and music.

Third: Go to the appstore (iOS or Android) and look up the app (see instructions in this chapter), look for these specific key phrases: the ability to chat with friends, finding nearby friends (aka: location services), "share" with friends, connect with friends, etc. Pay close attention to the permissions you

---

181 http://www.facebook.com/OvernightGeekUniversity

182 info@overnightgeek.com

183 http://www.commonsensemedia.org/learning-ratings

agree to when installing the app, most of the issues will reveal themselves during installation on that screen which most of us just blindly agree to

---

I DON'T MIND IF MY 4TH GRADER USES SOCIAL MEDIA, HE'S GOING TO HAVE TO LEARN SOMETIME

This is what I call 'The Song of the Dabbler". It basically goes like this (apply whichever tune comes to mind)....

Well, he's going to have to learn sometime.... I don't believe in keeping my kids in a bubble...They're going to do it anyway...I want to give them a chance to make their mistakes while they're young....I believe in letting her experiment with life experiences....

Before I launch into my anti-dabblers rant let me make it clear that I also believe in letting children make mistakes. I do not believe in sanitizing their universe. However, the mistakes that you allow them to make must be age appropriate, unless of course you believe that your 7-year-old should be allowed to toss back the beers since he's going to do it anyway when he's older. Or why not let the 10-year-old try driving the car? Maybe let the 12-year-old experiment with having sex with her teacher. I mean, you don't want to keep her in a bubble – right?

The Dabblers do not realize that the stakes are way too high, particularly when an unrestricted device is being given to young children. If you allow your young and immature children unfettered access to digital tools, you are also giving would-be predators direct access to your child. Are you okay with that? Some gross sweaty guy with his hands down his pants while he looks at your daughter's Science Fair photos? That's cool, right?

Do The Dabblers intend to have uber-sexualized and violent content normalized for their children? Do they see some benefit to exposing their children to videos of: mass executions, beheadings, sexual bestiality, and rape?

As a would-be Dabbler are you satisfied with the possibility that your child could lose his/her college acceptance or scholarship opportunity by engaging in sexting? How about prison? Is the concept of "prison" part of the Dabbler's Manifesto?

The Dabblers pose the greatest risk to the implementation of your digital safety plan because they're everywhere. Perhaps you're married to a Dabbler, or she's your child's teacher, or he's the parent of your child's best friend. These people appear to be educated on the topic, but they are clearly not educated.

Feel free to buy an extra copy of this book for your favorite Dabbler, or just hit her over the head with your copy. Either way. Win-win.

HOW DO I TELL MY CHILD 'NO'?

This is an actual question I was asked at a parent event by a lovely woman with tears in her eyes. At first I thought I had misunderstood her. She was asking the question through tears and a heavy Eastern European accent. I approached her and asked her to repeat the question, but by then "contagious crying" had taken hold of a little pocket of moms and I thought for sure that if I stood there long enough I would start blubbering as well.

Her question wasn't really, literally, "how do I utter the sound: no?" She was, I think, looking for me to validate the need for saying 'no'. This topic (of saying no to your children) can really fill the pages of an entire second book so here's my very abbreviated version.

REASONS WHY YOU NEED TO TELL YOUR CHILDREN "NO" – ESPECIALLY AS RELATED TO DIGITAL LIMITS AND CONSEQUENCES:

The real world will tell them "no" a great many times. Better they should learn coping skills while they have your love and guidance to fall back on. They can't develop coping skills if they've never had anything to "cope" with.

Adversity and scarcity build character, creativity, and resourcefulness. Some of the best childhood memories come from, inventing games and playing in the mud.

Avoiding 'no' in a misguided effort to make your children happy will only hurt them in the end. Children who are raised with a carefully cultivated sense of entitlement grow up to be self-centered a**holes who live in your basement until they're 35 years old. And that's too many years of chicken nuggets.

If you begin providing your children with "stuff" at very young ages, fairly soon they will age-out of child-like experiences. I know a young lady who was taken to Rome for 3 days by her mother for her 10th birthday. I'm not sure that this particular child will ever again be excited about a homemade cake and a party with five friends at a bounce house. A trip to Rome is wonderful, but what can possibly thrill this child later in life? Will she have peaked in life experiences by the time she turns sixteen? Just because you can doesn't mean you should.

If it's Christmas every day, Christmas becomes meaningless. When you say 'no' fairly often, the 'yeses' are that much more appreciated. And isn't that part of what we strive for as parents? To make them appreciate and value the good stuff?

I make you this promise – your children will not hate you for saying 'no'. Your children will not withdraw their love when you stop following the crowd. I promise.

Appendix 5

THANK YOU TO LAW ENFORCEMENT

(Originally appeared on my Facebook page on April 28, 2016)

I would like to take this opportunity to personally thank every single person connected to law enforcement - everywhere in the world. In my role as "speaker" - when I go out to school districts, very often (pretty much always) kids will come up to me after and ask me for help on very specific issues.

In the past month:
More than 20 kids asked for help with sexting issues - one 7th grade boy was terrified that what he had done would come back to haunt him and tried to explain his story to me through his sobs.

At least a half dozen asked for help with porn addiction - the most recent - a darling, sweet, and super-bright 8th grade boy who was terrified that his mother (who I had the privilege of meeting) would think less of him.

Several kids asked for help because they were in imminent danger - one 6th-grade-girl asked me to intercede because she believed that a sexual predator had her home address.

I even had a parent come up to me after a parent event to tell me that she was pretty sure that an acquaintance of hers was selling/giving her unborn child away to a man she met online who was probably connected to human sex trafficking. Oh and who should she call about that?

Here's what I've learned:

- I am the poster child for why civilians should not have guns (screw due process.)
- I am in continual awe of the work performed consistently by law enforcement personnel

DISCLAIMER: Are some police officers/prosecutors/detectives (etc) ... jaded/racist/criminal/douchebags who need to be fired? Yes, yes, and yes - Those individuals need to be rooted out and fired, prosecuted, and incarcerated, preferably. But I will tell you firsthand that this is the minority of the cases.

I have had the privilege to meet law enforcement folks who (primarily) work either sex crimes related to children, "internet crimes" related to children, or human sex trafficking. There are no words sufficient to describe what I feel for these people.

Here's the other thing I've realized about myself, and I'm sharing it here with you - there's no freaking way I could do their job - and you'll have to trust me on the fact that you wouldn't want to do it either. I barely brush up against these cases via the children who ask me for help.

After I complete a full day of back-to-back-to-back student presentations, I'm useless for 48 hours. I don't answer my phone, I don't socialize, and I don't even share what I've heard with my family. I watch Netflix, bake a cake (seriously), or paint/write/create something in order to reboot.

The faces of your children are permanently etched in my brain and on my heart, and it's hard for me to shake it. I see the kids who are hopeless and addicted to porn, the kids who think that a predator who threatened them will show up at their home at any moment, the 2nd grade boy who asks me why his aunt shows him porn every time he goes to her house, the 3rd grade little boy who asks me to explain to him why any of his so-called "friends" would call him stupid online, the tween girl who tells me that there is a man who is (right at this very moment) leaving Louisiana to come and "take her to lunch"....and oh yeah, that might not be such a good idea - so can I do something about that...

I hear their stories - one by one - and I try not to lose it, and then I refer them to law enforcement. Law enforcement comes to the rescue - *every single time* they are called. THEY are the ones who do the heavy lifting. They do ALL the lifting.

These brave and resilient cops/detectives/prosecutors face the absolute bottom of the barrel of humanity on a daily basis. They see the incarnation of evil wrapped up in mental illness, drug addiction, poverty, and some with no reason at all. They see the kinds of ugly that can't be articulated using language - it's a depth of fear and a darkness which can only be felt viscerally. And they do it EVERY DAY.

They do it, for you and for me - and for our children. There is NO doubt in my mind that they carry those children's faces around in their hearts as well.

There are very few jobs in the world where someone is told - "Yeah, so, you're only going to see the very worst of the world- like all day long. You're going to see the darkest side of people, and of humanity. Congrats, you're hired."

So, if you work in law enforcement - THANK YOU. Thank you for doing what you do, for showing up every single day, for not losing your humanity, for putting other people's safety above your own sanity, for trying every single day to see the good - please keep seeing the good. I know it's hard.

As for me - I have Patron tequila and all of you. PARENTS: Please get engaged in the safety of your children - we can't do this alone.

#BeFierceBeUnafraid.

ACKNOWLEDGEMENTS

I don't want to live in any form of humanity where public libraries cease to exist. My idea of heaven is sitting in a quiet library in the best seat near the fireplace, next to a stack of books, and a bottomless cup of coffee which never gets cold. At least half of this book was written within the walls of my favorite local public library. Thank you to all of the librarians in the Cuyahoga County Public Library system. Thank you to all of the librarians on the planet – after I die, I fully intend on reincarnating into either a librarian or an old, fat, bookstore cat. I haven't decided which is more awesome.

Thank you to the massive community support I have received throughout this entire journey. People I barely know have pulled up next to me at a red light to ask me about progress on the book. Friends and family members from all over the world (thanks to Facebook) have contributed news stories and articles. Jean Kanzinger, Erinne Clausen, and Rachel Crandall read advance portions of the book and offered me honest and helpful critiques.

Thanks to Brennan Donnellan, Katie Kessler, Danielle Sills, and the rest of the WKYC – Channel 3 crew. You gave me my first shot at appearing on the evening news as an internet-safety-phone-hammering "expert" and it has been an absolute blast to interact with you all. Thank you to Jen Donnellan who understands the solitary process of writers better than anyone I know. She left fresh baked cookies and coffee at my front door, rang the bell, and drove away. Jen, I wish I had five more of you in my life.

I have had the benefit and privilege to live with and learn from a long line of extremely strong women. Starting with my mother and travelling backwards, the women in my family were immigrants and cultural pioneers. Generation after generation they survived and thrived in an environment where failure was almost certain. There was zero whining and an almost cult fascination with education in all its forms. I can vividly remember being in high school and my mother catching me at the kitchen sink washing a few dishes. In Spanish she said 'What the hell are you doing?'I said 'Ummm, doing the dishes?' She responded: 'What the hell are you doing that for? Washing dishes won't get you anywhere in life, go study something'. So I did, and I haven't stopped yet; which coincidentally explains the pile of dishes currently in my sink.

The Sisters of Saint Joseph of Brentwood New York were my Catholic School educators for twelve years in Jamaica, Queens. Any success I have had is due almost completely to these brave, brilliant, and resourceful women. I was taught that failure is something that you choose to accept. I learned that education has intrinsic value and that if you want to live in a compassionate world that **you** need to make it so. Fix what you see wrong, whenever you see it. The religious women who do incredibly important and meaningful work all over the world are the main reason that these "institutions" still exist. They are the ones on the front lines doing the heavy lifting. They never ask for recognition, and they certainly never get any. For Sister Joan Petito, Sister Grace Avila, and the countless other religious who kicked my butt when it needed kicking, thank you. I love you all, still.

My family suffered immensely throughout this process. Their willingness to let me threaten their lives repeatedly is one of the reasons this book has been completed. To my amazing husband who brought me healthy food and smoothies every time I forgot to eat for an entire day, to my brilliant programmer-in-the-making teenage son who critiqued passages and gave me expert teen "hacking" feedback, and to my sweet and artistic tween daughter who drew hilarious characters from her imagination on my white board (most of which fart in rainbow colors – who knew?), everything I have ever done and will ever do is for the three of you. I love you to the moon and back….infinity.

Most importantly, thank you to all of the school districts and to all of the audiences large and small who have welcomed me so graciously into their communities. Thank you for sharing your stories, your worries, and your children.

I vividly remember a shy middle school student who waited to speak with me after a student presentation. She wanted to thank me, but immediately burst into tears. No one had ever told her that women should seriously consider becoming programmers. She was the only female member of her school's Computer Club and she consistently felt intimidated and self-conscious. I explained that if that's what she wants to do, that no human on this planet who stop her. I gave her a few websites where she could build her coding skills. Then I told her to stop crying, toughen up, and forge her own path. I handed her a written copy of my personal mantra:

"I'll consider giving up tomorrow. Today I am unstoppable."
I wish the same for all of you in this path towards digital safety for your family. **You** get to forge your own path. These are **your** children, in **your** home, with **your** devices.

Consider giving up tomorrow.
Today you are unstoppable.

For more by Jesse Weinberger

Internet Safety Blog: www.OvernightGeekUniversity.com
For video content: www.YouTube.com/OvernightGeekU

Connect on Social Media

- Facebook.com/OvernightGeekUniversity
- YouTube.com/OvernightGeekU

To hire Jesse Weinberger to speak to your: students, parents, school district, or organization please go to OvernightGeekUniversity.com

Made in the USA
Middletown, DE
21 January 2019